COLLEGE HISTORIES

TRINITY COLLEGE, DUBLIN

BY

W. MACNEILE DIXON

PROFESSOR OF ENGLISH LANGUAGE AND LITERATURE IN THE UNIVERSITY
OF BIRMINGHAM

AUTHOR OF 'IN THE REPUBLIC OF LETTERS,' ETC.

1902

Copyright © 2013 Read Books Ltd.
This book is copyright and may not be
reproduced or copied in any way without
the express permission of the publisher in writing

British Library Cataloguing-in-Publication Data
A catalogue record for this book is available from the
British Library

W. MacNeile Dixon

William Macneile Dixon was born in Bombay, India in 1866. The only son of the Reverend William Dixon, he returned to Britain as a young man to study at Trinity College, Dublin, where he excelled as a scholar. Dixon graduated with a first-class degree from the Modern Literature School and a second-class degree from the Mental and Moral Science School. Dixon also took part in the public life of the University with gusto: he was, amongst other things, President of the University Philosophical Society and auditor of the College Historical Society.

In 1891, Dixon was appointed Professor of English Literature in Alexandra College, Dublin; three years on, he was elected Professor of English Language and Literature in the Mason Science College, later Birmingham University. In Birmingham he was also made Professor of Literature to the Royal Society of Artists. During the 1890s, Dixon published various works of well-received literary scholarship, including *English Poetry from Blake to Browning* (1894), *A Primer of Tennyson, With a Critical Essay* (1896) and *In the Republic of Letters* (1898).

Dixon was chosen as President of the Library Association of the United Kingdom in 1902, and was re-elected in 1903. Lastly, on the transference of Professor Walter Raleigh to Oxford, Dixon received the appointment to the Regius Professorship of English Language and Literature at the University of Glasgow – a position he would hold for thirty years. During this time, while contributing articles to the *Quarterly Review* and other periodicals, Dixon published a slew of other works, both popular and academic: *Poetry and National Character* (1915),

The Fleets Behind the Fleet (1917), *The British Navy at War* (1917), *Tragedy* (1924), *Cinderella's Garden* (1927), *The Human Situation* (1937), *Thoughts for the Times* (1941) and *An Apology for the Arts* (1944). These various works marked Dixon as both a proud patriot, and an unrivalled academic expert on Hellenism, Classical Philosophy, and neo-Platonism.

Dixon died in 1946, aged 60. At this point, his work was hugely popular – *The Human Situation* (1937), for example, went through seven printings. The popularity of Dixon's work in the first half of the twentieth century has led many historians to wonder at the relative obscurity of his work today.

J. P. M.

ÆDIUM

HAUD MINUS AMATORI

QUAM DECORI

PREFACE

DURING the preparation of this volume I received kindly assistance from many friends. I am particularly indebted to Mr. John Wardell for a mass of material obtained from original sources, which a most generous expenditure of time and labour enabled him to place at my disposal. To Mr. E. J. Gwynn, Fellow of the House, I owe the critical estimate of the Irish MSS. in the library; to Mr. W. R. P. McNeight the account given of the College rowing clubs; to Professor Joly, the photograph of the Old Row in Library Square; and to Mr. John Cooke, Mr. R. P. Cowl, and Mr. Charles Exon I am indebted for much useful advice. The proofs have been read in part by Dr. Gwynn, Regius Professor of Divinity in the University, and throughout by Dr. Mahaffy, Senior Fellow and Registrar. To them, as well as to the above-mentioned friends, I wish here to express my warmest thanks.

I have drawn freely for my facts upon the existing histories of the University by Messrs. Heron, Taylor, and Stubbs; upon the *Book of Trinity College*; upon Mr. Urwick's *Early History of the University*; upon the pamphlets and the MSS. catalogued and uncatalogued in the College library; and I have incorporated some sentences from an article on 'Trinity College, Dublin,' written by myself in the *Quarterly Review* for July, 1892. Owing to the limits placed upon me by the character of the book, I have, however, been unable to make use of an immense body of material open to any historian who may project his work upon a nobler scale.

WHILE yet at sea the Athenian voyager,
Past Sunium, over the Myrtoan brine,
Full-hearted knew his home and Athens near;
And knowing watch'd, till by her pillar'd shrine
He saw Athena, helmeted, divine,
The city's warden, gloriously uprear
Her virgin front, and sun-illumined shine
The bright fierce point of her Olympian spear.
So gleams the spear of knowledge in thy hand,
For him who watches o'er a shifting sea
Its point of fire—across his troubled land,
Across the night of Ireland's agony;
Amid the storms by every passion fann'd,
Emblem of mind, and mind's supremacy.

INTRODUCTION

THE three centuries since the foundation of Trinity College, Dublin, have made of England the widest as well as the most powerful of empires, but they have brought to Ireland, once the star of Western civilization, the home of learning and the arts, neither prosperity nor contentment. Sharing in the fortunes of the country, impoverished by insurrection and civil war, hampered by their effects upon the early education of her students, exposed to the hostility of the Roman Catholic Church, the work of the Irish University has been done in face of disadvantages and discouragements the most formidable; and her success must be ascribed to the virtues and the vigour of the Anglo-Irish breed. That vigour and those virtues were early displayed within the College walls, for to the world of scholarship the University of Dublin gave in her infant years Ussher, *judicio singulari, usque ad miraculum doctus;* Dudley Loftus, the brilliant antiquarian and Orientalist; Ware, the historian; Dodwell, Camden Professor at Oxford and 'the greatest scholar in Europe.' The seventeenth-century drama owes to her Southerne, the author of *Oronooko* and *The Fatal Marriage*, while through

Congreve and Farquhar she reaped the laurels of Restoration comedy. For literature—apart from her greater names, like that of Goldsmith—she educated such men as Henry Brooke, the author of *The Fool of Quality*; Wolfe, who wrote the famous lyric on *The Burial of Sir John Moore*; Toplady, the hymn-writer; Malone, the editor of Shakespeare; and Parnell, the poet of *The Hermit*.

Though not infrequently attacked as the fortress of an alien race and an alien religion, these onslaughts have been made by men who would find it difficult to define the term 'alien,' and who had forgotten her share in every national movement in Ireland, the leaders she has given to every popular cause; nor can it be urged against her that she quenched in her sons the ardour of patriotism, the sacred love of country. Ireland has not yet produced a more vigorous champion of her wrongs than Swift, a more sagacious adviser than Berkeley, a more eloquent exponent of her political rights than Grattan, a more disinterested friend of her religion than Burke. Since the foundation of that ancient house, no generation of its students has failed to send recruits to the army which did battle for the amelioration of the conditions, religious, political and social, of the country. Flood, and Bushe, and Plunket, and Curran, and Foster, its Speaker, were not the least eloquent of the supporters of the Irish Parliament; there was nothing lukewarm in the patriotism of Sheil, of the Emmets, or of Wolfe Tone; Lefanu and Lever did not seek abroad for the subjects of their art, nor did Moore, and Davis and Ferguson chant the triumphs of the 'Saxon invader.' The Marseillaise of the Irish people, *Who fears to speak of Ninety-eight?* was written within the walls of Trinity College; the author of the phrase 'Home Rule for Ireland' was Isaac Butt, one of its Professors.

Though founded at the instance of English colonists, and ruled for long by statutes emanating from men like Laud and Stafford, her prejudices have been far less bitter, her attitude far less hostile to the aspirations of native Ireland, than her enemies have been willing to admit. True it is that she has not cared to neglect the proper sphere of academic work for the blinding arena of Irish controversies, but it ought to be remembered by her critics that in 1799 Trinity College called upon her members in the Irish Parliament to oppose the Union, which was vigorously and successfully supported by the Roman Catholic Bishops. The hope of Catholic emancipation was no doubt the motive of their action, but again it ought to be remembered that on the recall of Lord Fitzwilliam the students of Trinity College presented an address in favour of Catholic emancipation, the address which called forth the memorable words of Grattan: 'These young men in a few years must determine this question. . . . They will soon sit on these seats blended with Catholics, while we, blended with Catholics, shall repose in the dust.' In face of facts like these, it is at least futile to deny that Trinity College has been the intellectual nurse of political idealists, the fostering-mother of Ireland's patriot sons.

Yet this is not all. More than half a century before the Test Act which admitted Nonconformists to the membership of the English Universities, the degrees of the University of Dublin were thrown open to the world.

She was the first University to grant degrees to Jews. In 1854 she founded scholarships for students of any religious creed who declined to take the declaration at that time required from candidates for scholarships on the foundation. In 1858 she established studentships, open to members of any religious community, and five out of eighteen of those awarded in the first nine years went to Roman Catholics. In 1873 she gave her cordial support to the Act which abolished religious tests, and threw open to all comers her scholarships, her Fellowships, and her professorships, with the single and unavoidable exception of those in the Divinity School. In 1880, and again in 1890, she elected a Roman Catholic Fellow. These are the services rendered by Trinity College to the Liberal cause. She can do no more. That Roman Catholic Ireland does not now desire an 'open University,' but, rather, one in which education shall be rooted in theology and the dogmas of its own traditional creed, concerns not Trinity College—for she can do nothing to meet that desire— but Parliament and the English nation.

It may come as a surprise to some, that in the more strictly academic region the University of Dublin has more than once or twice been first to read the signs of the times, and show the way to her elder sisters. Hers were the earliest degrees ever instituted or conferred in Surgery, and hers the first degrees as well as the first University school of Engineering in the British Isles. Lectureships in Modern Languages, but recently admitted to most English Universities, were founded in Dublin as early as the eighteenth century, and English Literature, lately given reluctant place among the studies of Oxford and Cambridge, has for generations formed an important part of the Dublin undergraduate course. The Classical Moderatorship in Trinity College preceded the Cambridge *Tripos* by eight, the Mental and Moral Science Moderatorship the Cambridge *Tripos* in the same subject by seventeen, years; while Oxford as well as Cambridge followed the example set by Dublin in the development of new branches of study and the reconstruction of her final Honour Schools. The Natural Sciences, have long held an honoured place in the Dublin curriculum, and no Cambridge man will need to be reminded that the mathematical studies of his own University owe not a little to the work of Sir William Hamilton, of Lloyd, of McCullagh, and of Salmon.

Yet how little do facts like these weigh in the mind of youth fortunate enough to enter the charmed circle made by the ancient walls! They may serve to heighten the fame of the foundation in the eyes of strangers; for him they are unnecessary. He asks for no proof of the virtues that attend him there; the traditions, the companionships, the keen, intellectual air, these nourish his vitality, and in vitality is happiness. With him, though the world is wide and the intellectual horizon may broaden, there remains one unassailable and magnificent prejudice, and as a member of the College of Colleges, to the gracious figure of that august lady of many memories, he pays the passionate and unceasing homage of gratitude and affection.

CONTENTS

CHAPTER	PAGE
INTRODUCTION	ix
I. FOUNDATION AND EARLY YEARS	1
II. THE SEVENTEENTH CENTURY: PROVOSTSHIP OF TEMPLE — CHANCELLORSHIP OF LAUD — THE COMMONWEALTH	26
III. THE SEVENTEENTH CENTURY (*continued*): THE RESTORATION TO THE REVOLUTION	52
IV. THE SIXTEENTH AND SEVENTEENTH CENTURIES: LIFE IN THE COLLEGE—STUDIES	72
V. THE EIGHTEENTH CENTURY	94
VI. THE EIGHTEENTH CENTURY (*continued*)	126
VII. THE EIGHTEENTH CENTURY: LIFE IN THE COLLEGE—STUDIES	151
VIII. THE NINETEENTH CENTURY	178
IX. COLLEGE BUILDINGS—PICTURES—PLATE	199
X. THE LIBRARY	220
XI. DISTINGUISHED GRADUATES	234
XII. TRINITY COLLEGE TO-DAY	264

APPENDICES

A. THE CENTENARY	279
B. THE TERCENTENARY	282
C. COLLEGE DISCIPLINE	285
D. ARMS OF TRINITY COLLEGE, DUBLIN	286

ILLUSTRATIONS

I. ADAM LOFTUS, FIRST PROVOST	*Frontispiece*	
II. THE WEST FRONT	*facing p.*	22
III. THE LIBRARY—EXTERIOR	,,	108
IV. PARLIAMENT SQUARE AND CAMPANILE	,,	148
V. (*a*) DR. BARRETT. (*b*) OLD ROW IN LIBRARY SQUARE REMOVED TO MAKE ROOM FOR THE GRADUATES' MEMORIAL	,,	176
VI. THE PROVOST, DR. SALMON	,,	198
VII. PLAN OF THE COLLEGE, 1750	,,	208
VIII. THE SCHOOLS—INTERIOR	,,	214
IX. THE LIBRARY—INTERIOR	,,	224
X. PLAN OF THE COLLEGE, 1892	,,	264

CHAPTER I

FOUNDATION AND EARLY YEARS

IT was not permitted to the genius or fortune of Elizabeth to add the pacification of Ireland to the successes of her reign. In no slight measure were these successes the work of hardy adventurers, yet to the absence from Ireland of adventurers, military or political, few will incline to attribute the failures of the English rule. Conveniently situated for the purposes of the experimental English legislator in modern times as for those of the landless knight of earlier days, the value of such an island in the education of the Anglo-Saxon race has hitherto, perhaps, been overlooked. *In corpore vili*, runs the proverb, *fiat experimentum*. Here at least the race learned or might have learned the lesson, unpleasantly emphasized later in the American War of Independence, that Greek meets Greek when the English by birth encounter the English by blood. Occasionally, however, the ambitions of the colonists in Ireland met with favour in the hearts, or at least in the policies, of English statesmen, and to one of these fortunate conjunctions in the political firmament is due the foundation of Trinity College, Dublin.

Ireland might well indeed have possessed academies more ancient than those of England, for so far back as the eighth century her schools had been famous. Alcuin, the teacher of Charlemagne, in his life of the celebrated Willibrord, mentions his many years of study in Ireland, *inter eximios simul piæ religionis et sacræ lectionis magistros*. That immense services were rendered to civilization by the ancient Irish schools, which offered a haven for learning and literature while Rome was swaying to her fall, is indisputable, and we need not doubt the statement that in 901 under Cormac, King-Archbishop, there were 5,000 scholars and 900 learned works in Cashel, or that Clonard and Ross and Armagh were even more famous and frequented seminaries. To Irish scholars has been ascribed the foundation of some of the most ancient Universities of Europe, Paris and Pavia, and through that renowned Celt, Scotus Erigena, Oxford. But in 867 the galleys of the Norsemen grounded upon the Irish shore. Armagh was plundered and burnt, and the treasures of that great medieval home of learning submerged by this and succeeding waves of invasion. The Danes were followed by the Anglo-Normans, and the business of politics and war drove out indeed priestcraft, but with it arts and learning and the ancient civilization of the Celt.

In 1311 was founded the first University of Dublin by a Bull of Pope Clement V. The Bull, obtained at the suggestion of John Lech, then Archbishop of Dublin, established

' an university of schools (*scholarum universitas*), and moreover a general school (*studium generale*) in every science and lawful faculty, to flourish there for ever, in which masters might freely teach and scholars be auditors in the said faculties; and that such as might be thought worthy to be associated with the honour of doctors in any of the said faculties, might obtain the licence of any of the said schools for that end.'

At the death of Lech, however, in 1313, or upon the revolt of the clergy to the party of Edward Bruce in 1315, Pope Clement's University disappeared, and in 1320 Alexander de Bicknor, Lech's successor in the See of Dublin, applied for and procured a Bull from Pope John XXII., confirming the former Bull and the statutes drawn up for the earlier foundation.* De Bicknor's University was assisted by the pious bounty of Edward III.; its schools were connected with the Cathedral of St. Patrick, lectures were given in that building, and degrees were conferred. But, unsupported save by the goodwill of its ecclesiastical promoters and the commendations of the Papal See, this University of Dublin, like its predecessor, perished in undistinguished infancy. It seems, indeed, to have survived for a time the neglect of those for whose benefit it was designed, but it cannot have been in active existence late in the fifteenth century, for in 1475 the Dominicans and Mendicant Friars obtained from Pope Sixtus IV. a Bull decreeing once again the foundation of a University in Dublin.† In 1496 the Bishop and clergy of the

* John Clyn, Franciscan Friar of Kilkenny (who died about 1349), in his *Annals of Ireland* has this note:

'1320. *Incipit universitas Dublinia; universitas quoad nomen, sed utinam quoad factum et rem.*'

† Further evidence of its extinction or extreme debility is given by the Act passed in 1465 by the Parliament of Drogheda to found a University in that city. The statute begins by declaring that there was then no University in the kingdom of Ireland.

province in a synod held at Christ Church taxed themselves for the support of this University, which may have been in existence during part of the sixteenth century; but not until the necessity for such an institution had been widely recognised among the colonists, laymen as well as ecclesiastics, and a movement originating in Ireland had pressed the matter upon the attention of the English Government, was the time fully ripe for the establishment of a University, likely to survive the wintry weather of Irish history. By 1550 the more cultivated of the Dublin citizens and the more enlightened of the Lord Deputies had already given serious consideration to University projects, and various schemes were from time to time propounded and discussed.*

One of these schemes, which involved the transference of the lands and revenues of the Cathedral of St. Patrick to a new collegiate body, met with support from many influential persons,† and in the end might have been carried into effect but for the strenuous opposition offered by Adam Loftus, Archbishop of Armagh. Loftus, before his translation to the See of

* The foundation of Trinity College coincided with a period of considerable intellectual activity in Dublin, which in the early part of the seventeenth century displayed itself by the publication of a large number of scholarly books. The troublous times of rebellion interfered with the Dublin printing trade, which, however, recovered by 1650, and was fairly successful during the latter half of the century.

† It was chiefly supported by Sir John Perrot, when Lord Deputy, probably on the grounds that the ancient University of Dublin had been associated with St. Patrick's. Perrot was one of the most enlightened of the Lord Deputies, who, for his too sympathetic attitude towards Ireland and the Irish, was recalled, and died in the Tower of London.

Dublin in 1567, had secured for himself as a desirable town residence the Deanery of St. Patrick's, but it seems that the terms of the appointment involved his resignation if the University scheme proceeded.* By admirable zeal and enthusiasm in furtherance of the University idea, Loftus veiled his inability to discover any merit in the St. Patrick's plan, which was finally abandoned for another scheme, in the development of which the proposal in 1569, made by Stanihurst, three times Speaker of the Irish House of Commons, may fairly be regarded as the first step. In writing to the English Council, the Lord Deputy, Sidney, referred to the proposals made by Stanihurst in Parliament, and adds, 'The matter is so well liked as hath provoked many good men to offer very liberally to help it forward.'

* Loftus had come over to Ireland as chaplain to the Earl of Sussex, and obtained the primacy at the age of twenty-eight. 'But this post, though great in honour, was little in profit. Shane O'Neill was a most disagreeable neighbour in the north country; and, indeed, in 1566, burned the Cathedral of Armagh, lest it might serve as a barrack for the Saxon. Whereupon the indignant Primate excommunicated him, which censure from a Queen's Bishop, Shane, no doubt, held lightly. Altogether, the north was unsafe and unprofitable. So he preferred, to the barren honours of the primacy and the terrors of "the O'Neill," a comfortable residence in Dublin under the protection of the soldiers of the Pale' (Heron). Loftus, besides his deanery and translation to the See of Dublin, secured for himself the Lord Chancellorship of Ireland and other unconsidered trifles. 'Besides,' says Harris, 'his promotions in the Church and his public employments in the State, he grasped at everything that became void, either for himself or his family. Insomuch that the Dean and Chapter of Christ Church were so wearied with his importunities that on August 28, 1578, upon granting him some request, they obliged him to promise not to petition or become suitor for any advowson of any prebend or living, or for any lease of any benefice, nor for any fee or farm.'

For well-nigh twenty years no practical measures were taken, but in 1590 a petition was preferred to the Mayor and Corporation of Dublin by a group of prominent citizens, foremost among whom were Luke Challoner, a Cambridge man; Henry Usher, Archdeacon of Dublin, a graduate of both English Universities; James Fullerton and James Hamilton, Scotchmen who had probably studied at St. Andrew's, and were at this time the masters of the Grammar School in Dublin. The appeal to the Corporation produced a ready response, and it was resolved not only to present a petition from the city to the Lord Deputy, but to grant the land and disused buildings of the suppressed monastery of All Hallows, outside the city walls, for the proposed College. The prayer of the Corporation was entrusted by the Lord Deputy and his Council, together with a strong recommendation in its favour, to Henry Usher for presentation to the Privy Council in England, and private letters in its support were written by the Lord Chief Justice, the Archbishop, and others interested in the undertaking. Usher's mission proved successful, and a warrant was delivered to him empowering the Mayor and Corporation to proceed with the erection of the College. The charter which followed the warrant named Cecil as Chancellor, Loftus as Provost, Challoner, Fullerton and Hamilton as the first Fellows, and declared that the College should be 'the mother of an University, for the better education, training, and instruction of scholars and students.' The phrase here employed, *mater universitatis,* has been variously interpreted by the learned and by the ingenious, but we may take it that no strict or legal sense was intended, and that no more was understood by an expression so indisputably poetical than that Trinity, while it was the first College, might prove the nucleus of a University, the development of which could only be left to the future.

The original promoters of the University thus founded were men of culture and scholarship, for whom the word University had real meaning, and it is far from probable that they were in sympathy with the language of the Queen's warrant, which professed to find the newly-established College chiefly useful as a means of educating at home those students

'whereof many have usually heretofore used to travaile into ffrance, Italy and Spaine to gett learning in such forreigne universities, whereby they have been infected with poperie and other ill qualities, and soe became evill subjects.'

Loftus, as became a man of the world, appealed to the citizens of Dublin by recounting among others the advantages to trade which such an establishment in their midst might well provide, and added:

'I pray you consider . . . that the erecting of a College will not only be a means of civilizing the nation, and of enriching the city, as I have already observed unto you, but that your children by their birth in this place will, as it were, fall opportunely into the lap of the Muses, and that you need not hazard them abroad for the acquiring of foreign accomplishments, having a well-endowed University at your door.'

The land and buildings of the Augustinian Priory of All Hallows, situated outside the city walls, had become the property of the Mayor and Corporation of Dublin in 1538 on the dissolution of the monasteries by Henry VIII., as a reward for the loyal assistance they had given to the King at the time of the rebellion of Silken Thomas. The monastery, founded in 1166 by Diarmuid, son of Murchart, King of Leinster, had been distinguished and prosperous. Its Prior had been a member of the House of Lords, it had played an influential part in the religious history of Ireland, and in its later years found favour in the eyes of Norman Barons and of English Kings. The piety of wealthy donors had given dignity to the establishment, and the Geraldines had marked their reverence for its sacred traditions by making its cloisters the burial-place of the chiefs of their clan. No nobler or more fitting site for University purposes than that upon which Trinity College stands could now well be imagined, but at the time of the grant the old monastic buildings were dilapidated or in ruins, and the meadow-land and orchards of the Aroasian brotherhood let for grazing at a rent of £20 a year.

To raise funds for the necessary buildings and improvements was the first care of the promoters of the University scheme after the warrant and charter had been received. Lord Deputy Fitzwilliam accordingly issued a letter to all the Irish baronies, requesting the gentry to subscribe in money, lands, or chattels

'to the putting forward of so notable and excellent a purpose as' (he wrote) 'this will prove to the benefytt of the whole countrey, whereby knowledge, learning and civilitie may be increased to the banishing of barbarisme, tumults and disordered lyving from among them, and whereby their children and children's children, especially those that be poore (as it were in an orphants hospitall freely) may have their learning and education geven them with much more ease and lesser charges, than in other Universities they can obtain yt.'

The appeal thus made, it is important to note, without distinction of creed, was favourably received, and about £2,000,* a large sum in those days, contributed by the wealthier colonists. These gifts enabled the work of building to be taken in hand, and the foundation-stone of the College, *sacrosanctæ et individuæ Trinitatis, juxta Dublin*, was laid on March 16, 1591, by the Mayor; a seal was struck in which the arms of the city were combined with a device (not very successful from a heraldic standpoint), representing the royal, national, and academic character of the institution, and in January, 1593, the College was opened for the admission of students.

It was universally recognised that, to employ a phrase of Loftus, the College was 'raised out of the bowels of the city's bounty,' and the undoubted enthusiasm which its establishment evoked is sufficiently proved by the tradition recorded by Fuller:

'Nor must it be forgotten that what Josephus reports of the temple built by Herod—" During the time of the building it rained not in the day time, but in the night, that the showers might not hinder the work" (*Antiq. Jud.*, lib. xv., cap. 20)—I say what by him is reported hath been avouched to me by witnesses above exception, that the same happened here from the founding to the

* Equal to about £16,000 in our day.

finishing of the College; the officious heavens always smiling by day (though often weeping by night) till the work was completed.'*

Happy as were the auspices under which the College was thus founded, its prospects were far from bright. At the close of the century which gave to England her maritime supremacy by the defeat of the Spanish Armada, and her intellectual supremacy in Shakespeare and his contemporaries, Ireland was little more than the battle-ground of the Desmonds and O'Neills, and it seemed for a time far from improbable that the Elizabethan institution would share the fate of its medieval predecessors. A happy fortune preserved it during the precarious days of infancy, and until its roots had struck fast and far into the soil. The same dangers threatened this scion of English oak which had withered the plants set in the interests of religion and watered by words of Papal approbation. During the early years of its existence the College suffered from a plentiful lack of funds to carry on its work, and this despite the contributions from private persons towards its support, and the grants made from the royal revenues in Ireland. The rebellion of Tyrone rendered it impossible to obtain the rents from the province of Munster, where much of the College property was situated, and but for the special grants just mentioned the College must have closed its doors. These consisted of 'a concordatum of forty pounds per annum, and an allowance of six *morte payes* out of such charges as should be imposed on her Majesty's army,' and were

* Fuller's *Church History of Britain*.

REVENUE AND EXPENDITURE

renewed and confirmed by the Earl of Essex, the University Chancellor, when Lord Lieutenant. Elizabeth continued to show her interest in her own foundation by a fresh endowment in 1598 of £200 yearly under the Privy Seal; and James I. followed her example, when the importance of the College increased, endowing it with estates in the province of Ulster, and settling upon it a pension of £400 a year in addition to the gifts already made.*

* The total receipts of the College were in 1596 under £300; in 1615 they were something over £1,000. The items of expenditure in 1597 were as follows:

ORDINARY.

	£	s.	d.
The Provost	50	0	0
Three Fellows, £6 13s. 4d. each	20	0	0
Thirteen scholars, £4 each for twelve, and £10 for Mr. Shane's scholar	58	0	0
Butler's diet and wages	10	0	0
Cook's wages and his boy	8	10	0
A poor scholar towards learning	2	0	0
Firing, lights and other household charges, commonly called Decrements	20	0	0
Ordinary reparations of the house	13	6	8
Weekly sizings for the scholars	8	13	4

EXTRAORDINARY.

	£	s.	d.
Increase of charges for bread and beer above other ordinary years, from dearth of the time	40	0	0
Strengthening of weak and dangerous parts of the house	20		0
For travel into England, and continuing there suitors six months for enlarging our grant; for passing some part of said book, and some part of Mr. Shane's grant; and for Counsel in Laws for drafts of our several conveyances to the tenants	108	0	0
Total	£358	10	0

Loftus did not long remain Provost, surcharged as he was with the weight of other and more lucrative appointments, and on his resignation in 1594, the choice of the Fellows, in whose hands the election at that time lay, fell upon another Cambridge man, also of Trinity College, Walter Travers, a Puritan, a learned Orientalist, author of *Ecclesiastica Disciplina*, and a friend of Thomas Cartwright, the English Puritan. To Cecil, his friend and patron, Travers wrote, giving his impressions of the College:

'Being a quadrant of brick of three stories, and on every side within the court it is 120 feet broad; the west side which is of chambers, and the north side wherein are the chapel, hall, buttery, and kitchen, are orderly finished. The other two sides are only walls, having some little beginning of chambers, which for want of further means is yet unperfect. If the whole were finished it would conveniently lodge 200 scholars and twenty fellows.'

The small quadrangle of the Elizabethan College, with its buildings of red brick, surmounted on the north by the steeple, which had been part of the Aroasian priory, was certainly characterized by no architectural splendour. It was not until the beginning of the eighteenth century that the library, the first of the present great buildings, was erected, and the College began to take on the air of severe magnificence which now distinguishes it.

Between the gates of the sixteenth-century College and the castellated walls of Dublin lay the Green, upon which swine and cattle grazed, interfering with the comfort and security of pedestrians, hardly less than

EARLY COMMENCEMENTS

the sturdy beggars whose appeal for alms was liable by night to be associated with violence. A stream crossed the common, upon which there were then no buildings save a few cottages, to which early in the seventeenth century were added a hospital and a bridewell.

Provost Travers, zealous though he was in the discharge of his duties, found exile in a land vexed with civil wars too great a burden, and, losing his health, resigned the headship of the College in 1601. The Fellows chose as his successor a no less determined Puritan, Henry Alvey, also a Cambridge man, who became the first Vice-Chancellor of the University, and held office until 1609. The first public commencements seem to have been held in the first year of Alvey's provostship, but that degrees were granted before that date we gather from the description of Ussher as 'Sir Ussher' in 1599. A description of the ceremonies accompanying the conferring of degrees in the seventeenth century is given in *Desiderata Curiosa Hiberniæ*:

'The 18th of August, 1616, there was a great Commencement holden in the University of Dublin, but because the rooms in Trinity College were very small, they held their acts of disputation in the high choir of St. Patrick's Cathedral; and there proceeded that day five Doctors in Theology, videlicet: Dr. Jones, Lord Chancellor, and Dr. King, Bishop of Elphin, by grace; Dr. Ussher, Dr. Richardson, and Dr. Walsh, in public disputation; Bachelors of Divinity, 3; Masters of the Arts, 15; Bachelors of the Arts, 17. Being in all 38 graduates that commenced, with two others incorporated.

14 FOUNDATION AND EARLY YEARS

'The manner of this Commencement was accomplished in the following order:—First, Dr. Hampton, Arch Lord-bishop of Ardmagh and "Primate of all Ireland," who, having many years before proceeded Doctor in Theology, in the University of Cambridge, was now, at this Commencement, incorporated into the University of Dublin, and was Senior Doctor and Moderator of theological acts in the Commencement: so, upon the day appointed (18th of August), the said Dr. Hampton, Lord Primate, together with the Provost, Fellows and Scholars of the House, passed from the College, through the city of Dublin, in very stately order, for the Lord Primate, and other ancient doctors, and also those that were to proceed doctors, were every one attired in scarlet robes, with their doctors' hoods: also the Bachelors of Divinity, the Masters and Bachelors of Arts, were attired in such other scholar-like attire as appertained to them—which made a very beautiful appearance to the sight of all men; and they were farther graced with the presence of the Lord Deputy, the Lord Chancellor, Sir Thomas Ridgeway, Knt., Treasurer, and the Treasurer at War, with divers others of the council, who followed after them, and sate in the Cathedral to hear their disputations and discourses, which were performed as followeth: First, on entering St. Patrick's Cathedral, the Masters and Bachelors of Arts sat down in the places appointed for them, each according to his degree. Likewise Dr. Dunne, being a Doctor in the Civil Law, and Vice-Chancellor of the University, took his place which was appointed for him in the choir—and then Mr. Anthony Martin, Proctor for the College, ascended up into one of the pulpits, as Moderator of the Philosophical Acts; and the Lord Primate, who was Father for the day, of the Theological Acts, with those three who were to proceed in the public disputation, as also two Bachelors of Divinity, did ascend up to their places which were appointed for them on the right side of the choir; and when the Lord Deputy, and the Lord Chancellor, and the Council were placed, and all things in good order, Dr. Dunne, the Vice-Chancellor, began an oration in Latin, being as an introduction into all the Acts of that day's dispensation, which he performed learnedly; and when he had ended his oration, the Primate began another, also in Latin, commencing the Act of Divinity, and those that were to commence doctor. This oration contained a long discourse, in which he administered four academical consequences, as here do follow in order :—

'1st. He set them in his chair.
'2nd. He gave them square caps.
'3rd. He delivered to them the Bible.
'4th. He put rings upon their fingers.

'These ceremonies were administered separately to each of them—first to Dr. Ussher, then to Dr. Richardson, and lastly to Dr. Walsh; the Lord Primate expounding to them the signification of each ceremony.

'This manner of commencment was never used in Ireland before this time.

'Now all things being thus performed by the Lord Primate, Dr. Ussher went down into the choir, and ascended up into one of the pulpits, where he made a sermon-like oration upon the text, "*Hoc est corpus meum*," and after a long discourse thereon, the other two doctors (Richardson and Walsh) disputed with Dr. Ussher upon the same point; in which disputation, the Lord Primate, who was Father of the Theological Acts, was also Moderator; and having finished the Act, they rose up and returned to Trinity College, where a stately dinner was provided for the Lord Deputy and Council, and thus were completed all things concerning the Acts of Commencement in the

University of Dublin, to their high credit and commendation.'

Of the early Fellows, Luke Challoner seems to have been the ablest and most energetic. His learning, business capacity, and overflowing energy,* were of inestimable service to the infant College, of which, among those who knew, he was regarded as the virtual founder. The lines upon his tomb in the Chapel gave expression to this judgment among his contemporaries:

> *Conditur hoc tumulo Chaloneri triste cadaver*
> *Cujus ope et precibus conditur ista domus.*†

Challoner devoted a great part of his time to the direction of University affairs, and on several occasions visited England, once in connection with negotiations for an additional endowment, and on another occasion with Ussher to purchase books for the newly-founded library. Hamilton and Fullerton both attained to high social rank, the former being raised to the peerage under the title of Viscount Clandeboye, and the latter knighted and employed by James I. on important diplomatic missions.

With the accession of James I., who, whatever may be said of his strength or weakness as a King, acted as a generous patron of learning, the University became

---

* Sufficiently evidenced by his prowess as a preacher. 'From his own memorandum it appears that prior to 1607 he had preached no fewer that 1,428 sermons, of which number 379 were on the Book of Genesis.'—STUBBS: *History*, p. 23, note.

† On the wall beside the staircase to the gallery in the old chapel was written the following translation:

'Under this staircase lies Chaloner's sad carcase,
By whose prayers and entreaties this house now so great is.'

possessed of several important rights. In 1613 he conferred upon it the valuable privilege of returning two members to Parliament—a privilege curtailed by the Act of Union, but restored in the reign of William IV.—and to him the College owes its valuable estates in Ulster. Against these benefits may be set the general effects of his narrow ecclesiastical policy. Toleration was the note of the Elizabethan policy in Ireland, and before the accession of James I. Roman Catholics who abstained from politics were rarely called upon to answer for their faith. It was probably inevitable, however, that an attempt should be made to secure the triumph of Reformation principles in Ireland, foredoomed to failure as was that attempt. The existence of the Irish language was a greater bar to the progress of those principles than the most far-sighted politicians had foreseen, nor did Celt or Norman, native or English by blood, see anything attractive in the new heresy, which their natural enemies, the representatives of the English Government, so persistently forced upon their attention. The success of the Reformation in England, its failure in Ireland, and the consequent breach between the intellectual and religious ideals of the two countries, remains, as those who know Ireland are aware, the chief difficulty in the solution of all outstanding Irish problems.* It is none the less certain,

* As early as 1603 we have evidence that the College was looked upon with suspicion by some Roman Catholics. Dr. Mahaffy quotes (*Book of Trinity College, Dublin*, p. 16) from the Jesuit Father Fitzsimon's *Life and Letters* an interesting passage: 'A certain illustrious Baron,' he writes, 'whose lady, my principal benefactress, sent his son to Trinity College. Notwithstanding my obligations to them for my support, I, with the utmost freedom, earnestness

however, that the gruesome barbarity, wholesale and fraudulent confiscations of land, and abominable perfidy of the English Government in Ireland in the seventeenth century exacerbated the religious animosities of the time. In themselves, religious differences could never have given rise to that inextinguishable hatred of England of which Irish history gives unceasing evidence.*

Little printing was done in Ireland during the sixteenth century, and though there is proof that the College authorities were alive to the importance of establishing a University press, we may surmise from the few facts that constitute our only evidence that a printer's services were not easily obtainable. A paper is extant, bearing the date 1596, which sets forth the proposals made by the College to a printer named William Kerney, who had been sent over to

---

and severity, informed and taught them that it was a most impious thing, and a detestable scandal, to expose their child to such education. The boy was taken away at once, and so were others, after that good example.'

* See Lecky's *Ireland in the Eighteenth Century*. 'In Munster, after Desmond's rebellion, more than 574,000 acres were confiscated, and passed into English hands.' In Ulster, 'no less than six counties were confiscated, and planted with English and Scotch.' 'The project of making a plantation of Connaught similar to the plantation of Ulster was devised and adopted . . . when the death of James interrupted the scheme. It is not surprising, under these circumstances, that on the accession of Charles I. a feverish and ominous restlessness should have pervaded Irish life. The army was increased. Religious animosities became much more apparent than before. The security of property was shaken to the very foundation. The native proprietors began to feel themselves doomed to certain and speedy destruction' (vol. i., pp. 18 and 30).

Ireland by Elizabeth and the Lords of the Council for the purpose of printing the New Testament and other books in Irish for Church use, but it does not appear that the contract was ever carried out, though Kerney had already been employed as a printer in the College. The text of the proposals, quoted by Dr. Stubbs,* are of interest as showing the social position attainable by a capable printer in that age, equivalent to that of an artist in our own time:

'1. He (Kerney) should be allowed the use in the College during his life of a suitable chamber for his printing, and another for himself.

'2. Also for himself a Fellow's Commons during his life, at the Fellows' table.

'3. He should be allowed lodging for a boy, and his Commons at the lower Scholars' table, Kerney paying for it when he was able.

'4. The College issuing to him the balance of 200 marks, and even £20 besides, for the completion of his work.

'5. The College allowing him the benefit of all copies sold; and

'6. The College undertaking to help him in printing any other fit books for his own benefit.'

The teaching was, however, practically independent of books, for the simple reason that they were not obtainable by the average student. Nor was the library, when founded, open to them, for the statutes confined its use to the graduates of the University. We have, however, no reason to believe that the teaching of those days was meagre or the standard

* *History of the University*, p. 22.

low. Ussher's chaplain, Bernard, gives an account of the routine, which shows how progress in learning was made without books, and that both lecturers and students worked hard.

'Though at first there were but four Fellows,' he writes, 'yet the tongues and arts were very exactly taught to all the students, who were divided into several classes. Each tutor read Aristotle's text in Greek to his pupils; yea, each Fellow read three lectures a day, at each of which there was a disputation maintained either upon the present or the precedent lecture, and sometimes they were ordered to dispute *more Socratico*. On Saturdays, in the afternoon, each tutor read a divinity lecture in Latin to his pupils, dictating it (as they did all other their lectures) so deliberately that they might easily write after them, to their great benefit and advantage.'

The lectures of the time, always delivered in Latin, comprised prelections upon Divinity, Philosophy (chiefly, one imagines, Scholastico-Aristotelian), and Astronomy (the Ptolemaic system). Hebrew was regarded as of fundamental importance, but the study of mathematics, in the pursuit of which science the Fellows of Trinity afterwards achieved so great distinction, seems at this period to have been almost entirely neglected, and it was not until the reign of Henry Cromwell as Chancellor that serious attention was paid to it.* Judged by its results, the education given during the earliest years of the College was at least equal to that obtain-

* 'In Puritan times the mathematics were, comparatively speaking, neglected at Cambridge; and in the latter half of the following century, after the mathematical revivals about 1645 and 1708, metaphysical and moral questions began to monopolize the schools.'—WORDSWORTH: *Schola Academica*, p. 23.

able in any University of the time, and it is clear that in this, as in other matters, the University of Dublin owes not a little to the excellent policy which secured its early Provosts, and occasionally its Fellows, from among Oxford and Cambridge Dons, and so established from the first a high tradition of learning, while it led to the friendly usage, still in existence, which permits graduates of Dublin to become members of either of the English Universities without further residence or academical exercises, a privilege which is, of course, reciprocal.*

It may be well here to remark that any real distinction between Trinity College and the University of Dublin still remains to be drawn. During the provostship of Sir William Temple, and on his initiative, an attempt was made to secure separate charters for the College and the University. That attempt proved unsuccessful, and much ill-informed criticism has been directed against this academy of a single college on the assumption that its natural development has in some malign fashion been arrested. It is a common error to suppose that the ancient, and therefore presumably orthodox, type of University is that afforded by Oxford

* Fuller calls the University of Dublin a *colonia deducta* from Cambridge. This is true in a very partial sense; but Dublin certainly owes much to Cambridge, little to Oxford. The charter of Elizabeth recommends the adoption of the laws of Oxford and Cambridge, as do also those of Charles and of James. That this tradition was cherished and maintained we know from such entries as that (June 15, 1701) of a resolution of the Board to observe the *customs of Oxford*. Temple had been a Fellow of King's, and Challoner a graduate of Trinity, Cambridge; hence the close similarity between the statutes of Trinity, Dublin, and those of these Cambridge foundations.

and Cambridge,—the union of several Colleges under one Chancellor representing a central government. The Academies of Paris and Bologna did not provide for the students who frequented them any houses of residence, and the organization of the English Universities, whether prior to or following on the erection of Colleges, was entirely independent of all such private teaching-houses. Probably, therefore, in the constitution of the University of Dublin, which consists of but one College, that *sacrosanctæ et individuæ Trinitatis*, we have a more exact reproduction of the *Studium Generale* of the Middle Ages. The features of the younger sister reveal more truly the characteristics of a common ancestry. However desirable, then, may be the system of higher education, which in a diversity of parts retains an unmistakable individuality, no charge of arrested development can be laid against Dublin, because she has not increased her halls of residence. The attempts to alter the constitution made by her early heads, Oxford or Cambridge men, each of whom conceived, naturally enough, that in his own alma mater was to be found the most perfect type, and who were anxious to fashion the Irish University after the same model, all ended in failure.

A Trinity Hall, opened in 1617, served as a place of residence and tutorial instruction until the Rebellion of 1641, but it appears that it was found inconvenient, and

'in no wise fit to entertain students of the College, for there were so many buildings interposed between it and Trinity College that it was not possible in Trinity Hall to

THE WEST FRONT

hear Trinity College bell, by which the actual students thereof were summoned almost hourly to Divine service, meals, and exercises.'*

By 1640 the building had fallen into a dilapidated and ruinous condition, and was soon after occupied by Dr. John Stearne, one of the Fellows, who received permission to repair and use the building as a meeting-place for the city physicians. This was the beginning of the Royal College of Surgeons in Ireland, for which a charter was obtained after the Restoration.† The arrangement made with Stearne was

'that the College should have the nomination of the President of the College of Physicians, and that the President and Fellows of that College should give their professional services without fees to the Provost and Senior Fellows of Trinity College and their successors whenever they should require them to attend them during illness.'

It appears that the Hall was also to be used by medical students of the University, but there is no record to tell us whether there were any in residence there at

* See Stubbs' *History*, pp. 103-105. Trinity Hall occupied the site of a bridewell, sold by the city to the University for £30. It was built on Hoggin Green, lying between the present Trinity Street and Exchequer Street.

† A letter of Bedell's, dated 1628, to Archbishop Ussher, is of interest in this connection. 'At my being in Dublin,' he writes, 'there came to me one Dr. De Lanne, a physician, bred in Immanuel College, Cambridge, who in speech with me discovered their purpose to procure a patent like to that which the College of Physicians hath in London.' In another letter he adds: 'I suppose it hath been an error all this time to neglect the faculties of law and physic, and attend only to the ordering of one poor College of Divines.'

Stearne's death in 1669, and his project of a medical college or hall produced no permanent result.

Other attempts to add a College to the University were made in 1630. On the suppression of the Carmelite Seminary of Jesuits by Lord Ely in that year, their hall and property were handed over to the Fellows of Trinity College, by whom they were remodelled, and named the New College.* A Rector was appointed, and lectures were given, which, we are told, ' the Lords Justices often countenanced with their presence.' This Hall had also but a brief tenure of existence, and was eventually reconverted by Strafford to its original purpose as a Mass-house. Sir William Brereton, who visited Dublin in 1635, mentions this Hall, and also speaks of St. Stephen's Hall or Kildare Hall, in Bridge Street, which was acquired in the same year by the College, and seems for a time to have been occupied by scholars and other students.†

During the Commonwealth period the proposal to establish another College within the University of Dublin was again seriously considered, and the papers of Henry Cromwell include a complete and generous scheme, dated 1658,‡ for the expansion of the Uni-

---

* When in possession of the Jesuits this College had assumed the right of conferring degrees.

† The College accounts contain such entries as these (see Stubbs' *History*, p. 63, note):

'1630. The Rector of Kildare Hall and 9 or 10 Scholars are charged for Kitchen Buttery Sizings, and an extra dinner on Christmas Day.

'1633. Christmas Day. For College, Kildare Hall, and Bridge St., 10 Fellows, 22 Scholars, wine, £1 2s.'

‡ For the details of this scheme, see Urwick's *Early History of Trinity College, Dublin*, pp. 63-68.

versity by the addition of a new College, an increase in the number of 'public' Professors, and the establishment of a Free School. The site selected for the College was the Baggotrath land by Stephen's Green, and for the School, St. Sepulchre's, by St. Patrick's Church. In 1657 Cork House and Gallery were actually transferred to the Lord Deputy for the library. Archbishop Ussher's books, purchased by the army in Ireland, were to be placed there as the nucleus of the collection.

These and other similar schemes met, however, with no success, and since the reign of Charles II. the authorities of Dublin University have ceased to think seriously of assimilating that institution to the English model.*

* 'A scheme for establishing a new University in Armagh, chiefly for the benefit of the Dissenters, was under consideration in 1799, but was ultimately abandoned. The grounds on which the Duke of Portland principally objected to it are curious and significant. He thought that it was not desirable to stimulate Dublin University by the emulation of a second University, *as the students in Trinity College were already too apt to injure their health by overwork;* and he also thought it very desirable that, after the Union, the higher order of Irishmen should be educated as much as possible in England, or (if they were Presbyterians) in Scotland.'—LECKY: *History of Ireland*, vol. v., p. 170, note.

CHAPTER II

THE SEVENTEENTH CENTURY: PROVOSTSHIP OF TEMPLE—
CHANCELLORSHIP OF LAUD—THE COMMONWEALTH

WITHOUT doubt, the intention of Queen Elizabeth and her advisers was to establish in the University of Dublin a thoroughly national institution. Provision was made for the education of the 'natives,' aspirants after culture from beyond 'the Pale' of English civilization, and lectures in the Irish language were instituted in order that students who were ignorant of English might not thereby be excluded from the benefits of University teaching. It is not impossible that the true object of these benevolent provisions was the conversion of such Roman Catholic students as might stray into the educational net, but it ought to be remembered that Roman Catholics contributed liberally to the funds of the original endowment, that no religious tests were instituted,* that it was not incumbent upon the Fellows to take Orders, and that a number of the early students were Papists. In face of these facts it cannot be

* That Fellows must be members of the Established Church was first enacted by the charter of Charles I.

asserted that the Trinity College of the sixteenth century was under ecclesiastical dictation, or its policy governed by any exclusive system. Not until the accession of James I., who, while favouring the Universities in his realm, set his face against Dissent, was the campaign opened against Roman Catholicism in Ireland, which not only rendered nugatory all attempts to preserve a wide and unsectarian basis for higher education in the country, but so inflamed the religious animosities of the day as to postpone for centuries that fusion of the better-educated classes without which no settlement of the political problem in Ireland is, or can become, possible. It has been already remarked that the early Provosts sensibly inclined towards Puritanism, and the sagacious have suggested that Lord Burghley, in the exercise of his patronage, found the newly established College a convenient shelter for such of his friends as were debarred by the complexion of their religious convictions from promotion in England. Perhaps the same policy carried on by his son led, on Alvey's resignation, to the appointment in 1609 of William (afterwards Sir William) Temple, the first lay Provost, but none the less a Puritan. Temple, a man of considerable parts, who had been secretary in turn to Sir Philip Sidney and Robert, Earl of Essex, embarked, when he had taken over his new office, upon a career of enlargement and reform. Within five years he had achieved important changes, and had so skilfully ordered the financial affairs of the College that the revenue permitted of the increase of the Fellows from four to sixteen, and of the scholars from twenty-eight to seventy. Temple also planned an excellent scheme for the apportionment of the University business among a number of officials, whose duties were regulated and defined. These included a Professor of Theological Controversies,* now known by the less threatening title of Regius Professor of Divinity, two Deans, a Bursar, a Catechist, a Librarian, an Auditor, a Bedell, Lecturers, and other minor officers, many of whose titles and duties remain unchanged at the present time. Probably, however, the most far-reaching of the constitutional changes due to Temple was his introduction of a distinction between Senior and Junior Fellows, and the exclusion of the latter from any share in the government of the College. This change, despite some obvious advantages, proved in later years, and even down to the present time, a source of weakness to the corporation, and in Temple's own day gave rise to a violent controversy between the two bodies.†

In 1613 Abbot, Archbishop of Canterbury, who had become Chancellor, endeavoured to introduce some further alterations into the statutes, with which he was dissatisfied as 'flat puritanical.' He wrote that the King had been 'informed that the Provost and Fellows had refused to attend the chapel services on Sundays and holidays in their surplices,' and 'commanded them in the King's name to conform to the laws and decent regulations of the realm, upon pain of losing their places.' Temple replied that he had

* Joshua Hoyle, of Magdalen College, Oxford, afterwards one of the Westminster Assembly of Divines, was the first occupant of the chair.

† For the details of Temple's and those of Challoner's rival and unsuccessful scheme for the organization of the College, see Stubbs' *History*, pp. 39-41.

accepted the provostship on 'Dr. Challoner's protestation that the Provost was a mere civil officer, and that he should not be tied for any respect of the same either to enter the ministry or to use the habits and vestments of ministers,' and it does not appear that the recalcitrant members of the body were forced to assume the hated habiliments. It is certain that many of the Fellows, including Ussher, sympathized with Temple's attitude, and a firm resistance was offered to the Archbishop when, in 1616, he proposed that the Elizabethan charter should be surrendered for another. Their suspicions of the Chancellor's policy were probably well grounded, for there seems little reason to doubt that their resistance to his authority would in the new charter have been visited with a serious curtailment of their dignities and privileges.

While, however, rejecting the proposal as made by Abbot, Temple and his colleagues were anxious to provide for the University administration as distinct from that of the College, and statutes were drawn up and approved for that purpose; but there the matter ended. The statutes under which both the College and the University are governed were in large measure modelled upon those of Cambridge, from which University so many of the early rulers of Trinity College were drawn. Temple as well as others paid several visits to Cambridge for the purpose of studying the regulations there in force. Had lack of statesmanlike foresight not appeared in Temple's later policy, his name might have been venerated as one of the greatest benefactors of the College, as he was beyond doubt one of the most capable of its early governors. But his proposals for the leasing of the estates, which would have resulted in some immediate profit at the expense of the future of the institution, were vigorously and most properly opposed by the Junior Fellows, and the concluding years of his life spent in bickerings which greatly impaired his reputation. Justice, however, requires the fact to be mentioned that his financial schemes were approved and supported by Ussher and Challoner—good men are not necessarily financiers—and that of the charges made against him of selfishness and nepotism no very damaging case can be built up.

The spirit of sturdy independence and devotion to literary and scientific freedom of thought which have from the first been the distinction of Dublin among British Universities owes not a little to the Puritan atmosphere of the College in its early career. Ecclesiastical methods or traditions never captured the citadel of Irish education; the attacks of Laud upon its liberties, though in a measure successful, effected no drastic change in the dominating principles of the University; and to the Puritans of the Commonwealth period must be ascribed the honour of preserving the academic cosmopolitanism of thought and feeling which served to protect it down to the present day from the follies of party politics and the transient phases of religious dogmas.

An interesting episode of Temple's period connects the College with the Papal Inquisition. In the MS. records of the Inquisition brought from Italy to France at the close of the last century, and preserved in the library of Trinity College, appears the statement of a certain Thaddæus O'Farrihy, a Roman Catholic priest,

THE COLLEGE AND THE INQUISITION 31

who voluntarily gave himself up to the Court for the reasons which appear in the following extract:

'I am the offspring of Catholic parents, and as I was brought up, so to the present time I have lived in a Catholic manner; but two years ago from the month of April I entered the College of Heretics in the City of Dublin in Ireland on account of poverty, and I was received because I signified to the Heads of that College that I would follow their Sect or Religion, saying also that I was a Catholic priest. Whereupon they received me kindly, and supported me, so that I was in want of nothing; and they instructed me in the doctrine of a certain author Ramus, in the Science of Logic, which author is a Heretic; and I used to be present at their sermons and prayers, and in all respects I lived outwardly according to their custom; and I continued in the said College during the space of about ten months, eating flesh on every day without distinction, neither celebrating Mass nor hearing it, and not confessing my sins sacramentally.'*

For this scandalous sojourn in the tents of wickedness O'Farrihy was sentenced by the Holy Office to visit seven Privileged Altars, to fast on Fridays upon bread and water for three years, and once in the week to recite the seven Penitential Psalms.

Before Temple's death, the name of Richard Sibbes, Preacher at Gray's Inn, was mentioned in connection with the provostship, and supported by the Chancellor, who took occasion in recommending him to take a verbal revenge upon the recalcitrant Temple. 'I send

* Extract from *The Holy Office's Book of those appearing voluntarily in the Year* 1628, fol. 929, translated from the original Latin by Dr. Gibbings, formerly Professor of Ecclesiastical History in the University.

unto you Mr. Sibbes, who can best report what I have
said to him. I hope the College shall in him have a
very good master, which hitherto it hath not had.'
Sibbes visited the College, and, though possessed of
some Puritan sympathies, was seized by no enthusiasm
for the place, and, returning to England, wrote declining the appointment. Ussher, the Vice-Chancellor,
who had recommended Sibbes to the Archbishop, thereupon wrote suggesting the name of William Bedell, of
Emmanuel College, Cambridge.* The Fellows in the
meantime played at a harmless game of election among
themselves, the Seniors choosing Mede, and the Juniors,
who by charter had an undoubted right to participate
in the election, selecting Ussher. An opportunity was
thus given to the Chancellor to override the charter by
bringing in the King's authority, and Bedell was appointed in August, 1627.† Like Sibbes, Bedell seems
to have had some inkling that the post was not altogether a pleasant sinecure, for it seems that the Archbishop found it necessary to strengthen his resolution
to accept the office by the Scriptural exhortation, 'I
will go in the strength of the Lord God,' and the
accompanying less spiritual encouragement that once in
Ireland he might hope for further preferment. The
provostship led shortly to the See of Kilmore, but
Bedell fairly earned his promotion. His righteous soul

* To whom is attributed the famous remark: 'The island was
almost entirely Popish, and its Protestant establishment had as
little effect on the religion of the people as a chariot, lashed upon
the deck of a ship, has in directing her course.'

† The Caroline statutes, to avoid such controversies in the
future, transferred the right of election to the Crown, where it still
remains.

BEDELL'S REFORMS

was not a little troubled when he entered upon his duties by the disorderly condition of College discipline and finance. 'For the College,' he wrote, 'I find a world of business.' The entries in his diary prove that he set about the task of reformation with great zeal.* The management of the College estates was utterly unregulated—'all this is nothing to the trouble about suits of land which none of the House knows what they are'—proper collegiate discipline had long been disregarded, the Fellows engaged in private quarrels to the neglect of their duties, the observances of religion had been disregarded for years, the very statutes existed only as a bundle of loose papers, 'part English, part Latin, all out of order.' The new Provost's first care was for the spiritual welfare of his charge. His diary records :

'All the Fellows and Masters absent from prayers (being Sunday), the Dean bidden to look to his duty.'

'Mr. Travers for omitting his commonplace (sermon) the second time appointed, punished 13s.'

'Mr. Tho. for omitting prayers reading, 5s.'

The Communion, discontinued for some years, was again regularly administered in the College chapel, and an arrangement for catechizing the scholars after dinner

* Among Bedell's reforms it is noted that he drew up a statute ordering that 'Noe marryed man should be a Scholar or a Fellowe.' The Elizabethan charter contained no celibacy clause, and celibacy does not seem to have been strictly enforced even after it had been ordered by the Caroline statutes drawn up by Laud in 1637. The stringent statute of 1811 put an end to further unions, though it made an exception in favour of Fellows who were at the time actually married. All restrictions on marriage were removed in 1840.

on Sunday was established. An important part of Bedell's new policy was the promotion of the study of Irish among the undergraduates. He undertook the instruction of the 'native' students in the Irish language, and arranged for a lecture in Irish and Irish prayers.* The conversion of the natives of the country from Roman Catholicism by preachers who spoke their own tongue was a cherished scheme with Bedell, as it

* Before the foundation of the College similar efforts had been made. Nicholas Walsh, Chancellor of St. Patrick's, and afterwards Bishop of Ossory, who was murdered in 1585, had interested himself in the attempt to educate and civilize the natives through their own language, and a fount of Irish type was procured from Elizabeth in 1571 and sent to Dublin. In 1573 Walsh set about translating the New Testament into Irish. In this work Trinity College took part. The types and press sent over by Elizabeth were set up in the College, under Kerney, a printer, educated at Cambridge. Kerney (see p. 18) was promised certain collegiate privileges in return for his work, but a dispute seems to have put an end to the alliance between him and the College. William Daniel, a Fellow of the College, and afterwards Archbishop of Tuam, published a translation of the Book of Common Prayer, and of the New Testament out of the Greek into Irish, which was printed, in 1602, with the dedication to King James, who had always displayed a keen interest in the religious instruction of the natives through their own language. These efforts to promote the study of Irish came to an end under Chappel. They were revived under Marsh in 1680, who himself engaged and paid for teachers, whose lectures were attended by as many as eighty students; and again, at a later period, by Vice-Provost Hall, who supported a private lecturer in Irish, and by Archbishop William King, who engaged a public teacher of Irish in the College.

Huntingdon, a friend and successor of Marsh in the provostship, had a translation of the Old Testament into Irish prepared, which was printed at the expense of the Hon. Robert Boyle in 1686. It contained only the canonical books and a preface in English by Bishop Martin. See *Hon. Robert Boyle, his Works and Life*, by Th. Birch, D.D., London, 1744.

The present Professorship of Irish was not founded until the middle of the nineteenth century.

was later with Marsh also, who had Irish sermons preached in the chapel once a month, but it seems to have found little or no favour among the English colonists. Bedell's tenure of the provostship, though short, was marked by other no less important reforms. He collected and revised the statutes, introduced an orderly system of accounts, endeavoured to place the finances on a secure basis, and to extend the scope of the College work, unwisely narrowed to the 'ordering of one poor College of Divines.' It is interesting also to note that he resisted what seemed to him the dangerous decline into luxurious habits of Dublin society, 'the newfanglednesse in apparel and long hair and ruffles wherein this city and the very greatest of the clergy are methinks very exorbitant.'

Despite his determined Protestantism, Bedell was beloved by all classes. When the rebellion headed by Phelim O'Reyly broke out in Cavan, and gave the country to fire and sword, Bedell, then Bishop of Kilmore, alone of Englishmen was permitted by the insurgents to remain at peace in his own house, which became an asylum for the homeless. He continued to preach and administer the Sacraments unmolested. When he died, O'Reyly and his followers marched to his funeral, allowed the English Church Service to be read over his grave, and fired over it a military salute, with the parting words, *Requiescat in pace ultimus Anglorum*—a magnificent tribute no less to the nobility of the man than to the generosity of the Irish nature.

In 1629, when Bedell was advanced to the bishopric of Kilmore, he was succeeded by Dr. Robert Ussher, who, according to Primate Ussher, 'albeit a very honest man, and one that minded the good of the house, yet was of too soft and gentle a disposition to rule so heady a company.' Ussher's government was marked by a continuation of Bedell's policy in promoting the study of the Irish language, and enforcing the due observance of religious duties among the Fellows. Like Bedell, of whom it is on record that he found a curious difficulty in obtaining their 'consent that punishment should be inflicted on themselves either for absenting themselves from the church, or lying out of the house, or frequenting taverns, or other such enormities,' Ussher also found his subordinates 'factious,' and within a year or two Lord Deputy Strafford, with the approval of Laud, who in 1633 became Archbishop of Canterbury and Chancellor of the University, took the advice of Primate Ussher, that his kinsman should be promoted, and that 'a man of more rigid temper and stouter disposition' should be appointed to the provostship.

The new man was William Chappel, Dean of Cashel, who had been Fellow of Christ's College, Cambridge, and who, perhaps, is best known as having been Milton's College tutor and the *Damoetas* of the elegy on King. At Cambridge he had acquired a great reputation as a 'close Ramist and a notable disputant.' He seems, indeed, to have been an unusually formidable opponent in syllogistic warfare, for an account of Commencements in Cambridge, at which James I. was present, records that 'Dr. Roberts, of Trinity College, being respondent in St. Maries, this Mr. Chappel opposed him so close and subtilely, that the Doctor, not being able to unloose the arguments, fell into a swounding in the pulpit, so as the King, to hold up the Commencement, undertook to maintain the thesis, which Mr. Chappel, by his syllogisms, prest so home, *ut rex palam gratias ageret deo, quod opponens ei fuisset subditus, non alteri; alias potuisset in suspicionem adduci perinde throno suo atque cathedra submoveri debuisset.*' 'This kind of subtlety,' says Dr. Mahaffy, commenting upon the years of misery following Chappel's nomination, ' may have enabled him to reconcile his various breaches of statute with his sworn obligations.'

It was clearly from the first the intention of Laud to effect through the agency of his nominee Chappel in the provostship, and the support of his friend the Lord Deputy, such changes in the constitution as would withdraw from the College the extensive powers of self-government it had hitherto enjoyed, but enjoyed without conspicuous advantage to itself or benefit to the country in which it had been placed. Strafford, through whom the Chancellor's policy was to be effected, had already exhibited the witchery of his methods. Ireland had never known a rule so magical in its effects. The island, though it supported a large army, supplied the Lord Deputy with an unexampled revenue; the Irish Parliament ceased to care for debate when it heard his wishes; the landlords of Connaught, members of the most ancient Irish houses, whose tenures were as old as their lineage, began to make search for their title-deeds; the Scottish settlers in Ulster accepted that accursed thing—the episcopal system. These miracles were wrought by a genial disregard for any code of morals, human or Divine, with which the islanders were acquainted, but they were none the less astonishing. And when Strafford turned his attention to the affairs of the College much was naturally expected. On the day following his election as Chancellor, Laud wrote to the Lord Deputy, 'Since they have made me Chancellor, and your Lordship approves them in so doing, I will begin to take them to task.' The College had already some experience of the persuasive methods of the Viceroy. In June, 1634, he had directed the choice of the College in the matter of its representatives in the Irish Parliament, naming Sir James Ware and James Donellan to the Provost as the burgesses whom he desired to see elected, and it was probably without surprise that the Fellows received his commands in respect of the provostship on Ussher's promotion.

'I went down to the College myself,' he wrote to Laud, 'recommending the Dean (of Cashel) to the place, told them I must direct them to choose the Dean, or else stay till they should understand his Majesty's pleasure, and in no case to choose any other. They are willing, so on Thursday next he will be Provost, and your Grace shall not need to trouble the King about it.'

For 'so heady a company' the Fellows seem to have been singularly open-minded in the presence of good arguments. Such an election opened not unfittingly an era of the most flagrant violation of statutes and impudent interference with College liberties. Chappel, who avoided taking, as Provost, the oath of adherence to the charter and statutes, made haste to take advantage of his immunity in the sight of heaven. At an election to Senior Fellowship in 1635, he passed over the three senior candidates on the ground of their declining to wear the surplice or neglecting the services in the chapel, and with the assent of two of the seniors abrogated an important statute in order to legalize his conduct. Complaint was made to the Visitors, the Provost censured, his further proceedings inhibited, and his partners in the malpractice deprived of their Fellowships. The Lord Deputy in great annoyance wrote to Laud: ' Methinks the act of the Visitors was very precipitate so sharply to expel two of the Senior Fellows, and all this for a fellow's sake that never wore a surplice.' The expelled Fellows were restored by Laud, who replied:

' That College, as your Lordship hath often acknowledged unto me, both by letters and otherwise, having been as ill governed as any in Christendom, or worse, will never be able to recover or settle . . . if both the power and credit of the Provost be not upheld by his superiors ;'

and again suggests to the Lord Deputy

' to keep a continual eye upon the malady in the College, till we shall be able to place the Provost elsewhere, and have another fit man ready to succeed him.'

Strafford, however, having found Chappel a useful instrument, was not anxious to remove him till the scheme of ' Thorough ' had been completed. A sentence in a letter to Laud is noteworthy:

' I have so great an opinion of his government and integrity that I am putting my son thither, under his eye and care, by which you will judge I purpose not to have him one of Prynne's disciples.'[*]

[*] Prynne's *News from Ipswich, discovering certain late detestable Practices of some domineering Lordly Prelates* had just been published.

There is little doubt that Chappel was in sympathy with that part of the Chancellor's policy which confined the benefits of the University to members of the established Church. In his autobiographical verses he laments the difficulties of his position:

> *Ruunt agmine facto*
> *In me profana turba Roma Genevaque;*

but there is not much evidence, despite the subsequent proceedings against him in Parliament, that he was actively interested in the affair of the new constitution. He did not, however, fail in obedience to his patrons when Laud and Wentworth proceeded with their scheme of forcing upon the College a new charter and statutes. In order to procure the assent of the governing body, of whom two only, beside the Provost, were willing to sign away their privileges, two new Fellows, Harding and Marshall, Cambridge men, were appointed by *mandamus*, and Kerdiffe, one of the existing seniors, removed to the rectory of Desertcreight. The charter was then presented to the Board, and, of course, received with becoming pleasure and gratitude, though, as was shortly apparent, there were some among the juniors who were preparing a counter-stroke.

By the new constitution, which was afterwards embodied in a charter of Charles I., the number of Visitors, hitherto inconvenient champions of the old régime, were reduced to two, the Vice-Chancellor —whose appointment now rested with the Chancellor —and the Archbishop of Dublin; the tenure of Fellowships was extended from seven years to an optional tenure for life, the appointment of the

Provost and the power of making statutes reserved to the Crown, and the authority of the Chancellor and of the Provost considerably extended.* The increase in the number of Fellows from three to sixteen, and of scholars from three to seventy, was approved and made permanent, and the government of the College was committed entirely to the Provost and seven Senior Fellows, who were empowered to make new statutes in cases not provided for in, and not repugnant to those granted by the King. Shorn as it thus was, and in the most indecent fashion, of its early liberties, it cannot with justice be asserted that the College suffered from serious evils as the result of Laud's legislation. The verdict of time—for Trinity College is still governed in the main by letters patent obtained in this reign—may even be cited in its favour, and but for the narrowing effect of the clauses introduced with the object of excluding the Junior Fellows from all share in the government, and debarring Roman Catholics from the Fellowships, might be regarded as almost wholly favourable.

The arbitrary doings of the Chancellor were not yet, however, at an end. Chappel, as a reward for his admirable docility, was in 1638 appointed to the bishopric of Cork, and, in accordance with the regulations of the new statutes, offered his resignation of the provostship. But despite the earnest remonstrance of Primate Ussher, who wrote, 'The eluding of oaths in this manner I do consider to be a matter of the most pernicious consequence,' Laud peremptorily refused to

* The Elizabethan statutes at Cambridge followed the same policy of increasing the power of the heads.

accept Chappel's resignation. Two years later, however, permission was given him to resign, and the following piece of unctuous flattery appears in the College Register:

'The Right Rev. Father in God, William, Lord Bishop of Cork, being chosen Provost 21 August, 1634, after he had graciously reformed the Students, happily procured new Statutes and rich amplifying of the buildings, beautified the Chapel, Hall, Provost's Lodgings and the Regent House, with the garden and other places, by the good advice and assistance of our worthy, learned and pious Vice-Provost, Dr. Harding, and wonderfully increased the College plate and stock, reduced all things into a blessed order, and faithfully governed by the space of six years as a glorious Pattern of sobriety, justice, and godliness, resigned his Provostship this day.'

This view of Chappel's doings as Provost and the 'blessed order' which he had established was not widely shared, and he was soon to have less pleasant phrases fall upon his ear. There were some among the Junior Fellows who possessed sufficient influence to procure a Parliamentary inquiry into his conduct, and on March 4, 1640, the Irish House of Commons proceeded to an investigation.

It was complained that the government introduced into the College by the late Provost, and used there since the procuring of the late charter, had 'subverted the ancient and first foundation thereof, and doth wholly tend to the discouragement of the natives of this kingdom,' that he had 'put back the natives who ought to be preferred to Scholarships and Fellowships, and fetched strangers of his pupils in Cambridge though less learned than the natives, and preferred them to the Fellowships and Offices in the College and Scholars' places,' that, in addition to dispensing with the mathematical and Hebrew lectures, he had abolished the Professorship of Irish, originally intended to be one of the most important of all, that he had assisted in the alteration by which 'the Mayor of Dublin, at whose instance the College was founded, and the site and lands on which the College stands by him given, was ungratefully put forth from being a Visitor,' that after his acceptance of the bishopric of Cork he had continued Provost of the College for two years, 'contrary to the statutes to which he was sworn,' and, finally, that the College property was so mismanaged at his hands as to suffer serious diminution.

On June 9, 1641, the Commons, after an investigation of these charges, voted *nemine contradicente* that

'all and every the proceedings of William Chappel, late Provost of Trinity College, Dublin, and now Lord Bishop of Corke, since he assumed upon himself the office of being Provost of the said College, and during his continuance in the said office, are great grievances and fit to receive redress.'

The Commons also voted that the new charter should be discharged, and the first foundation and charter re-established, and empowered the Committee of the House then in England to supplicate His Majesty for speedy redress. These motions were carried in June, 1641, but in October of that year the Irish Rebellion broke suddenly and fiercely forth, giving to the Government more serious matter for deliberation than even the mismanagement or spoliation of the University. Chappel was imprisoned for a few months by order of the Upper House, but was set at liberty in December, and fled to England like many other Englishmen who held official posts in Ireland. Nor did he find it expedient to return even when in 1647 the Parliament, before its dissolution by Cromwell, found time for further orders and investigations in connection with the charges made against him.

Though originally founded for the education of Irishmen without distinction of creed, it is hardly surprising that Trinity College should have become almost exclusively a University for members of the Established Church. Upon the shoulders of Laud the responsibility for the legislation which excluded Roman Catholics must indeed rest, but though the gates had not been absolutely shut against members of alien creeds, the statutes from the beginning of the seventeenth century had been so framed as practically to exclude both Roman Catholics and Protestant Dissenters from the scholarships and Fellowships. By the Caroline charter the oaths administered to Fellows and scholars, which in Bedell's statute-book did not differ, were altered so as to exclude all Roman Catholics from Fellowships, but left it possible for such scholars as were prepared to deny the Pope's temporal power in the English realm to subscribe and receive the emoluments. It was not to be expected, however, that many Roman Catholics would enter the University in the face of such clauses as the following :

'Moreover it shall be the duty of the Provost and Senior Fellows to take heed that no opinion of Popish or

ATTITUDE TOWARDS NONCONFORMISTS 45

heretical doctrine be supported or propounded within the boundaries of College, whether publicly or privately. Which, if it shall happen, we will that the progress of the impious doctrine be intercepted as soon as possible. Besides that no one shall be elected into the number of Fellows who shall not have renounced the Popish religion (so far as it differs from the Catholic and Orthodox) and the jurisdiction of the Pope, by a solemn and public oath.'

These clauses fairly represent the policy of Laud, but, in spite of regulations sufficiently explicit, the authorities of the College studiously avoided any public inquiry into the religious tenets of undergraduates. Until 1794 no student was required to make any declaration of his creed at entrance, and it appears that even those who lived within the walls were not forced to attend the services of the chapel if known to be Dissenters. While, therefore, the undergraduate courses were virtually open to all comers, and even scholarships obtainable by Nonconformists whose consciences were not too nice, the oath of supremacy and declaration against Transubstantiation barred the gate of graduation against all who were not members of the State Church. When the movement for the abolition of the penal laws against Roman Catholics achieved its slowly-won success, it naturally brought in its train the removal of their educational disabilities, and in 1793, the disabling Acts having been abolished by Parliament, a King's letter altering the statutes was obtained, and the degrees in the University of Dublin thrown open to all comers.

Richard Washington, Fellow of University College, Oxford, who succeeded Chappel in 1640, remained in

Ireland for one year, and then, following the example of his courageous predecessor, fled to England in October, 1641. The affairs of the College now became very critical. In England the year 1641 saw the execution of Strafford, the impeachment of Laud, and the abolition of the Star Chamber and the Court of High Commission. The 'Root and Branch' Bill, which split the Parliamentary party, had brought some hope into the Royalist camp, which was dispelled, however, by the rebellion in Ireland. The removal of the iron hand of Strafford gave the opportunity against the hated yoke. The Anglo-Irish Catholics of the Pale joined with the natives. In Ulster a number of the colonists were butchered by Sir Phelim O'Neill and his followers. Many thousands more were driven from their homes into obscure hiding-places, to perish of cold or of famine. A letter purporting to have come from the King was shown by O'Neill as a warrant for his rising to support the royal authority against the Parliament, and fuel was added to the Puritan indignation by the proof thus offered of the King's duplicity and treachery.

On the outbreak of the rebellion it became impossible to collect the rents of the College estates in Ulster and Munster, many of which were in the hands of the insurgents, and it was soon found necessary to pawn or sell the valuable plate presented in better days by the noblemen and gentlemen whose sons had passed through the University. By the money thus raised, by occasional State grants,* and by public subscription,

* The petition of the College for assistance was referred to Sir Francis Willoughby, Sergeant-Major-General of the army, on whose

THE COINAGE OF COLLEGE PLATE 47

the College was with extreme difficulty preserved from ruin for the following ten miserable years. The straits to which it was reduced are abundantly proved by the entries in the Bursar's books from 1642 to 1649. A few will serve as examples :

1645, Dec. 24. Received for one College pott	£7 14 0
1646, May 28. Received for a Spanish cup coined	6 8 6
1646, Aug. 16. Received for Mr. Courtney's flagon which was coined ...	15 16 6
1646, Oct. 3. Received for a piece of plate which was broken up and coined to supply the College with provisions against the approaching siege (it had been presented by Sir Robert Trevor of Trevillin, Co. Denbigh, Governor of Newry, a former benefactor of the College)	30 19 8
1646, Oct. 10. Received for Sir Richard Irven's College pott	18 3 6
1646, Oct. 17. A candlestick coined ...	15 17 3
1646, Nov. 30. do. do. ...	15 15 0
1646, Nov. 27. Received for Sir William Wentworth's basin and ewer, weighing 128 oz. 4 dwts.	30 19 8

On Washington's desertion of the College the Council appointed Dr. Faithful Taite, a former student, and

---

advice the Lord Lieutenant and Council discharged one man out of each of the thirty-five companies, and directed that the pay of these soldiers, amounting to £3 10s., should be paid to the Bursar. Other small grants were from time to time made.

Dr. Dudley Loftus, Master in Chancery, as *temporarii subrectores*, but by an Order in Council dated April 25, 1643, Taite as being a Parliament man, and 'ill-affected to his Majesty's government,' was subsequently removed, and shortly afterwards, on the petition of Vice-Provost Hoyle and the Fellows, Anthony Martin, formerly a Fellow and at this time Bishop of Meath, but unable to reside in his diocese, owing to the rebellion, was appointed to the provostship. The Lord Deputy Ormonde, who throughout the troubles of the University remained its stanchest friend, was admitted Chancellor in 1644 in succession to Laud, then in prison, and within a year of sharing the fate of his friend Strafford upon the scaffold.

In 1647 Ormonde surrendered Dublin to the English Parliament, but Bishop Martin was left in possession of the provostship* until his death from the plague in 1650, though he declined to substitute the Directory for the Book of Common Prayer in the College chapel, and seems to have made no secret of his theological opinions.

* Martin, like most of the early Provosts, had his troubles. He expelled Richard Coghlan, a Fellow, appointed by King's letter in 1646, for the following offences:

'1. Coming to a meeting of the Board without being called when he was only a Junior Fellow.

'2. Disturbing the members of the Board with improper language.

'3. That he hath often abused Fellows and others.

'4. That his habit of dress was unstatutable.

'5. That he exhibited to the Lord Lieutenant, the Chancellor of the University, a petition against the Provost and Senior Fellows.

'6. That he did not take Priest's orders.

'7. That he publicly charged the Provost and Fellows with great offences, called the Provost a fool and a knave, and swore he would kick him.'

In 1649 the English Parliament found time to pass an Act relating to Trinity College, 'for the encouragement and increase of learning,' which vested 'all castles, lands, tenements, rents, which did heretofore belong to the late Archbishop of Dublin, the Dean and Chapter of St. Patrick, and the farm of Ardbracken, with the parsonage of Trim,' in certain trustees, among whom were named Henry Ireton, Henry Cromwell, and Ralph Cudworth.* The property was to be applied to the maintenance of Trinity College, and 'for the erecting, settling, and maintenance of one other Colledge' in the city of Dublin, and of a free school. John Owen, Cromwell's chaplain in Ireland, who was also named a trustee, resided for some time in the College, and reported on its condition to the Parliament. In 1651 we find, from a letter addressed to Owen by the Parliamentary Commissioners, that they proposed to close the College for a time, and introduce important alterations in its administration and curriculum.

'We have enquired' (the letter runs) 'into the present state of the College of Dublin, and do find it furnished with very few officers, the consideration whereof (and the House being at present visited with the pestilence) move us to dissolve that Society until it shall please God to remove the sickness.'

On Bishop Martin's death the Parliamentary Commissioners appointed Samuel Winter to attend to the College affairs, and he was regularly installed as Provost by a warrant under Cromwell's hand and seal in

* The author of *The Intellectual System of the Universe*.

THE SEVENTEENTH CENTURY

June, 1652.* Winter was an Englishman, a Cambridge graduate, and is described 'as a faithful preacher of the Divine Word and an acute vindicator of true religion.' He set vigorously about the task of restoring order and rescuing the College from its financial embarrassments. Henry Cromwell, the Lord Deputy, was chosen as Chancellor in 1653 in the place of Ormonde, who had been driven abroad by the wind of political tempest. Winter encouraged some of the old Fellows to return, and some eminent scholars among the Nonconformist ranks were elected to Fellowships.† He also on several occasions visited the estates both in the North and South to recover the rents long unpaid and due to the College. Carte in his *Life of Ormonde* senselessly describes Winter and his associates 'as intruders, and for the most part insufficient, disloyal, and eminently active in spreading faction, schism, and rebellion,' and the same tone is taken by other of the loyalist historians, but no greater service was ever rendered to the College than that performed by its rulers of the Commonwealth. Winter gave considerable sums out of his own pocket for the support of

* 'The war ended at last in 1652. According to the calculation of Sir W. Petty, out of a population of 1,466,000, 616,000 had in eleven years perished by the sword, by plague, or by famine artificially produced; 504,000, according to his estimate, were Irish, 112,000 of English extraction. A third part of the population had been thus blotted out.'—LECKY: *History of Ireland*, vol. i., p. 104.

† Henry Jones, Vice-Chancellor, who abandoned his episcopal style, and Dr. Stearne, were retained in office. Among the distinguished Nonconformists connected with the College during the Commonwealth were the Mathers, Samuel, Increase, and Nathaniel —of whom the first two were graduates of Harvard—Edward Veal, Stephen Charnock, Robert Norbury, and Jeremiah Marsden.

poor scholars, encouraged the study of the Irish language, was indefatigable in his efforts to place the University on a sound financial basis, and was instrumental in helping to establish the great mathematical school.* The Directory was of course substituted for the Liturgy, and special regulations were made affecting the religious life of the students, who were encouraged to a strict devotional life. An order made by the Lord Deputy and Council in 1654 sounds a familiar note:

'The Lord Deputy and Council being desirous to give all due encouragement to the advancement of learning, and to promote Godliness, and on the contrary to discontinue vice, and what hath a tendency to looseness and profaneness; it is therefore thought fit and ordered, that Dr. Winter, Maister of Trinity College, Dublin, do call the respective Fellows, students, and other members of the College together, exhort them to a careful walking, becoming the Ghospel, and to build up one another in the knowledge and fear of the Lord, and diligently to attend public prayer, preaching the Word, expositions and other religious duties; and also by encouraging and countenancing private Christian meetings together in the College or elsewhere, for the edifying and encouraging one another in conference, and repeating what they have heard preached of the Way of the Lord, and by frequent seeking God by prayer instructing and admonishing one another, to edify each other that they may increase in the saving knowledge of Christ.'

Such Orders in Council need not be dated; they possess the unmistakable inflection of the Puritan voice.

* The Donegal Lectureship in Mathematics was founded in 1660.

CHAPTER III

THE SEVENTEENTH CENTURY (*continued*): THE RESTORATION TO THE REVOLUTION

ORMONDE, wisest and most generous of Chancellors, returned with the Restoration to the duties of his office. A reconstruction of the governing body was inevitable. 'The pretended Provost' Winter, as the zealous royalist, Carte, styles him, and his Genevan associates, were removed, the Puritan régime abruptly terminated, and Anglican doctrine was re-established in one of its most eloquent and least bigoted representatives, Jeremy Taylor, Bishop of Down, who was chosen by Ormonde to be Vice-Chancellor. A new Provost, Thomas Seele, the first 'home' graduate who attained to the dignity, and five Senior Fellows, were appointed by a King's letter.[*] By degrees the vacant Junior Fellowships were also filled up, and by 1663[†] the

---

[*] Two of the existing Senior Fellows were retained in office—Nathaniel Hoyle, who had been Vice-Provost during Washington's absence, and Cæsar Williamson. John Stearne, M.D., a former Junior Fellow, was also appointed.

[†] In this year a Fellow named William Leckey was executed in Dublin for his part in a plot against Charles II.

number of scholars was once more brought up to the full number of seventy. Bishop Taylor, who during his visits to Dublin occupied ' the great middle chamber in Sir Richard's Scot's buildings adjoining unto the steeple,' seems to have given up much of his time to academic affairs. His affectionate interest in ' the little but excellent University of Dublin '[*] was of the utmost value at a period in its history only less menacing than 1688. It is not surprising that Taylor found 'all things in perfect disorder—indeed, as great as can be imagined to be consequent on a sad war, and an evil incompetent Government set over them ;' but the College rapidly recovered its efficiency despite the remediable lack of funds and the irremediable lack of ability and learning among the Fellows of the time. Seele, who was Dean of St. Patrick's as well as Provost, seconded the efforts of Taylor by attention to discipline, which had become relaxed,[†] to an improvement of the chapel services,[‡] to the affairs of the library, and the reconstitution on a more liberal basis of the more important chairs in the University. The Professorship of Civil and Canon Law was founded in 1668, the endowment of the Professorship of Divinity[§] increased in 1674, and the Donegal Lectureship in

[*] Preface to London edition of his *University Sermon*, 1661.
[†] That is to say, the Bachelors refused ' to cap ' the Fellows, the students haunted the town and returned to College at unstatutable hours and by unauthorized routes ; and it appears that some of the scholars were so far lost to the sense of wisdom and decency as to denounce the government of the College.
[‡] The appointment of an organist and the annual election of University preachers date from the provostship of Seele.
[§] Constituted a Regius Professorship in 1761.

Mathematics* incorporated with the Chair of Mathematics.

It would be unpardonable to omit a mention of Seele's claim to the gratitude of the eighteenth-century undergraduate. He first planted, 'upon consideration of the want of water in the College,' in its commanding position in the centre of the early quadrangle the famous College pump, which from 1670 for one hundred and thirty years was the rallying-point for the lords of misrule and their stalwart followers. With the removal of the pump to an inconspicuous site behind the chapel opened the era of a more diffused boisterousness, and a transference of many illegal student activities to the forbidding shades and horrid desolation of 'Botany Bay.'

We learn from a MS. preserved in the Bodleian† that Seele restored and beautified the old steeple, which was the only part of the ancient All Hallows' Monastery then standing, and we may conjecture from the record of various private donations for an extension of the College during his provostship that he inaugurated the building policy which in the eighteenth century gave to the University its noblest architecture. The gratitude of the College finds expression in his epitaph:

Tecta Chalonerus pia condidit ; obruta Seelus Instauravit.

Up to the end of the seventeenth century most of the public offices in Ireland were conferred upon Englishmen disappointed of promotion in their own country,

* This was founded by the Earl of Donegal about 1660, who nominated to the lectureship during his lifetime, and bequeathed his patronage to the Board.
† Smith's MSS., vol. xxi.

and little opportunity had been afforded to native talent. With Seele's appointment a new era opens. Irishmen could now receive in their own country an education which fitted them to hold the highest offices in Church and State, and the distinct type of culture which prevails at and distinguishes the University of Dublin begins to be apparent, and to receive its due recognition. No one can now pass from an experience of the life in Trinity College, Dublin, to that of Oxford or Cambridge without becoming sensible that the atmosphere is that of another climate and country.* On the whole, the Dublin man finds himself more at home on the Cam than by the Isis, but there are few who do not know the change and feel it, who are not conscious that in leaving Trinity they have left an irrecoverable something that helped to sweeten the springs of life. To define such differences as I have noted is difficult, but perhaps humour, that subtle solvent, plays a proportionately larger part in the life of the old Irish College. By sentiment, on the other hand, the conduct of the Irishman is less regulated than the Saxon mind supposes. But his refusal to regard life and his own part in it as of transcendent seriousness and importance, his far-darting imagination, his habit of playing over the surface of things with a gentle irony, his capacity for enjoyment, his conservation of energy which men call indolence, his rapid transitions from dejection to gaiety, from gaiety to dejection

* The distinction between the manner of an Oxford or Cambridge and that of a Dublin undergraduate has been aptly defined: The former assumes the air of a man to whom the world belongs, the latter that of one who doesn't care a d——n to whom it belongs.

—these are qualities which render him something of an enigma to the Englishman. With more delicately poised faculties and quicker apprehensions he suffers reverse in a world through which the momentum given by a fixed purpose weighted with stupidity carries a more vulgar soul in triumph. For him the laughter-loving gods have decreed a hard fate, that he should hew the oak in the forest and quarry the granite of the mountain with the steel of a Toledo blade.

Provost Seele died in 1674, and his place was filled by another 'home' graduate, Michael Ward, of whom we are told that 'besides his accomplishments in learning he was esteemed a person of fine conversation, and of great sagacity in dexterously managing proper conjunctures.'* Ward's career was, if brief, brilliant, for he died as Bishop of Derry, to which he was translated from Ossory at the age of thirty-nine. Thus did preferment in Ireland knock in those days at the doors of youth.

Dublin was not at the moment rich in scholars who were qualified to follow Ward. The names of men whose reputation survives are few and honourable. Dudley Loftus and Henry Dodwell were both in Ireland, but neither was available for the vacant post, and Ormonde reverted to the wise policy of securing a man of high academic qualifications and experience, even if he had to be brought from an English University. It happened that he was at this time Chancellor of Oxford as well as of Dublin, and had some years previously appointed Narcissus Marsh, a sound scholar of unusual parts, Principal of St. Alban's Hall. Marsh

* Harris's *Ware*.

was now induced to accept the Irish post, and for five and a half years filled his office with universal approbation. But the provostship, though it led directly to the highest ecclesiastical preferment, was never a sinecure, and Marsh passed to the archiepiscopal See of Dublin, and later to the primacy, through a strait gate of labour which he found extremely irksome. In his diary* he wrote :

'Finding the place very troublesome, partly by reason of the multitude of business and important visits the Provost is obliged to, and partly by reason of the ill education that the young scholars have before they come to the College, whereby they are both rude and ignorant, I was quickly weary of 340 young men and boys in this lewd, debauched town, and the more so because I had no time to follow my dearly beloved studies.'

The reason suggested in the last sentence was that which really weighed with Marsh, whose whole heart was given to the cause of learning and scientific investigation. He built a noble monument to his own memory in the library which bears his name in Dublin, where his body now rests, and had the fates been kind he might have been remembered as the founder of a Royal Society. In conjunction with Molyneux, Sir William Petty, and men of like tastes, including some Fellows of the College, he inaugurated meetings for scientific discussion which were held in his own lodgings, and himself contributed many valuable papers,† which were

* Preserved in MS. in Marsh's Library, Dublin.

† Professor Mahaffy (*Book of Trinity College, Dublin*) mentions a paper on 'Musical Sounds,' and remarks that his library contains a collection of ancient music, which proves his interest in that subject.

afterwards conveyed to the London Society and published. The Irish branch of this learned body was, however, rudely parted from the parent tree by the gale of the Civil War, which was nowhere felt more severely than in Ireland. Besides his interest in these matters, and in the cultivation of the Irish language, to which he gave unremitting attention, Marsh found time to publish a text-book of logic, the first book specially prepared for the use of undergraduates, long familiarly known as *The Provost's Logic*; he also carried on the building policy inaugurated by Seele.

'Whilst I was Provost of the College,' he wrote, 'both the Hall and the Chappell being too little and straight to receive the number of Schollers that was then increasing very much each year, I resolved upon building a new Hall and Chappell (as well as enlarging the College, to which considerable accessions y^r made to the value of above 6,000^{lb}, nearer 7,000^{lb}). But I thought it most proper to begin with the house of God, and thereupon caused the foundation of a new Chappell (much larger than the former) to be laid, and before the Structure was half finished I was removed, and Dr. Huntingdon (who succeeded me) compleated the work, the College Treasury being at that time sufficient to pay all charges. In the meantime the Schollers were forced to attend prayers in the College Hall. When the Chappell was finished the next work was to build a larger Hall, and because the old one could not be conveniently enlarged as it stood, it was necessary to pull that down, and to build a larger in its place, both in length and breadth, which was the work of some years. Whilst this was doing the Schollers having no place to eat in, they were forced to make use of the Library for yt purpose, and because the books were not chained, 'twas necessary that they should remove them into some other place . . . they laid them in heaps in some void rooms.'*

Marsh was succeeded by Huntingdon, another Oxford man, a Fellow of Merton, and an Orientalist of high attainments.† Apart, however, from his interest in the translation of the Old Testament into Irish, and the decent discharge of his duties, Huntingdon made no mark in the history of the University, and in 1688, when the College was seized by the King's troops, with an overpowering regard for his own safety, and a corresponding indifference to the fate of the College, beat a pusillanimous retreat across the Channel. The troubled affairs of the University were nobly held together by the Vice-Provost Acton, and three Irish Fellows, Thewles, Allen, and Hall, natives respectively of Meath, Down, and Kerry. When the crisis was over Huntingdon returned to Ireland, but he never resumed the duties of his office, and was rewarded for his previous services by the See of Raphoe. It appears that an interchange of civilities took place between the College and its late head, whose gift of a salver engraved with his arms is still preserved among the plate. A note of what reads like irony occurs in the

* The following entry in the Register of the Diocese of Dublin records the conclusion of part of Marsh's design:
'1684. 5 Oct. The ABp consecrated ye New Chapel of ye College of ye H. Trinity, extending from E. to West 82 feet and from N. to South 38 feet, reserving to himself and his successors ye right of visiting ye same manner as by the Statutes he has a right to visit the College at large.'

† He had been chaplain at Aleppo, and had lived eleven years in the East, during which time he collected many valuable MSS., now in the Bodleian.

address with which the Fellows accompanied their testimonial to Huntingdon, which speaks of his 'great care and kindness to the Society, and the members of it, especially in their necessity, lately in England,' but no doubt the Provost endeavoured to make up for his desertion by such services as he could safely render.

It was during Huntingdon's provostship that the first rumble of the approaching storm was heard which so nearly overwhelmed the College.* On August 7, 1686, a royal letter reached the Provost and Senior Fellows ordering them to admit Arthur Greene, a convert to Roman Catholicism, and a Bachelor of Medicine, 'to the place of Irish Lecturer, founded by Sir Thurlough O'Neill, for which lands were settled upon the College, which was bound to pay £30 a year to the lecturer.' On the explanation being given that no such endowment or lectureship existed, and that the post held by Higgins in Marsh's time had been maintained by private subscription now withdrawn, Tyrconnel,† the Lord Deputy, contented himself with a demand for a copy of the College statutes, and the matter dropped. But the unfriendly spirit displayed in the attitude of Tyrconnel seriously, and with reason, alarmed the authorities, and on the occasion in September, 1687, of the King's visit to Chester, when the Lord Deputy crossed to meet him for instructions as to the policy to be adopted towards the Protestants of Ireland, the College commissioned two of its Fellows to convey to James an address assuring him of the Society's

* See *Case and Conduct of Trinity College, Dublin, 1686-90*. Compiled and written by Venerable A. B. Rowan, 1858.
† Colonel Richard Talbot, created Earl of Tyrconnel in March, 1686.

allegiance and prayers for his welfare. To this deputation the King returned the ominously brief reply: 'I thank you for your address, and I don't doubt of your loyalty, or of any others of the Church of England.' The attitude of James towards the English Universities was already pretty clearly defined. In 1686 he had appointed a Roman Catholic to the Deanery of Christ Church, Oxford; in 1687 he endeavoured to force his nominee, Anthony Farmer, as their President, upon the Fellows of Magdalen College; and in the same year the Court of High Commission deprived of his office Pechell, the Vice-Chancellor of Cambridge.

The storm was now about to burst upon the Irish sister of the English Universities. In 1687 James issued a mandamus to admit Doyle, a Roman Catholic of doubtful learning or parts, and, it was asserted, of more than doubtful character, to a Fellowship in Trinity College. Doyle refused to take the usual oath, and was refused admission. The King took no further proceedings in this case, but through Tyrconnel devised other means of enforcing his wishes. The Concordatum Fund of about £400 a year paid by the Exchequer was suspended from Easter, 1688, and the permission obtained from Lord Clarendon, Tyrconnel's predecessor, to sell some of the College plate—about 5,000 ounces[*]—in order to defray the expenses of the buildings then in progress was cancelled, and the part already shipped

---

[*] Plate seems to have been regarded as a good and easily realizable investment, and a sum was set apart from all admission fees for its purchase. Much, as we have seen, was sold to supply the necessities of the College between 1641 and 1649, but a considerable quantity seems to have been accumulated in the intervening years.

for England seized by the Lord Deputy, and only restored on condition that no attempt to send it out of the country should again be made. It was consequently brought back from the Custom-house and placed in 'a closet in the Provost's lodging.' Attempts were subsequently made to purchase lands in Queen's County with money raised from the sale of plate, but Tyrconnel was inexorable.* In 1688, however, the affairs of the College grew desperate. Various retrenchments, including the abolition of supper in the hall as an 'expensive meal by reason of coals,' were agreed upon, and eventually, as the Fellows were, as they said, 'resolved to keep up the Society as long as possibly we can,' it was determined that, as soon as the College money failed, the plate should be pawned or sold. A request was accordingly preferred to the Lord Deputy that, since sale in Ireland would involve great loss, leave might be given for its shipment to England. Tyrconnel, however, remained unmoved, and the entry in the Register runs, 'The Lord Deputy refused leave.'

The remainder of the story of the College, until the Battle of the Boyne decided the question 'Under which King?' is best told in the graphic directness of the entries in the Register:

'Feb. 19, 168$\frac{8}{9}$.—It was agreed on by the Vice-Provost and Senior Fellows that two hundred pounds of the College money should be sent into England for the support of those Fellows that should be forc't to fly thither. At the

* In the Diary of Clarendon, Tyrconnel's predecessor, there is told a ridiculous story of a plot among the students to murder Tyrconnel. See *Diary of Henry, Earl of Clarendon*, pp. 147-149. Stubbs gives some details in his *History*, pp. 123, 124.

same time the dangers of staying in the College seemed so great that it was judged reasonable that all those who thought fit to withdraw themselves from the College for their better security might have free liberty to do so.'

'Feb. 25, 168$\frac{8}{9}$.—All the Horse, Foot and Dragoons were drawn out and posted at several places in the town, from whence they sent parties, who searcht the Protestant houses for arms, whilst others were employed in breaking open stables and taking away all their horses. Two Companies of Foot, commanded by Talbot, one of the Captains in the Royal Regiment of Foot Guards, came into the College, searcht all places, and took away those few fusils, swords, and pistols that they found. At the same time a party of Dragoons broke upon the College stables, and took away all the horses. The Foot continued in the College all night; the next day they were drawn off. On the same day it was agreed on by the Vice-Provost and Senior Fellows that the Fellows and Scholars should receive out of the College trunk (the two hundred pounds not being sent into England as was design'd) their salaries for their respective Fellowships, Offices, and Scholarships, which will be due at the end of this current quarter, together with their allowance for Commons for the said quarter.'

'March 1, 168$\frac{8}{9}$.—Dr. Browne, Mr. Downes, Mr. Barton, Mr. Ashe, and Mr. Smyth, embark't for England; soon after followed Mr. Scroggs, Mr. Leader, Mr. Lloyd, Mr. Sayers, and Mr. Hasset. Mr. Patrickson soon after died; and (of ye Fellows) only Dr. Acton, Mr. Thewles, Mr. Hall, and Mr. Allen, continued in the College.'

'March 12, 168$\frac{8}{9}$.—King James landed in Ireland; and upon the 24th of the same month, being Palm Sunday, he came to Dublin. The College, with the Vice-Chancellor, waited upon him, and Mr. Thewles made a speech, which he seemed to receive kindly, and promis'd 'em his favour and protection ;* [but upon the 16th of September, 1689, without any offence as much as pretended, the College was seized on for a garrison by the King's order, the Fellows turned out, and a Regiment of Foot took possession and continued in it].'†

'June 13, 1689.—Mr. Arthur Greene‡ having petitioned the King for a Senior Fellowship the case was referred to Sir Richard Nagle; upon which he sent an order to the Vice-Provost and Fellows to meet him at his house on Monday the 17th, to shew reason why the aforesaid petition shud not be granted. The reasons offered were many, part of 'em drawn from false allegations in the petition, part from the petitioner's incapacity in several respects to execute the duty of a Senior Fellow; and the conclusion was in these words: There are much more important reasons drawn, as well from the Statutes relating to religion, as from the obligation of oaths which we have taken, and the interests of our religion, which we will never desert, that render it wholly impossible, without violating our consciences, to have any concurrence, or to be any concerned, in the admission of him.'

'July 24.—The Vice-Provost and Fellows, with consent of the Vice-Chancellor, sold a peece of plate weighing about 30 ounces for subsistence of themselves and the Scholars that remained.'

'Sept. 6.—The College was seized on for a Garrison by the King's order, and Sir John Fitzgerald took possession

* 'He promised that he would preserve them in their liberties and properties and rather augment than diminish the privileges and immunities granted to them by his predecessors.'—KING: *State of Protestants*, sec. lxxix.

† As Dr. Mahaffy remarks (*Book of Trinity College, Dublin*, p. 40), 'This entry must have been made subsequently and separately.'

‡ See p. 60.

of it. Upon Wednesday the 11th, it was made a prison for Protestants of the City, of whom a great number were confined to the upper part of the Hall. Upon the 16th the Scholars were all turned out by souldiers, and ordered to carry nothing with 'em but their books. But Mr. Thewles and some others were not permitted to take their books with 'em. Lenan, one of the Scholars of the House, was sick of the small-pox, and died, as it was supposed, by removing. At the same time the King sent an order to apprehend six of the Fellows and Masters, and commit 'em to the main guard, and all this without any provocation or crime as much as pretended; but the Bishop of Meath, our Vice-Chancellor, interceded with the King, and procured the last order to be stopt.'

'Sept. 28.—The Chappel-plate and the Mace were seized on and taken away. The plate was sent to the Custom-house by Colonel Lutterel's order; but it was preserved by Mr. Collins, one of the Commissioners of the Revenue.'

'Oct. 21.—Several persons, by order of the Government, seized upon the Chappel and broke open the Library. The Chappel was sprinkled and new consecrated, and Mass was said in it; but afterwards being turned into a storehouse for powder, it escaped all further damage. The Library and Gardens and the Provost's lodgings were committed to the care of one Macarty, a Priest and Chaplain to ye King, who preserved 'em from the violence of the souldiers, but the Chambers and all other things belonging to ye College were miserably defaced and ruined.'

That the College suffered severely from the military occupation by James's soldiery is clear from the account given of the time by Archbishop King :*

* *State of the Protestants*, sec. lxxix.

'Many of the chambers were turned into prisons for Protestants. The Garrison destroyed the doors, wainscots, closets, and floors, and damnified it in the building and furniture of private rooms, to at least the value of two thousand pounds.'

The entries in the Register make no reference to the appointment in 1689 by the King's order of a secular priest of the Roman Catholic Church, Dr. Michael Moore, to the general charge of the College. Probably but for this appointment, and that of another priest, Teigue Macarthy, the King's chaplain, to the custodianship of the library, little would have escaped the ruthless pillage and destruction. Trinity College owes much to the affection and generosity of her own sons, but perhaps none of those bound to her by filial ties have a better claim to her remembrance than these strangers within her gates to whom at an evil hour her fortunes were committed. To Moore whatever honour we can give is due for his exertions, not only to restore order, but on behalf of the Protestant prisoners, and for the use he made of his influence to restrain the more vindictive action of James and his agents. Good service was also done the University by another Roman Catholic—Coghlan—who was its representative at that time in the Irish Parliament. He was successful in a stratagem by which Trinity College escaped inclusion in the Bill of Attainder.* Moore forfeited the royal

---

* Taylor's *History of the University*, p. 55. Stubbs' *History*, p. 133: 'Mr. Coghlan was one of the representatives of the College in that Parliament, and being disgusted with the proceedings he absented himself from the House; he was sent for and asked to supply the names of the absent members of the College, in order that their names should be inserted in the Bill. He thereupon went out to

favour soon after his appointment to the headship of the College by his opposition to the scheme of the Jesuit Father Petre, that the University should be handed over to that society,* and he retired to Paris,

---

consult Dr. Acton, the Vice-Provost, and on returning he moved that the Clerk of the Buttery should be sent for in order that the College books should be before the House. The Serjeant-at-Arms proceeded to the College to bring up the Clerk of the Buttery, but that officer, having received a hint from Mr. Coghlan, could not be found, and was absent for some days until the Bill was passed.'

* That there was some competition among those who expected to fall heirs to the property of the University, then apparently *in articulo mortis*, is seen by the following petition which appears (*Dublin University Magazine*, August, 1762) to have been presented to the King about this time by the Roman Catholic prelates of Ireland:

'Humbly Sheweth

'That the Royal College of Dublin is the only University of this kingdom, and now wholly at your Majesty's disposal, the teachers and scholars having deserted it.

'That before the Reformation it was common to all the natives of this country, as the other most famous Universities of Europe to theirs, respectively, and the ablest Scholars of this Nation preferred to be professors and teachers therein, without any distinction of orders, congregations, or politic bodies, other than that of true merit, as the competent judges of learning and piety, after a careful and just scrutiny did approve.

'That your petitioners being bred in foreign Colleges and Universities, and acquainted with many of this Nation, who in the said Universities purchased the credit and renown of very able men in learning, do humbly conceive themselves to be qualified for being competent and proper judges of the fittest to be impartially presented to your Majesty, and employed as such directors and teachers (whether secular or regular clergymen) as may best deserve it, which as is the practice of other Catholic Universities, so it will undoubtedly prove a great encouragement to learning, and very advantageous to this Nation, entirely devoted to your Majesty's interest.

'Your petitioners therefore do most humbly pray that your Majesty may be graciously pleased to let your Irish Catholic sub-

and afterwards to Rome. His career was throughout a distinguished one, and it is interesting to record that, after holding some educational posts in Italy, he was finally chosen to fill the Rector's chair of the University of Paris, while he held in addition the Principalship of the College of Navarre and the Professorship of Philosophy, Greek, and Hebrew.

The Register of 1689 mentions that the Vice-Provost Acton and the Fellows presented a petition to the King, pointing out the losses the College had incurred, and praying for a redress of their grievances. To this petition no answer appears, and the Register may be permitted to bring the history of the crisis to a conclusion:

'Nov. 20, 1689.—The Vice-Provost and Fellows met together, and elected the same officers that were chosen the year before.'

'December.—About the beginning of this month Dr. Acton died of a fever.'

A demand was made by an Order in Council for the keys of the College in April, 1690 :

---

jects make use of the said College for the instruction of their youth, and that it may be a general Seminary for the clergy of this kingdom, and that either all the bishops, or such of them as your Majesty will think fit (by your Royal authority and commission), present the most deserving persons to be directors and teachers in the said College, and to oversee it, to the end it may be well ruled and truly governed, and pure orthodox doctrine, piety and virtue be taught and practised therein, to the honour and glory of God, propagation of His true religion, and general good of your Majesty's subjects in this realm, and as in duty bound they will ever pray,' etc.

ACCESSION OF KING WILLIAM

'Upon receipt of this Mr. Thewles and Mr. Hall consulted the Vice-Chancellor, and delivered the keyes.'

'June 14, 1690.—King William landed at Carrick Fergus, and the same day Mr. Thewles died of a fever.'

'July 1, 1690.—The armies of the English and Irish engaged at the Boyne, and the Irish being routed, King James returned that night to Dublin, and commanded his army not to plunder or do any harm to the city, which order was observed by ye Irish.'

'July 15, 1690.—Mr. Scroggs landed, and immediately after Dr. Browne, and then Mr. Downes, Mr. Reader, the Provost, etc.'

The Fellows and Scholars that returned were allowed their Commons, but their salary was reduced by agreement to the old statute allowance, both for Fellowships and places, till the College revenues shall increase.

'Before King William left Ireland he gave order to ye College to seize upon all books that belonged to forfeiting Papists; but the order not being known till about half a year after, the greatest part of the books were lost, but those which were recovered, and worthy anything, were placed in the Countess of Bath's library.'

With peace renewed Trinity College rapidly regained the prosperity it had enjoyed before the outbreak of the Civil War, and in 1693 the first centenary was celebrated with considerable solemnity.* Soon after King William's accession the number of students had so greatly increased that new buildings were found necessary, and by means of grants from the Irish House of Commons, and the generous contributions of the

* See Appendix.

ecclesiastics and gentry of the country, many architectural improvements were made.

Despite the Treaty of Limerick, the reigns of William III. and of Anne, far from emancipating the Roman Catholic community in Ireland from the disabilities under which they had so long suffered, greatly increased both the number and the severity of the laws directed against them. Not only were members of the obnoxious Church debarred from all high offices and many honourable professions, but inducements of a degrading character were held out to converts, of which the transference of his father's property to a son who conformed to the doctrines of the English Church was the most scandalous.* By an Act of 1709 Roman Catholics were forbidden to teach either in public or private, and £30 per annum was offered as a bribe to any Romish priest who embraced Protestantism.

In times such as these, it will be easily understood, the doors of the University were made strong against Dissent, and the original intention with which it was constituted was even more completely lost sight of than during the early years of its existence. But it ought to be borne in mind, as already stated, that it pressed no inquiry into the religious faith of its undergraduates, and in many cases overlooked absence from the chapel services. That previous to 1794 Roman Catholics could, and did, receive their education in Trinity College, although they could not graduate, nor obtain any of the higher distinctions, is certain. Whatever may have been the motives of the authorities in thus

* Act of 1704.

violating the spirit and letter of the statutes—and it is not urged that proselytism may not have entered into the mental scheme of some—Trinity College, at least, added nothing on its own initiative at any period of its history to the intolerable burden of Roman Catholic Ireland.

CHAPTER IV

SIXTEENTH AND SEVENTEENTH CENTURIES: LIFE IN THE
COLLEGE—STUDIES

THE sixteenth century was a period of tribulation and trial to the English Universities. The ancient régime was rudely shaken by the expulsion of the religious Orders; new ideals were abroad, and students of a type hitherto unknown, sons of gentlemen who desired neither to take Orders nor to undergo the severe discipline of the scholar, began to form a considerable section of the undergraduate population. Patronage, too, filled the more lucrative posts, and the rewards due to learning were not infrequently bestowed upon the friends of the wealthy and well connected. As Latimer declared, 'talent, learning, poverty and discretion went for nothing in the College where interest, favour and letters from the great exerted their pressure from without.' Dr. Caius, the founder of the College that bears his name at Cambridge,[*] on revisiting his University, after the accession of Elizabeth, makes complaint of the changes that had come about since his

[*] Caius, *Historia*, pp. 94-96.

own day. No longer, he tells us, were the students serious-minded seekers after knowledge, or respectful to the seniors who imparted it. Frivolities had taken the place of the old strenuous devotion to study, instead of books fine clothes were purchased, and the time gained from the neglect of their proper studies was spent by the modern undergraduates in town and tavern, gambling and hatching mischief.

'An Englishman Italianate is a devil incarnate' ran the Elizabethan proverb, and Renaissance influences in the van of the new spirit of liberty produced a ferment in the medieval cloister. With the accession of Elizabeth, however, and the enforcement of a definite political and religious policy, matters began to improve; but the stern pre-Reformation ideals of plain living and high thinking in almost monastic seclusion from the gay world never quite re-established themselves. The horizon of the scholar was extended; he fell heir to new intellectual territory, to the emotions and ambitions of the modern man, as the new world began to take shape under the powerful and contending forces of the time.

The College system in the English Universities was nevertheless so firmly rooted and so admirably adapted to the work it had to do, that without serious alteration it survived, and the founders of Trinity College, near Dublin, could find no better model for the Irish University. Nor was the old rigorous discipline at once relaxed. The day's work of the earnest but poor students of the sixteenth century is described in a sermon, appealing for their necessities, by Thomas Lever, of St. John's, Cambridge:

'There be divers there which rise daily betwixte four and five of the clock in the morning, and from five until six of the clock, use common prayer with an exhortation of God's word in a common Chapel, and from six until ten of the clock use ever either private study or common lectures. At ten of the clock they go to dinner, when as they be content with a penny piece of beef amongst four, having a few porage made of the broth of the same beef with salt and oatmeal and nothing else.

'After this slender dinner they be either teaching or learning until five of the clock in the evening, when as they have a supper not much better than their dinner. Immediately after the which they go either to reasoning in problems or unto some other study until it be nine or ten of the clock, and then being without fire are fain to walk or run up and down half an hour to get a heat on their feet when they go to bed.'

At Dublin the College day began at six with service in the chapel, followed by lectures at seven. Morning prayers were read at ten o'clock, and on certain days were followed by declamations in Hall. The afternoons from two o'clock until four were occupied by disputations in syllogistic form upon subjects in the case of junior students selected from Logic, in the case of seniors from Natural History or Metaphysics. Evening prayers were held at four o'clock, and on Sundays and Fridays one of the resident masters was required to deliver a short sermon or 'commonplace'* in chapel after the service, a custom which was maintained until the year 1836. Religious duties were strictly enforced,

* A Cambridge custom, to which it appears that Archbishop Abbot (Chancellor 1613-1633), being an Oxford man, objected. See Stubbs' *History*, p. 98.

as is proved by an order of October 23, 1623, which enacted that

'whoever shall neglect to receive the Holy Communion once a quarter (unless he shall have given to the Provost a satisfactory reason) shall be fined 5s. if he be M.A.; 2s. 6d. if he be Fellow Commoner or Scholar; and 2s. if he be Pensioner.'

From the first all students dined and supped together in Hall, presided over by the Vice-Provost (who was by statute required to be present), and during dinner listened to a passage from Scripture, or the works of one of the Fathers read aloud by a scholar.

No provision seems to have been made until late in the seventeenth century for any form of exercise or recreation—the story goes that an ancient statute forbade the playing of marbles in the courts and the shooting of snipe in the park—and its place was taken by a rapid 'constitutional' either in the hall or court, between supper and bedtime to circulate the blood and warm the feet. The games that enter so largely into the life of the modern University were entirely unknown, nor was the leisure afforded from study sufficient to permit of any organization of sport.

- 'In Brooking's map of Dublin there appears to have been, in 1728, a quadrangular walled-in court on the site of the present new square, for the recreation of the students. There were two gates giving access to this in the arches under Nos. 23 and 25 in the Library Square, which is the oldest existing part of the College, and which was erected after (or about) 1700.'*

* See Stubbs' *History*, pp. 144, 145.

In 1684 a bowling-green was laid out, and in 1694 a fives court built, the former on the site of the present tennis courts, and the latter in the Fellows' garden. Thus the poet's history is at fault by nearly a century:

> 'Three hundred years have modified the scene
> Since cattle grazed knee-deep in College-green:
> Since Senior Fellows shared exciting sports,
> Bowls in the orchard, marbles in the courts.'*

Some idea of the College diet may be obtained from a MS. in Chaloner's hand preserved in the library:

'The Colledge revenew of £400 st. per annum will mayntayne yearly:—

'A Provost havinge a good diet dayley as after apeares £6 and £14 yearly.

'Ten Fellowes havinge a good diet dayley and £10 yearly; forty Scolers having a good diet and 20s. yearly. The diet must be £133 6s. 8d. for which wee are to receve victuals at prices:—

'A mutton alive with the wool at 26½d. the pece, ...	320 a year.
'A befe large and fatt alive at 16s. the pece	54.
'Corne at 5s. the peck, market mesure, ...	200 pecks.
'half whete and bear malt; half ote malt	

'A Fellowes diet shall be 6 ounces of Manchet a mele a pint and halfe of good bear the pece, three quarts in the mess, and a sholder of mutton, and at night a good pece of beath and porage, more than they can ete, enowe for

* Prologue to the Tercentenary play, by Edwin Hamilton.

ech, the bread (beare) a farthyng, of mutton 2d., befe 2d., and the heth [they had] a Second . . . they have £4 a year a mess besid, for the former make but £4.

'The Scolers diet is 6 ounces good cheet [*i.e.*, 2nd sort of wheaten] bread for ech, pint of ber the pece, pottell a mess, a joynt of mutton at supper a mess—and a good pece of befe at dinner at 12 peces in the quarter.'*

Undergraduates of Dublin, then as now, were divided into four classes, Junior and Senior Freshmen and Junior and Senior Sophisters—a nomenclature borrowed from Cambridge. Each student entered, as at present, under one of the Fellows as Tutor, who acted *in loco parentis*, and was responsible, not only to the College for his pupil's fees, but also for the debts he incurred during his undergraduate career. Some kind of entrance examination appears to have been early instituted, but public entrance examinations at fixed times were first established in 1759, when the number was fixed at four—February, Easter, July, and November. In the early days of the University, however, as the average age of students was about sixteen, no very severe test can have been imposed. Goldsmith, in his *Life of Parnell*, speaks of the entrance examination as more difficult than that of Oxford or Cambridge, a statement not altogether incredible.

The Laudian statutes forbade the authorities to make any changes in the curriculum laid down in 1637, and it remained practically unaltered for a hundred years. During the four years of study required by them from the student before he presented himself for his degree, Logic was specially pressed upon his atten-

* Quoted by Stubbs, *History*, p. 41.

tion; the whole of the *Isagoge* of Porphyrius was 'to be read twice a year at least.' Aristotle's Physic and Metaphysic being the work of the senior classes, beginning with the *Organon*, 'not running away from the text,' said the statutes, 'after commentaries.' All undergraduates were, of course, lectured in Greek and Latin, and English essays were required from them every week upon subjects treated of in the lectures. To students backward in classics special instruction was given by the College schoolmaster, in order that they might benefit from the lectures of the ordinary undergraduate course.

In 1659 it was resolved by the Provost and Fellows that

'no student be admitted B.A. unless he produce the Senior Greek Lecturer's certificate of his competent proficiency in the Greek tongue. Nor any admitted A.B. from the 8th of next July, unless he produces two certificates, one from the Hebrew Lecturer,* the other from the Rhetoric Professor, of his diligent attendance upon those lectures and considerable progress in those studies. Nor that any be admitted A.M. from same date unless he produce a certificate from the Hebrew Lecturer of his competent skill in that language.'

It is evident that the studies of a student were not then, as now, regarded as complete when he had reached the standing of a Bachelor.† Post-graduate work

* In June, 1628, appears an order enforcing attendance upon Hebrew lectures for Bachelors. The first endowment for a Professorship of Hebrew was given by Henry Cromwell in 1658. John Stearne, M.D., was the first lecturer appointed.

† A somewhat fuller account of the curriculum may be of interest. The regular academic exercises imposed upon all undergraduates

leading to the Master's degree formed part of the normal scheme, and was provided for in the curriculum. It is not, indeed, improbable that it was looked upon as entirely necessary for such youths as proposed to enter upon professional life. No special examination seems to have been required in the seventeenth century as a preliminary to graduation, but each candidate for the Bachelor's degree prepared or delivered two declamations, one in Greek and one in Latin *in laudem philosophiæ*, and was also required to act as respondent or defendant in a logical disputation. Prizes for pro-

---

during term were *commentaries, themes,* and *declamations*. Declamations were delivered in public in the hall *Memoriter*, on some subject *e morali aut politica disciplina*. The *first class* studied dialectics, and were required to furnish weekly an analysis of invention and rhetorical elocution, *analysin aliquam inventionis elocutionis rhetorica*. The *second class* was lectured in logical controversies, *controversa logica disciplina capita*. Students at this stage were required to send in weekly an analysis of invention and judgment, *aliquam inventionis et judicii analysin*. The *third class* read Aristotelian physiology, *præcepta physiologiæ de elementis, de corporibus mixtis, sive imperfectis, qualia sunt meteora : sive perfectis, qualia sunt metalla, planta, animalia*.

The *fourth class* was lectured on psychology and ethics. The third and fourth class students attended disputations weekly, the former concerned with some logical, the latter with some philosophical, thesis. A thesis was delivered by the respondent *oratione perpetua, adhibito vario argumentorum genere, et elocutionis rhetorica ornamentis*.

The study of mathematics was not then taken up until after the B.A. After graduation students attended lectures *in mathematicis et politicis,* and disputations took place in mathematics or physics.

M.A.'s were required to deliver *commonplaces*, and were exercised in theological disputations after the Cambridge practice, the Professor of Theological Controversies acting as *Moderator*.

Locke's *Essay on the Human Understanding*, published 1690, was introduced into the curriculum by Provost Ashe immediately on its appearance, and has retained its place down to the present day.

ficiency were not offered in the early history of the University, but care was taken to prevent idling by the institution of examinations held at the end of each term. A student who failed to display a competent knowledge of the work done in his class was liable to be *cautioned* (rejected), or at least *warned*. The latter term, still in use, notifies to the candidate that his work has not been satisfactory, and that he may look to have it made the subject of special inquisition at the subsequent term examination. The roll of Easter Term, 1685, gives *pessime, male, vix mediocriter, bene, optime*, and *negligenter*, as terms of discrimination.

During the seventeenth century the average number of students who entered Trinity College in each year was about fifty. Provost Marsh, writing about 1678, mentions the number of residents in the College as 340. From the first the custom prevailed in Dublin of allotting sets of chambers to two students who shared a sitting-room with each other and kept house together. This feature of student life in Trinity College, Dublin, though it still prevails, is now less characteristic, as sets of single rooms have been from time to time added, and the number of students accommodated within the walls has decreased while the number of undergraduates has largely increased. In the seventeenth century there were no extramural students,* and permits to visit the town were given sparingly. These sanctioned a two hours' absence from College, from two till four, or seven till nine, and any transgression of the time-limit was

* 'The proposal to recognise as students those who had matriculated, but lodged in the city of Dublin, is as old,' says Professor Mahaffy, 'as Bedell's time, who favours it. *Cf. College Calendar* for 1833, Introd., p. xxvi.'—*Book of Trinity College, Dublin*, p. 46 (note).

visited with severe admonition or punishment. The College gate was kept locked, and even within the College the students were expected to preserve a strict sobriety of manner, even aimless loitering being definitely forbidden by statute. As was natural, the bolder spirits chafed under the severe discipline, and occasionally broke through its restraints. It was not unknown for an undergraduate to display a preference for the amusements and alehouses of the town to the College sermons and the lectures of the Catechist; and for playing at cards 'in the porter's lodging under the steeple' to attendance upon the necessary declamation. He escaped for a glad hour from College discipline by climbing the wall, and was fined for breaking the Provost's or a Fellow's windows. We are recalled to the fact that he was a student of 300 years ago when we read that he was sometimes punished by confinement in the stocks during supper-time, or had a public whipping administered to him at 'Corrections.'

The earliest mention of punishment occurs in 1599 :*

'16 July, 1599.—Whereas Nicholas Smith and Andrew Donellan, Scholars of the College, by their many jars and several quarrelings have troubled and molested the same; notwithstanding public admonition heretofore given to them by the Provost and Fellows, have yet of late in most furious and disordered manner assaulted each one the other with weapons within the said College to the great contempt of the authority of the same and bad incouragement of the rest of the Scholars to the like lewd practices—it is therefore ordered by the fellows upon due examination

* MS. History in library, Trinity College, Dublin.

of the said matter that both the Parties for their Presumptions shall be punished with sitting in the stocks all supper time.'

The following entries appear in the Book of Censures during the provostship of Temple:

'Aug. 4, 1617.—Gower and Tolles punished with the rod for going into the country and lodging in the town all night. Gower censured for his negligence in his studies, which was by the Examiners of the Midsummer Term discovered and complained of. Patrick Smith removed from the College for non-proficiency and incapacity of learning.'

'Nov. 21, 1617.—Mr. Taylor, Senior Fellow and Dean, severely censured and punished for a wound committed upon the person of Gower, a Scholar of the House.'

'June 2, 1619.—Thomas Cuff and Jos. Travers for abusing M. Middop's servant, and for their irreverent and savage carriage in the presence of Sir John King, to make three public acknowledgments of their faults at three several times in the Hall; to forbear going out into town for six months except to hear sermons; and for six months not to keep company with each other. Cuff for wounding with a knife the scullion of the kitchen to lose his privilege of adult age, and to rest subject to the rod until he graduates.'

'Sept. 15, 1619.—Rowland Eustace, for his drunkenness and other misdemeanours, was punished with a public acknowledgment of his fault in the Hall at dinner, to be performed for three days together on his knees, from the beginning of dinner to the end; his several offences to be set down in writing, and delivered to the Senior Fellow that sits in the Hall, and pronounced and confessed before the whole company present. On the 17th of September the same man, and Sir Dowman, were enjoined to declaim in the Chapel for drinking in an ale-house. Also the same punishment was inflicted upon Sir Toller and Sir Hallowell. Sir Underwood for going to an ale-house, and coming in after the shutting of the gates, was punished by declamation openly in the Hall during dinner. Hogan, Hurley, and Lisragh severely punished with the rod for going out into town without leave, and tippling in ale-houses. Sir Holland confessed that he was late out of College at night and came into the Chapel by breaking a bar of the window in the steeple. Beere, Temple (son of the Provost), and Paget were sharply corrected for departing from the Sermon (at Christ Church) to go a-walking, and for consenting to the plucking of cherries from a tree of Dean Wheeler's garden hanging on the wall. One Life, a lewd boy, and an instrument for them, was banished the College.'*

The following entries in Bedell's Register are also of interest:

'1628, Sept. 23.—Deane and Wilson mulcted a month's Commons for their insolent behaviour, assaulting and striking the butler, which was presently changed into sitting at the lower end of the Scholars' table for a month and subjecting them to the rod.'

'1628, Jan. 28.—Tho. Walworth refused to read Chapter, and enjoined to make a confession of his fault upon his knees in the Hall, which he disacknowledging, he had deserved expulsion.'

'1628, July 23. — Sir Walworth said to have sold his study to haunt the town. Somers, Deane and Elliott appointed to sit bare for going out of the Hall before

* The 'Sir' appended to the surname designated the Bachelor and corresponds to the 'Ds.' (*Dominus*) in the Calendar. It was quite generally in use until a few years since.

grace, and not performing it, made to stand by the pulpit.'

'1628, April 11.—Mr. Travers for omitting his Commonplace the second time appointed, punished 13s. Mr. Tho. for omitting prayers reading, 5s.'

'1628, May 12.—The Sophisters proposed supper to the Bachelors: prevented by sending for them and forbidding them to attempt it.'

'1628, July 11.—The Fellow Commoners complain of Mr. Price for forbidding them to play at bowls in the Orchard; they were blamed, and it was shown that by Statute they could not play there.'

'1628, July 29.—Six natives, Dominus Kerdiffe, Ds. Conway, Ds. Baker, Ds. Davis, Ds. Kerdiffe, jun., and Burton, admonished for being often absent from Irish prayers.'

'1629, Aug. 19.—The natives to lose their weekly allowance if they are absent from prayers on the Lord's Day.'

'1629, Aug. 29.—Sir Springham said to keep a hawk. Rowley for drunkenness and knocking Strank's head against the seat of the Chapel, to have no further maintenance from the house.'

'Booth, for taking a pig of Sir Samuel Smith's, and that openly in the day time before many, and causing it to be dressed in town, inviting Mr. Rollon and Sir Conway (who knew not of it), was condemned to be whipped openly in the Hall, and to pay for the pig.'

The somewhat elliptical entry—*Sir Springham said to keep a hawk*—suggestive of contempt of College discipline on Sir Springham's part, must be read as a note of luxurious and censurable extravagance. The sumptuary laws were strict, and hawking, besides being an expensive sport, could not have been indulged in by Sir Springham without neglect of the lectures and religious services with which the College day was filled. Lectures, it must be borne in mind, were necessarily very numerous, for, owing to the scarcity of books and the inadequacy of preparatory schools, most of the students were largely dependent upon oral instruction for whatever proficiency they attained during the undergraduate course, which comprised, in addition to the usual subjects, a study of the elements, nowadays acquired before matriculation. It is noteworthy that no text-books are specified in the Caroline statutes, and probably, indeed, none were available.

'Dudley Loftus' *Logic* and *Introduction*, printed in 1657 (Dublin), seem to me,' says Dr. Mahaffy,[*] 'the earliest books likely to have been used as text-books in Trinity College. Strange to say, there is no copy of either in our College library.'

In 1636 the attention of Lord Deputy Wentworth was called to the fact that

'some of the Youth sent to study in the University and College near the City, called Trin. Coll., are often misguided and drawn away to mispend their precious time in Taverns, tippling houses, and such other disorderly Places as gives them Opportunity of idle Company, drinking, and gaming.'

An order was accordingly issued at Dublin Castle (February, 1636), forbidding tavern or inn keepers to allow a student to make any stay without notifying the

[*] *Book of Trinity College, Dublin*, p. 26.

Provost, or to run a score against him, or take anything in pawn from him. In May, 1638, we read that a student named Daniel Weld repaired about ten o'clock at night to the house of Elizabeth Jones

'(being a house where Ale or Beer is sold by retail), and there lodged till about 2 or 3 o'clock in the morning of the next day; and then that the Watch, imployed (as it seems) in search of disordered places and persons, came to the chamber where the said Weld lodged, and there found him, and albeit the said D. and E. endeavoured to excuse the matter, yet it may well be conceived that they intended Lewdness and Folly therein.'

It was therefore ordered that Weld should be punished, and that the said Elizabeth should

'for her offence stand fined in £40 to his Majesty, and stand on a Market day at the Market Cross from 9 till 10 o'clock in the forenoon, and a paper on her head with these words written thereon:

'" For harbouring a Collegian contrary to the Act of State";

which part of this order, for her standing at the said Cross, the Sheriffs of this city are required to see executed.'*

In the case of Bachelors, who were probably permitted more freedom than undergraduates, the Board claimed, and occasionally exercised in the interest of discipline, the power of suspension from degrees. A reference to

* Stubbs' *History*, Appendix, p. 406.

this subject appears in a pamphlet in the College library:*

'1665, Oct. 7.—The Bachelors behaving insolently to the Junior Fellows, and not capping to them, the Provost and Senior Fellows convened them in the Hall, and declared that those who hereafter offended therein should be suspended of their degree.'

And the latest instance is perhaps that of Forbes in July, 1700, except only this:

'17$\frac{21}{22}$, March 22.—John Smith, A.B., having fraudulently obtained his Testimonium, and taken his name off the Books, and having after this committed some offence in the College, the Board resolved that he should never be readmitted or allowed to take an higher degree.'

The rigours of University discipline seem at Christmas to have been somewhat relaxed. Permission was given to play cards on that day in the hall, and the only dramatic performance sanctioned during the year took place, as is shown by an entry in the Register: 'The Senior Sophisters exercise dominion over the Junior Sort, this Christmas, a Comedy acted by them and a play by the Bachelors.' We find that this relaxation was not, however, viewed with favour by some of the Provosts. In Ware's MSS., it is said of Ussher, Bedell's successor in the provostship, that he was 'an enemy to all theatrical representations, and would not admit them into the College, *according to the usual practice*, until commanded by the Lords Justices to allow them.'

* See *Postscript to an Examination of the Charter and Statutes* (Pamphlets), Coll. Lib., 29, c. 12.

Some license was given at great University functions to the University Merryman, or *Terræ Filius,* known at Cambridge as *Tripos* or *Prevaricator.** On the occasion of the centenary celebrations in Dublin, 'a very diverting speech' is said to have been made by the *Terræ Filius;* and Dr. Barrett, in his *Early Life of Swift,* has published 'Sir Jones' *Tripos,'* or satire upon the University, on the ground, apparently, that so Rabelaisian a composition could have had no other author than Swift. A brief extract will suffice to indicate the character of this exquisite piece of work:

'THE SCENE—DROGHEDA.

'*Enter* MR. DOYLE *and his damsel,* NELLY; *after them the Tapster, with a Porringer of burnt Brandy and a Mutton Pie.*

'DOYLE. Come, Nelly, sit down, and give me a kiss.

'NELLY. Faugh, Sir, stand off! I protest you smell so strong of brandy and tobacco a body can't endure you. . . .

'DOYLE. But won't you hear me? I tell you, woman, as simple as I stand here, I'm to be a Fellow of Dublin College.'

'The heads at Oxford, holding public acts in 1712, stopt the mouth of the *Terræ Filius* (who is called a *statutable* orator at this solemnity), having intelligence

---

* The term *Tripos* is derived from the three-legged stool upon which the Merryman sat as 'master of the disputations.' His speech was printed upon a slip, and the habit grew up at Cambridge of giving the names of successful candidates for the degree on the back of the same paper—hence the title of the class lists in that University.

that he designed to utter something in derogation of the Reverend Mr. Vice-Chancellor'; * and no mention of such a functionary occurs in the Dublin records later than the seventeenth century.

A MS. in the library gives an interesting account of the forms employed at seventeenth-century Commencements. The occasion was the conferring of a honorary degree upon the Earl of Ossory in 1646 (*circa*).

'1. All the Doctors and Masters of the University are to meet here, hence to go formally in hoods and caps to the Castle; thence to attend his Lordship so as the Bedel may go first, after him all the Candidates bare, the Juniors first, then the Sword and my Lord's personal attendants, after them my Lord himself, then the Pro-Vice-Chancellor and the Provost, after them the Lords of the Council, then the Doctors in their scarlet, then the two Proctors, the Senior carrying his Book, after them the Bachelors of Divinity and the Masters according to their seniority.

'2. As my Lord comes into the Hall, Mr. Boyle is to receive him with a short speech by way of salutation, which done his Lordship is to pass through the Hall to the Regent House, there to take his seat, then to give oath to the Pro-Vice-Chancellor, and after to the Proctors. The Vice-Chancellor, after his Oath, is to sit on a chair placed below my Lord's to the right hand, the Provost to the left, both with a table and cushion before them. The Proctors after their Oath are to take their seats on the two sides of another table, so as their faces must be towards the Chancellor. This table is to stand in the middle of the house, the Register at the further end of the table. The candidates are to be uncovered.

* Dr. Mahaffy in *Book of Trinity College, Dublin*, p. 53.

'3. The Earl of Ossory's supplication is to be made by my Lord of Meath in such form as his Lordship shall think fit, and then to be presented after the placets are gathered by my Lord of Meath, and after he leads him to the Pro-Vice-Chancellor, who admits him, and then the Bedell leads him to an empty chair which stands besides the Proctors. Then the Bedel shall say this: "Pone manum in manu magistri," which done the Bedel shall say: "Respondebis questioni in aure Magistri sedendo." This he must do; have his Cap sent on by the Proctor, and after he shall be led by the Bedel to his first seat.

'4. Then Mr. Bishop leads all the Supplications for the Doctors of Divinity, and by the Vice-Chancellor's direction the Bedel is to cry, Ad Scrutinium 1º. After a pause he cries, Ad Scrutinium 2º. Then both the Proctors gather placets on both sides the house, and meeting at the end consult. And the Senior Proctor answers Placet or Non-Placet as they find it. If Placet, the Bedel goes down and brings up the Candidates, and leading them round about the Regent house salutes all the University, and brings them down again. Then he cries, Ad Scrutinium 3º. Then the Proctors gather Placets again and return Placet; and after a pause demands, "Placet ut intrent"; after Placets the Bedel leads the præcentor down, and both bring up the Candidates; the father presents them. All the Masters, after they are presented, are to do as the Earl of Ossory, before as the Doctors of Divinity.'*

By the charter of James I. provision was made for the holding of Commencements once in the year, in the month of July. The College Register for 1613 (January 28) records a resolution of the Provost and Senior Fellows to hold Commencements on the first

* MS., F. 1, 21. Quoted by Stubbs, p. 404.

SERMONS AT CHRIST CHURCH 91

Monday after the end of Trinity term. While the number of students was but small,* the necessity for a graduation ceremony more than once a year was not felt, and the College finances probably did not admit of unnecessary expenditure. 'In 1611 there was a charge of disbursements for the scaffolding at Commencements, £7 11s. 1d.; for borrowing the cushion at St. Patrick's, 3s.; do. at Christchurch, 1s.'† Commencement fees are first mentioned in the year 1608, when the College received from two Doctors 40s., four Bachelors of Divinity 13s. 4d., nine Masters £3, seven Bachelors of Arts, 35s. In the sixteenth century the College cook appears to have been paid 7s. per week, the gardener 20s., the men and women who weeded the garden 6d. a day. The early College accounts also show the payment of 1s. to the woman who swept the College seat in Christ Church, for

'it appears from early records that the students of the College regularly attended sermons in Christ Church Cathedral, where the heads of the Government constantly worshipped. They were assigned certain seats, which were both inconvenient for hearing and exposed to the extremity of the wind and weather, and where they could not attend to the sermons with any edification. The Fellows consequently, in December, 1615, asked permission of the Lords of the Council "to seat themselves and the students in the Cathedral in such places as they can hear the sermons best, until convenient seats shall be assigned to the members of the College." '‡

* The greatest number of degrees conferred in the seventeenth century was seventy, in 1699.
† Stubbs' *History*, p. 25 (note).
‡ Stubbs' *History*, p. 35 (note).

It is unfortunate that the records of the University examinations during the seventeenth century have not been preserved. The names of all the students who entered after 1637, however, were registered in the Senior Lecturer's books, of which the muniment-room possesses a complete set from January, 163⅞, to November, 1644, and from January, 1652, down to the present day.

Society was picturesquely varied in Trinity College during the first hundred years of its existence. Raw lads, natives of the West and South, mingled with the sons of English settlers in the Pale, and youths from the English counties bordering on the Irish Sea. A note in Temple's hand gives in one year of his provostship the following particulars as to the membership of the College: 'Irish by birth, 44; Irish by habitation, 16; Irish Fellow Commoners and Pensioners, 18; Strangers of Derbyshire, 12; Strangers of Cheshire, 8.' From Temple's time the College seems to have been supported by the nobler families of the country, who entered their sons there in preference to sending them to England. Strafford, when Lord Deputy, set the example by sending his two sons in 1637; Lucius Cary, afterwards Lord Falkland, graduated in Dublin in the days of his father's viceroyalty; while many other notable names are to be found in the College register of these its early days.* The order made by

* Class distinctions were, of course, preserved. The *Filius nobilis* and the Fellow Commoner possessed special privileges not granted to the ordinary pensioner, and wore a distinguishing academic dress. A moderate disrespect of the authorities was permitted to members of aristocratic families—*e.g.*, it was ordered in 1632 that ' everyone under the degree of M.A. (*noblemen's sons and heirs of Privy Councillors excepted*) shall uncover their heads when they see the Provost in the quadrangle.'

the Court of Wards, founded in 1617, that the sons of the important families should be educated at Trinity College, also assisted to bring about a close connection between the University and the nobility and gentry throughout the country. Thus, boys from the middle class of Dublin citizens and members of the great Irish families meeting on common ground prepared in company for the business of the great world, and Trinity College rapidly developed into a great national institution intimately associated with the social and political movements which make the history of Ireland.

CHAPTER V

THE EIGHTEENTH CENTURY

DURING the reign of William III., the provostship, and even a Fellowship, was the most direct avenue to the Episcopal Bench. St. George Ashe, who in 1692 succeeded the nominee of King James, Michael Moore, was promoted to a bishopric within three years, as was Peter Browne,* appointed Provost in 1699, and at one time there were ten Irish Bishops who had been Fellows of Trinity College. With no good feelings, however, Primate Boulter did the University an unconscious service. He disliked the College, affected to regard it as 'a nest of Jacobites,' dammed the stream of promotion which flowed through it, and again and again urged the necessity of vacant sees 'not being filled with a native of the country.' To the policy of Boulter Baldwin's long and active provostship is due, of whom it has been said that ' it astonished everyone that he could

* Ashe was followed in the provostship by George Browne in 1695, who, it is said, died of the effects of a well-directed brickbat in a College skirmish, and Peter Browne was succeeded in 1710 by Benjamin Pratt, an easy-minded straggler through life, who directed the affairs of the College largely from England, fell in consequence out of rank, and died ingloriously as Dean of Down.

not get out of the provostship, as much as it did to know how he got into it.'* Nor could he bear with patience the growing power and independence of the University, which had now established a firm place in the hearts of the people, and had won the sympathy and support of the Irish Parliament. Swift, the champion of Irish rights, was the object of Boulter's especial aversion, and we may regard the latter as an early representative of the long line of English politicians who, hating while they governed, laboured earnestly against the emancipation of Ireland. A sentence from one of his letters is significant:

'I cannot help saying it would have been for the King's service here if what has lately been transacting in relation to the Professors had been concerted with some of the English here,† and not wholly with the natives, and that after a secret manner; that *the College might have thought it their interest to have some dependence on the English.*'

* 'The long quarrel between Archbishops Boulter and King arose in a great degree,' says Mr. Lecky (*History of Ireland*, vol. i., p. 208), 'from the bitter language in which the latter prelate censured the conduct of the Primate, who had ordained and placed in an Irish living a man named Power, who had been one of the famous Hampshire deer-stealers known as the Waltham Blacks, and had only saved himself from the gallows by turning informer against his comrades.' This recalls Swift's sarcasm on the Englishmen appointed to Irish sees. 'Excellent and moral men have been selected on every occasion of vacancy. But it unfortunately has uniformly happened that as these worthy divines crossed Hounslow Heath on their way to Ireland, to take possession of their bishoprics, they have been regularly robbed and murdered by the highwaymen frequenting that common, who seize upon their robes and patents, come over to Ireland and are consecrated bishops in their stead.' It is noteworthy that the policy of appointing Englishmen to the highest judicial posts was no less consistently followed.

† That is, English by birth.

This insane dislike and jealousy of the English by blood displayed on the part of the English by birth who were sent over to fill the important offices in Church and State was naturally productive of a policy intensely exasperating to the Irish people. Disloyalty to the English rule at the Castle was construed as a deeper disloyalty to the Crown and to the Union, and upon the very endeavours to exterminate it the spirit that was dreaded fed and strengthened. Though a Whig, Boulter made no effort to have Provost Baldwin, a no less vehement Whig than himself, appointed to any episcopal see, and commented with some cynicism upon the elevation of the 'good Berkeley,' a former Fellow, to the bishopric of Cloyne.*

* 'I wish the Dean's promotion may answer the expectation of his friends in England.' With Boulter's policy it is instructive to compare that of the wise patriot, Ormonde, who, as Chancellor, when an Englishman was unnecessarily brought over, wrote to the Secretary of State: 'It is fit that it should be remembered that near this city there is an University of the foundation of Queen Elizabeth, principally intended for the education and advantage of the natives of this kingdom, which hath produced men very eminent for learning and piety, and those of this nation, and such there are in the Church: so that, while there are such, the passing them over is not only, in some measure, a violation of the original intention and institution, but a great discouragement to the natives from making themselves capable and fit for preferment in the Church, whereunto, *if they have equal parts, they are better able to do service than strangers, their knowledge of the country and relations in it giving them the advantage.* The promotion, too, of the already dignified or beneficed will make room for, and consequently encourage, students in the University; which room will be lost, and the inferior clergy much disheartened, if, upon the vacancy of bishopricks, persons unknown to the kingdom and University shall be sent to fill them, and be less useful there to Church and kingdom than those who are better acquainted with them' (Taylor's *History*, p. 43). That Ormonde

The indolent rule of Provost Pratt made difficult the task of Baldwin, whose severity cut at the roots of his popularity, and obscured in some measure his many services to the College. He had first to deal with internal discipline.

'The lecturers seldom attended lectures, even the public ones. The Fellows were seldom seen at prayers. Commons was greatly neglected by them. There were Deans who never once attended dinner in the Hall during an entire year.' *

But the Jacobite sympathies of an ardent section of the society constituted a more serious problem. Baldwin grasped the nettle of disloyalty firmly, and the College retained its reputation as a fortress of Whiggery, in spite of the occasional outbursts which gave evidence of the presence of disaffection beneath the surface. In 1708 a certain Edward Forbes, a student, had been expelled by the act of the Provost and Senior Fellows for an expression of opinion at the Commencement supper that the Queen's right to the throne was no better than that of her predecessor, and *eodem nititur fundamento*—no very revolutionary sentiment. The expulsion of Forbes led to a curious passage of arms between the Lords and Commons of the Irish Parliament. Fearing that the disloyalty of one of their number might be predicated of the whole body, the Senate of the University prepared a document declara-

---

did not hesitate to select Englishmen for posts when he judged their qualifications higher than those of available ' natives ' was shown by his appointments as Chancellor.

* Pamphlet, Coll. Lib., P. ii. 31.

tory of the firmness of their allegiance to the reigning house. The Commons, in an address to the Throne, through the Lord Lieutenant, petitioning for a grant to Trinity College for the erection of a new library, took occasion to strengthen the case by a mention of the stable loyalty of that corporate body. This proceeding found no favour, however, in the Upper House, which passed, and embodied in the address, a resolution censuring the grounds upon which the petition was partially based. The Commons, in turn, taking advantage of the granting of the petition, expressed their indignation at the censure, and voted:

'That the Lords in the Address have highly infringed the rights, privileges, and liberties of the Commons, misrepresented her Majesty's condescension to their humble application, and have unjustly insinuated (to the dishonour of this House) that the principles for encouragement of which the aforesaid application was made were such as her Majesty disapproved.'

The heads of the College deemed it wise on several subsequent occasions to assert their adherence to the Hanoverian House as against the Stuarts. The reverberations of the storm raised by the expulsion of Forbes sounded all through the reigns of Anne and George I., and various efforts were made to procure a repeal of the sentence passed upon him. His 'wicked words,' as Archbishop Synge called them, 'which placed the title of the late Queen on the same foot with that of her glorious predecessor,' echoed in the memory of the College, and fed the evil imaginations of succeeding generations of undergraduates. In 1710 a student

A NEST OF JACOBITES

named Harvey 'was convicted of inflicting an indignity on the memory of King William by wrenching the bâton out of the hand of his equestrian statue in College Green.' For this act he was expelled, together with two aiding and abetting accomplices.

'In 1713 Theodore Barlow was expelled for drinking in the rooms of one of the scholars to the memory of the horse from which King William was thrown, to the great danger of his life, and also to the health of the Pretender, and for denouncing with a curse the Hanoverian succession.'

On April 8, 1715, 'a student named Nathaniel Crump was expelled for saying that Oliver Cromwell was to be preferred to Charles I., and in May

'A Master of Arts, a Bachelor of Arts, and an Undergraduate, were publicly admonished for reading a scandalous pamphlet reflecting on the King, under the name of *Nero Secundus;* and a notice was placed upon the gates of the College denouncing this pamphlet, and threatening the expulsion of all students who should read it or make a copy of it.'

In June a Master of Arts was expelled for making the forbidden copy, and two Bachelors expelled for using language disrespectful to the King.* In the same year Archbishop King† wrote to Addison, then Chief Secretary for Ireland:

'The business of the College gives a great deal of trouble to every honest man, and a peculiar pain to me. 'Tis plain there's a nest of Jacobites in it; one was con-

* Stubbs' *History*, pp. 154-156.
† King was at this time one of the Lords Justices.

victed last term, two are run away, and, I believe, bills are found against one or two more. But we can't as yet reach the fountains of the corruption; but I assure you no diligence is wanting, and everybody looks on it to be of the last consequence to purge the fountain of education. I believe next Parliament will look into the matter.'

The unpopularity of their rulers increased among the students, but the causes can hardly have been to any extent political. Riots and disorders were of frequent occurrence, the ringleaders being in many cases sons of noblemen or gentlemen of position. Between 1725 and 1734 Lords Tullamore, Mount-Cashel, Strangford, Massarene, and Lord George Sackville, the son of the Duke of Dorset, then Lord Lieutenant, were members of the College, while there were almost a hundred Fellow Commoners on the books. In a *Letter to the Students of the University*, published in 1734, we read of one of the tumultuous outbreaks by which at this time the collegians greatly added to their reputation as organizers of magnificent mischief. One of the undergraduates, having insulted the Junior Dean, was publicly censured. His friends stoned the Dean, and reduced his rooms, into which forcible entry was made, to a condition of elemental chaos. Fired by the unholy joy of destruction, they proceeded to other parts of the College, and achieved similar successes.

'The Board offered considerable rewards for the discovery of the perpetrators of these riotous proceedings; the Students retorted by offering higher rewards to anyone who would bring in the informer dead or alive. A

RIOTS AND DISORDERS

threatening letter was sent to the Provost. Strangers from town, as was usually the case, came into the College to assist in the pillage. One of these attempted to set fire to the College gates; and had not some of the well-disposed Students prevented this, they would have laid the College in ashes, as the flames would have caught hold of the ancient buildings, extravagantly timbered after the old manner, and would have reached the new buildings, and the flames could not then have been extinguished.'

A pamphlet in the College library* published in 1734, refers to the constant disorder and the difficulty felt in attempting to control it:

'When the Board meets to inquire into a violation of the Statutes on the part of the students, the young gentlemen assemble in the Courts below; they have secured a number of their friends; they are surrounded by a great crowd of their brethren; how many they may have engaged to be of their party is not to be discovered, and they give, perhaps, plain intimations that they will not suffer them to be censured. Trusting in their numbers, they will not suffer any one man to be singled out for an example.'

From Primate Boulter's letters we learn of the escapade of a scholar named Annesley, a relation of Lord Anglesea. It was customary for the porter to lock the College gate at night, and carry the keys to the Provost. The Provost had retired to bed, when he was roused by an outrageous knocking, which continued and forced him at length to rise. It appeared that Annesley had been entertaining some friends in College, who had remained beyond the statutable time. The

* P. ii. 31.

keys were demanded that they might be let out of College, and the demand was accompanied by threats to break down the gates. The impudent request was very naturally refused, and Annesley called on for an apology next day. This he refused, put on his hat before the Provost, and walked off. He was expelled, but restored later through his influence with the Lord Lieutenant and the Visitors.

During Baldwin's provostship one of the best disliked of the Fellows was Edward Ford,* a martinet whose interference with student doings was judged by some to have passed the bounds of unprotesting toleration. One evening a number of gownsmen who felt themselves aggrieved proceeded to display their annoyance, in the ineradicable fashion of all ages, by throwing stones at his windows. Ford, a man with no reputation for suffering insults gladly, lost his self-control, seized a loaded gun, and fired upon his assailants below. The superiority of his arms challenged the undergraduate resources. In a few minutes firearms were upon the spot, and Ford, who persisted in remaining at his window, was shot at and mortally wounded. As might be expected, intense excitement prevailed, not only in College, but throughout the city, after this tragic occurrence. The five students suspected of the act were expelled, and prosecuted for the murder. But the authorities of the College were at this time far from popular. Public sympathy was largely on the side of the students, especially among ladies, while

* In the late Isaac Butt's *Chapters of College Romance*, a tragic story is founded on this occurrence, in which, however, an imaginary colouring is given to the facts.

'one noble lord declared that a Fellow's blood did not deserve an inquisition which might detain a man one day from his ordinary business.' The students prosecuted by the Board were acquitted by the Court of Commission, which conducted the trial.

After the death of Ford, the prevalent disorder seems greatly to have diminished, and no other riot of any consequence occurred within the College walls until 1747, when the last serious outbreak on record took place. A scholar of the household had been arrested by bailiffs within its sacred precincts, hitherto inviolable. A studied revenge was taken by a band of gownsmen. They sought through the whole city for the offender, and when found conveyed him to College, when by a free use of the pump, celebrated by Lever in *Charles O'Malley*, he was supposed to be cleansed of his guilt. Some bold spirit suggested that, to celebrate the great day of justice, an attempt should be made to break open Newgate and set free all the prisoners. The attempt ended in failure, but not until several citizens had lost their lives in the affray to which it gave rise.*

Richard Baldwin, Senior Fellow for twenty, and Provost for forty-one, years,† must take rank as one of the most striking figures in the succession of its rulers. To his parentage and early life, and the influence to which he owed his promotion, a mystery attaches. He was a contemporary and schoolfellow of Swift, for whom he

---

* Among those students who were publicly censured for aiding and abetting this riot by their presence the name of Oliver Goldsmith occurs.

† 1717 to 1758.

entertained a personal, added to a political, dislike.* Baldwin's intellectual strength fell far short of that of his character, and Swift looked with disdain upon the man, while he expressed at the visitation of 1734 the opinion that the government of the College stood badly in need of reformation. Baldwin's tyrannical methods could hardly, perhaps, commend themselves to any except those whose interests they served. 'The power he has,' wrote Boulter, 'is indeed beyond anything any head of a College has in Oxford, but is little enough to keep the College from being a seminary of Jacobitism.'

It was Baldwin's custom to nominate the members for the University constituency, which became for the time the Provost's pocket borough. In the year 1728 a vacancy occurred in the representation by the death of Molyneux. Baldwin wished Palliser to have the seat, sent for the scholars, and ordered them to vote for Palliser. Among those who promised their support was a scholar named Skelton. The rival party now withdrew their candidate, proposed a Dr. Ellwood, and managed to induce the Provost to transfer his support from Palliser to the new man. The scholars were again sent for, and this time ordered to vote for Ellwood. Skelton declined to break his promise for Palliser. 'Sirrah,' said the Provost, 'you are an obstinate fellow, and I never can get any good of you, but I'll make you repent of it yet.'

On another occasion Skelton was summoned before

* He said of Swift that ' he was remarkable for nothing else while a student than his skill in kindling a good fire, and that he would never allow his College woman to do it for him.'—BURDY: *Life of Skelton*.

Baldwin and charged with Jacobite sympathies. His protestations of innocence were in vain. Baldwin believed himself to have a sure nose for the political taint.

'"Child," he cried, "I'll ruin you for ever!"
'"Will you damn my soul, sir?" said Skelton.
'"No," said the Provost; "but I'll ruin you in the College here."
'"Oh, sir," replied Skelton, with sang-froid, "that's but a short 'for ever'!"'*

Another, the martial, side of Baldwin's character is displayed in Skelton's account of his conduct in one of the many conflicts between the undergraduates and their hereditary enemies, the butchers of the city :†

'He ran out before the students. "Follow me, my lads, and I'll head you! I am appointed by your parents and friends to take care of you, and I'll fight for you till I die!" He would have done so,' adds Skelton, ' for he was as brave as a lion.'

Of the brawls and riots which in the eighteenth century were common in the streets of Dublin, the records supply details almost too vivid to be credible. Between the Liberty Boys, or tailors and weavers of the Coombe, and the Ormond Boys, or butchers who lived in Ormond Market, an irreconcilable feud raged,

* Burdy's *Life of Skelton*. Wesley had a great admiration for Skelton. 'When there is occasion he shows all the wit of Dr. Swift, joined with ten times his judgment' (*Journal*, June, 1771).

† On account of these butchers' quarrels an Act of Parliament was passed dispensing with the attendance of students at St. Patrick's.

and Homeric battles, at times occupying several days, took place, not without wounds and bloodshed.

'The butchers used their knives, not to stab their opponents, but for a purpose then common in the barbarous state of Irish society, to hough or cut the tendon of the leg, thereby rendering the person incurably lame for life. On one occasion, after a defeat of the Ormond boys, those of the Liberty retaliated in a manner still more barbarous and revolting. They dragged the persons they seized to their market, and, dislodging the meat they found there, hooked the men by the jaws, and retired, leaving the butchers hanging on their own stalls. The spirit of the times led men of the highest grade and respectability to join with the dregs of the market in these outrages, entirely forgetful of the feelings of their order, then immeasurably more exclusive in their ideas of a gentleman than now; and the young aristocrat, who would have felt it an intolerable degradation to associate, or even be seen with an honest merchant, however respectable, with a singular inconsistency made a boast of his intimate acquaintance with the lawless excesses of butchers and coal-porters. The students of Trinity College were particularly prone to join in the affrays between the belligerents, and generally united their forces to those of the Liberty boys against the butchers. On one occasion several of them were seized by the latter, and to the great terror of their friends it was reported they were hanged up in the stalls, in retaliation for the cruelty of the weavers. A party of watchmen sufficiently strong was at length collected by the authorities, and they proceeded to Ormond Market; there they saw a frightful spectacle—a number of College lads in their gowns and caps hanging to the hooks. On examination, however, it was found that the butchers, pitying their youth and respecting their rank, had only hung them by the waistbands of their breeches, where they remained as helpless, indeed, as if they were suspended by the neck.

'The gownsmen were then a formidable body, and from a strong *esprit de corps* were ready, on short notice, to issue forth in a mass to avenge any insults offered to an individual of their party who complained of it. They converted the keys of their rooms into formidable weapons. They procured them as large and heavy as possible, and, slinging them in the sleeves or tails of their gowns or pocket-handkerchiefs, gave with them mortal blows.'*

Even the Fellows participated, it appears, in this *esprit de corps*, and we have seen that Provost Baldwin was at times inflamed with a similar martial ardour. Unpopular though he was in his own day, Baldwin was a good lover of the College. To him it owes the present library, completed in 1724, the dining-hall, erected between 1740 and 1745, and many improvements of a less important character. It is true that learning owes little to Baldwin, and his rule was marked by no important intellectual developments. Harsh, imperious, often unjust, his qualities were those of a man of action, and if he possessed the faculty of amassing wealth, the body corporate reaped the enduring advantage forbidden to the mortal, for at his death he bequeathed to it £24,000, together with all his real estates in various parts of Ireland.† The monument erected to his memory by the grateful foundation over which he had ruled so long keeps his memory green, for it occupies a commanding position where all must see. 'None of us ever can for-

* *Ireland Ninety Years Ago.*
† In all the value of the bequest was about £80,000.

get the marble angels round the figure of the dying Provost on which we used to gaze during the pangs of the Examination Hall.'*

To the stern and academic Baldwin succeeded the polished courtier and gentleman, Francis Andrews, a Senior Fellow, though a layman. Distinguished by the versatility and elegance rather than by the depth of his learning, and by a pronounced taste for the pleasures of accomplished society, witty discourse, and a good table,

* Sir Robert Ball in *The Book of Trinity College.* Taylor's *History* breaks into poetic rapture over this monument.

' In this work the Provost is represented in a recumbent position, resting on his left elbow, and holding in his hand a scroll supposed to represent a will. . . . His head, which is of a dignified character, is thrown a little backward, and looking upward with an expression of pious resignation, which is admirably represented. . . . A female figure, emblematic of the University, bends over him in an attitude and with a countenance expressive of the most tender grief; at his feet is an angel approaching him, holding in her left hand a wreath of palm, and looking on him with a countenance of ineffable benignity, points up to heaven.'

The strength of Baldwin's character is well brought out in the story told of him in Hutchinson's MS. Delany, the friend of Swift, a Junior Fellow and politician of the opposite camp from Baldwin, took occasion to preach at the Provost in chapel. Baldwin remained indifferent, but a little later Delany handed him a copy of the sermon. 'You did then, sir, preach this sermon against me?' inquired Baldwin. 'You must, then, beg my pardon publicly in the College Hall, or I will expel you.' Delany, a favourite with Lord Cartaret, the Viceroy, refused, and his patron sent a message to the Provost that the matter must go no further. His advice was declined, whereupon a messenger was sent to deliver a stronger mandate. 'Tell the Provost that his house is made of glass, and that I have a stone in my sleeve.' Baldwin replied, 'Tell his Excellency that if Dr. Delany does not beg my pardon in the College Hall to-morrow, I will expel him there at twelve o'clock.' It is said that the apology was given and the Provost left master of the field.

THE LIBRARY—EXTERIOR

'Frank with many friends' inaugurated a new régime. The year after his elevation to the provostship he entered the House of Commons, and until his death in 1774 played a conspicuous part in the fashionable life of the capital. To his friend Rigby, the Irish Secretary of the day, 'a gay, jovial, and not overscrupulous placeman,' the secretary and favourite of the Duke of Bedford, Andrews probably owed the appointment which proved of no little advantage to the College. His influence and popularity had much to do with the magnificent grants made by the House of Commons for the erection of the new and splendid buildings by which during this period the University was ennobled. There is little doubt also that the reputation and policy of Andrews assisted in drawing into bonds of closer sympathy the academic circle within the walls and the larger political and civic society of Ireland, a service of the utmost importance. Neither academies nor nations profit when savants cease to be gentlemen and good citizens, or the leaders of public opinion are lacking in their appreciation of learning and of culture. It appears 'from the information of the late Duke of Leinster, and many gentlemen who lived much with him at Rome,'[*] that Andrews charmed his Italian acquaintances with the purity and elegance of his conversation in Latin, and there is good evidence that his type of scholarship served to attract many students from the best families in the country. Few of the young men of good birth in Ireland thought it necessary to cross the Channel

[*] Hardy's *Life of Charlemont*.

for their University education during the eighteenth century, and it is noteworthy that few of those who did so in the nineteenth achieved in after-life very brilliant reputations.

The most important ceremonial occasion during Andrews' tenure of office was the installation of the Duke of Bedford as Chancellor on the death of Frederick, Prince of Wales, in 1751,* which was marked by unusual pomp and circumstance, and is of interest, among other reasons, in that it gave the Earl of Mornington, father of the famous Duke of Wellington, a graduate, and the first Professor of Music in the University, an opportunity to compose the music for an ode written for the occasion, together with a *Te Deum* and *Jubilate* for the service on the succeeding Sunday in the chapel.† To the versatile culture of the Provost both the foundation of the School of Music and the selection of the Earl of Mornington as the first Professor are due. A College organist appears to have been first appointed at the Restoration, and a regular choir and choral service instituted in 1762, the latter under the direction of the Professor. A number of musical societies, a public garden in which musical entertainments were given, a music-hall, and an academy, of which Lord Mornington was president, give evidence that the taste for music, even at this time, was general in the Irish capital, and it will be remembered that Dubourg, the violinist, came to Dublin in 1728, and

* For a full account see Stubbs' *History*, p. 217. The fine portrait of this Chancellor by Gainsborough, now in the Provost's House, dates from this time.

† These compositions have all been lost.

lived there many years, and that Handel's *Messiah* was first produced before a Dublin audience.*

The provostship of Andrews was distinguished, as might be expected, by a large and growing expenditure by the House upon entertainments, always carried out in a handsome and dignified fashion. But that his interest in, and zeal for, the College, to which all contemporary records bear witness, were not confined to a care for hospitality or the arts is seen in the record of the additions made under his direction to its teaching power. The Chairs of Mathematics and Hebrew were founded in 1762, and the Chair of Modern History separated from that of Oratory, and thus increased in importance. Men of real ability and eminence were appointed to the new Chairs, among whom Dr. Leland,† who filled the Professorship of Oratory for twenty years, achieved an enviable distinction as a scholar and man of letters. Kearney, Professor of History, whose name is known to readers of Boswell; Hugh Hamilton, Professor of Natural Philosophy, author of an original and important treatise on conic sections; and Murray, afterwards Provost, whose name is familiar as the author of a once-famous textbook on logic, were among the scholars and teachers who give distinction to the reign of Andrews, and co-operated with him in building up the high reputation which Trinity College so rapidly achieved during the eighteenth century. More than a century and a half of

* See Lecky, *History of Ireland*, vol. i., p. 327. Mr. Lecky also reminds us of the interesting fact that ' Garrick acted Hamlet in Dublin before he attempted it in England.'

† Author of editions and translations of Demosthenes, of a *Life of Philip of Macedon*, and a well-known *History of Ireland*.

storm and trial successfully encountered had laid firmly the foundations of that prestige, intellectual and social, upon the enjoyment of which it now entered. Vexed as Ireland still is by religious differences, there are few Irishmen, of whatever creed, and those only among the ignorant, who are unwilling to acknowledge its claims to the gratitude and admiration of their country.*

The obligation to celibacy, strictly enforced during the earlier years of the century, began about this time to be frequently evaded, and the Fellows, who were supposed to be bachelors, had many of them contracted marriages which were an open secret. Society recognised the position of their wives, who (prefixing Mrs.) retained their maiden names, and the violation of the statute was deliberately overlooked. Previous to 1812 a Fellow was not bound to declare the fact of his marriage, nor the Provost required to ask for a resignation on the ground of marriage unless it were brought officially to his notice.† The obligation to celibacy

* To give an example. In reply to some attacks on Trinity College in the *Irish National Press* and *Freeman*, a writer in the *Daily Independent* said (April 22, 1892): 'We are not concerned to defend the governing body of Trinity College in the anti-Home Rule policy which they have unfortunately pursued, but we think it unworthy of journals professing to be national to belittle the work done by Irishmen and members of an Irish University which has shed a brilliant lustre upon this country.'

† A story is told of the resignation in 1709 of a Mr. Squire, a Junior Fellow. He was engaged in a conversation with Provost Browne in the garden, when a gentleman of his acquaintance in the city came up to him with congratulations on the birth of a son. The untoward intimation of the happy event led to a hasty letter of resignation. Theophilus Swift, in his *Animadversions*, prepares a simple dilemma for the married Fellows: 'Now, either Dr. Shuffle is married or he is not married . . . the holy sinner may cleave to either side of the question: I leave him to embrace either his wife or his mistress.'

was not removed, save by special dispensation, until 1840. A brilliant *jeu de mot* of the late Cardinal Newman on this subject is on record. On one of his visits to Ireland not long after his secession to Rome, a clergyman of the then Established Church, in a conversation with him, introduced the subject of the celibacy statute, and deplored its repeal.

'But,' asked Dr. Newman, 'is it not the fact that the statute was evaded?'

'Well, yes,' admitted his interlocutor, 'no doubt it was. G—— was privately married, M—— was privately married, and many others. My own tutor, Elrington, the Bishop of Ferns, was privately married.'

'Naturally,' remarked Dr. Newman, 'one expects to find Ferns among the Cryptogamous.'

In his will Provost Andrews made provision for the erection and endowment of an astronomical observatory in connection with Trinity College, a project which had long possessed his mind. Certain technical difficulties arose which occasioned long delay, and a reduction of the amount originally bequeathed to the College, but the board at once proceeded to select a Professor of Astronomy and to choose a site for the observatory. Dunsink, where the building now stands, about five miles to the north-west of Dublin, was regarded as the most convenient and suitable of the accessible places then considered, and Dr. Henry Ussher, the first occupant of the new Chair, proceeded to plan the dome and meridian-room, and equip them with the necessary instruments. Ussher accomplished some useful work, and upon his death, in 1790, was succeeded by Dr. Brinkley, a Caius College, Cambridge, man, and a

Senior Wrangler. Two years later, by letters patent, the Andrews Professor of Astronomy became the Astronomer Royal of Ireland. Eighteen years, however, passed before the new Professor obtained the great telescope with a graduated circle 8 feet in diameter which he employed in his subsequent important observations. But in 1826 Brinkley exchanged his Chair for the bishopric of Cloyne, and was succeeded by a lad who, at seventeen years of age, had paid him a visit bearing with him two mathematical papers entitled 'Osculating Parabola to Curves of Double Curvature' and 'On Contacts between Algebraic Curves and Surfaces.'

At twenty-two years of age William Rowan Hamilton, still an undergraduate, was elected to the Chair, although Airy was a candidate, and at once gave himself up to that series of profound researches which culminated in the discovery of the system of Quaternions, and placed him among the greatest mathematicians of any age or country. The marvellous genius of Hamilton in the realm of abstract science was combined with a singular personal charm, and with a deep love and considerable aptitude for poetry. He became the friend, not only of men like Herschel and De Morgan, but of Coleridge and Wordsworth, and was visited by the latter poet at Dunsink, where a shady avenue still bears his name. Before Hamilton's death, the present magnificent equatorial, with its 12-inch object-glass, was erected, and an equally fine meridian circle was added in 1873, during the tenure of the Chair by his successor, Dr. Francis Brünnow. Among the later names associated with Dunsink, that of Sir Robert Ball, now

Lowndean Professor of Astronomy at Cambridge, is probably the most widely known.

During the last illness of Andrews, candidates for the Provostship were already anxiously at work, and in the end, through the influence of Sir John Blacquiere, Chief Secretary, the coveted preferment fell to a Dublin barrister, John Hely Hutchinson, Prime Serjeant and Alnager of Ireland. The appointment created bitter hostility, as did the new Provost's tyrannical methods, and a shower of pamphlets attacking the Chief Secretary and his nominee issued from the press. Of Blacquiere it was said, 'who he was, save that he had been an officer of dragoons, no man could certainly tell; his origin, like the source of the Nile, was only guessed at.' And of Hutchinson it was remarked by Lord North, in answer to an inquiry by George III., that if the King were pleased to bestow on him England and Ireland, he would ask for the Isle of Man for a potato-garden.' A Junior Fellow of the time, a bitter enemy of Hutchinson, describes him and his methods in the well-known *Lachrymæ Academicæ*.[*] Here we learn that he

'bought a seat in Parliament for a borough; that immediately after taking his seat, having the advantages of strong lungs, a copious flow of words, and a sufficiently

---

[*] 1777, by Dr. Patrick Duigenan. He was also the author of a once famous reply to the address published by Grattan on his secession from Parliament in 1797. Of this pamphlet, which ran through five editions in a few weeks, Mr. Lecky says: 'A reader who is exempt from the passions of that time would find it difficult to conceive a grosser or more impudent travesty of history. The calamities that had befallen Ireland, in the opinion of Duigenan, were mainly due to two men — Burke and Grattan' (*History of Ireland*, vol. v., p. 109).

graceful delivery, he commenced a most violent and obstreperous patriot. Luckily, in respect to his own advancement, he had a very confined understanding, so that he could thunder forth nonsense for whole days together with the most furious distortions of his visage and the rest of his body.'

Another attack upon the Provost, entitled *Pranceriana,** contains a series of letters, dialogues, and verses, scurrilous but amusing. Among the descriptions given of him, the following, perhaps, best sums up his versatile attainments and capacity for acquiring offices:

' A Harlequin genius, Cognomine Prancer,
A Duellist, Scribbler, a Fop, and a Dancer,
A Lawyer, Prime Serjeant, and Judge of Assizes,
A Parliament man and a Stamper of Frizes,
A Chancellor Privy, a Cavalry Major,
A Searcher and Packer, Comptroller and Guager,
A Speecher and Critic, Prescriber of Rules,
A Founder of Fencing and Equestrian Schools:
If various employments can give a man knowledge,
Then who knows as much as the head of the College?'

Though by no means 'ridiculously illiterate,'† as he was described, and beyond question a man of vigorous

* 1784. Mr. Jack Prance or Prancero were names given to Hutchinson in allusion to the riding-school which he attempted to establish in the College. Hutchinson is represented in this volume as trampling on Newton's *Principia* in the act of making a lunge; a sarcastic reference to the fencing school.

† No. 40 of *Prancerians*. *The Rook and the Blackbirds* contains these lines, in which by the Rook Hutchinson is designated:

' No lawyer in a triple major
Could look more reverend or sager,
Than he declaiming in a ring
And teaching Blackbirds how to sing.

intellect and powers of initiative, Hutchinson, who had never been a Fellow or scholar, for thirty years had taken no interest in the College, and had sent his eldest son to Oxford, was in no way qualified for the post he had secured. Despite the unpopularity of his appointment, however, as a man of the world he understood how to take advantage of the formidable powers now in his hands. He could give or refuse to the Fellows leave of absence even during vacations, could grant or refuse chambers, remove pupils from their tutors and transfer them to others, and withhold many privileges, some of them of pecuniary value, from such of the Fellows and scholars as offended or crossed him. In consequence he was successful in securing the adhesion of a considerable section of the society, which did not care or dare to forfeit the goodwill of the Provost, while the Fellows who were privately married contrary to statute were entirely at his mercy. It was well, as Dr. Mahaffy says, that Hutchinson did not set himself to plunder the College for his family,* and confined his efforts to the attempt to secure political power, and to make of the University constituency a pocket borough for his family. In 1776 he secured the return of his eldest son by intimidation and bribery, only to have him unseated on petition, and in 1790 renewed the attempt, this time for a

For he had store of learned words
Which sounded sweet with simple birds,
And could discourse of Rome and Greece,
Of Jason and the Golden Fleece;
Had read, which proved him learn'd enow,
Demosthenes, peri Stephanou.'

* *Book of Trinity College, Dublin*, p. 78.

younger son.* A petition was again lodged against the election, and was heard by a committee, upon which Lord Edward Fitzgerald and the future Duke of Wellington had seats. There is little doubt that the case against the Provost was complete, but his face was saved, and his son's election confirmed by the casting-vote of the chairman.†

Among the uncatalogued MSS. in Trinity College library is a volume described on the front-slip as 'Papers relating entirely to Disputes with Provost Hutchinson.' Many of these arose out of mere personal animosity, or distaste of the Provost's high-handed methods in matters clearly within his rights. But on two occasions he was called to account for serious

* The wife of the Provost was created a peeress with remainder to her son, who on her death became Lord Donoughmore.

† A number of College songs of the period refer to these elections. One has the refrain:

> 'For in spite of oath,
> Or promise or both,
> I'll vote for honest Frank Hely, oh.'

Another contains the following stanza:

> 'Now I've got a scholar's gown
> I'll quit reading for the town;
> Learn good breeding, get a coat,
> Visit Lords, and sport my vote;
> Caper, vapour, swagger, swear,
> Bully porters, charm the fair.
> Three cock'd hat
> And all that;
> Powder'd hair
> Boots, a pair;
> Fop, Sir;
> Pop, Sir.
> My books at the pawnbroker's shop, Sir

Another runs:

> 'Comrades, to make a tedious story short,
> For Frank I voted, and have nothing for't.'

breaches of statute. In 1775 the Vice-Chancellor, as Visitor, decided in favour of the appeal of a scholar whom Hutchinson had deprived, and in 1791 another visitation, held by Lord Clare, refused him the right of negative which he claimed in every election. The less serious charges levied against Hutchinson merely prove his disregard of academic tradition and contempt for the conservatism of the Fellows. His departure from all recognised principles in the establishment within the University of a gymnasium, a fencing and a riding school is tearfully bemoaned.

'The College walks and gardens, heretofore sacred to the exercise and contemplation of sober academick, are now infested by himself and military officers mounted on prancing horses; his wife and adult daughters, with their train of female companions; and his infant children, their nurses and go-carts, who, by their clamour and pomp, have banished the Muses, and may probably be the authors of greater and more serious evils.'*

It was also asserted that the duel which he fought with a Mr. William Doyle, Master in Chancery, had encouraged the practice of duelling among the students.

'Scarce a week passes,' we read in the same pamphlet, 'without a duel between some of the students; some of them have been slain, others maimed; the College Park is publicly made the place for learning the exercise of the pistol; shooting at marks by the gownsmen is every day's practice; the very chambers of the College frequently resound with the explosions of pistols. The Provost has introduced a fencing-master into the College, and assigned him the Convocation or Senate House of the University

* *Lachryma Academica*.

for a school, to teach the gownsmen the use of the sword, though the use of swords is strictly forbidden in the College by the statutes.'*

It is clear, both from the complaints of his enemies and from the account of official acts of the Provost, that he was anxious to modify the curriculum and life of the University in view of what seemed to him the requirements of the time. He aimed at the education of the man of fashion and the gentleman, the sons of the aristocracy of Ireland, and with these in mind would naturally seek to provide for such accomplishments as riding, fencing, and a conversational knowledge of modern languages. It ought to be remembered that Dublin was at this its most brilliant period the second city in the empire, crowded with an intellectual and fashionable society, in which it was Hutchinson's natural ambition that the University should play a leading part. Nor was his experience as a man of the world entirely at fault, nor the changes he introduced the result of mere caprice and without knowledge. By the establishment, for example, of professorships in French and German, he laid the foundation of a school of modern literature, which has since done important service in the cause of higher education. He so skilfully managed the estates of the College as to increase their annual value by £5,000 per

* The author is himself credited with one or two duels. The above-quoted statememt with regard to duelling among undergraduates may be an exaggeration, but there is abundant evidence that it was not unusual; *e.g.*, in Burdy's *Life of Skelton* we read, p. 269: ' He had a quarrel there (Trinity College, Dublin) with one of his fellow-students, which they thought fit to determine at St. Stephen's Green with small swords.'

annum. He built the present Examination Hall, one of the finest in this or any other College, and it must always be recalled to his honour that he was a strong advocate of Catholic emancipation, that as a member of Parliament he urged the admission of Roman Catholics to degrees in Trinity College, and that it was on his motion that the Honorary Doctorate of Laws was conferred upon the greatest of her then living sons, Edmund Burke. Burke's reply, accepting the proffered honour, is worthy quotation, alike for its pathetic dignity and for the gratitude to his *alma mater* which it expresses.

'I received,' he says, 'this most honourable testimony of your approbation just as I was going to the House of Commons yesterday to commence my tenth year's warfare against the most dangerous enemy to the justice, honour, morals, and Constitution of this country, by which they have ever been attacked. I mean the corruption which has come upon us from the East, and in which I act with everything respectable in every party in the House. Although I have been for some days ill in health, and not very full of spirits, your letter enabled me to go through a long and fatiguing day, if not with strength, at least with resolution. I thought that the University which had bred me called upon me not to disgrace in my last stage the lessons she had taught me in the early part of my life; and I hope, old as I am, I shall prove as docile to her lessons as when I was subject to her discipline.'

Before Hutchinson's death, intrigues for the provostship began. The Fellows were anxious that a member of their own body should be appointed, and feared that the post might be given to a creature of the Government. Burke, who was himself spoken of for the place, exerted his influence to secure the appointment for Murray, the Vice-Provost, a man of considerable learning and parts. A letter written on this matter* by the most shining representative of disinterested statesmanship of that age is of interest:

'A strange and unfounded report is, I find, rife all over Ireland, that I am to be made Provost of the University of Dublin. If my Richard had lived, for whom alone I could bear to take any charge, I would not accept it on any account. But it is not for that reason I mention it, but most earnestly and pressingly to put it to your conscience not to suffer this great, important, and (just now) most critical of all trusts to be jobbed away in any manner whatsoever. It ought not to be suffered to enter into any sort of political arrangement. . . . The Provostship ought to be given to a member only of the body, and for a thousand reasons to an ecclesiastic. . . . I have no favourite, no connection, political or personal, to warp my judgment in this point. The law is wiser than cabal or interest. . . . If I saw you I could say much more on this subject, for though my heart is very sick, it has these things in it.'

In the end Murray was appointed,† and the anxiety of the society relieved. From this time onward, as Dr.

* To Mr. Wyndham.
† The uncatalogued MSS. in the College library contain the following letter from Dr. Hall, who was in London as representative of the Fellows, to Murray:

'*To the Rev. Dr. Murray.*

'MY DEAR SIR,—While I was kissing the King's right hand at Levee to-day, I saw him deposit our Petition in his Pocket with his left, and am, Dear Sir,

'Yours affectionately,
'Mail Coach Office,   'GEO. HALL.
 'Anniversary of the Irish Rebellion, 1793.'

Mahaffy says, the practice of promoting 'the Senior Major of the Regiment' was regularly followed. But as the provostship now again became a direct avenue to the Episcopal Bench, its heads ceased to take that exclusive and paramount interest in the concerns of the College which they demanded, and 'the history from the appointment of Murray to that of Bartholomew Lloyd in 1837 is probably the least creditable in all the three centuries.'* Neither from the Provosts nor Fellows came any learned or intellectual work, though their leisure was ample, nor was the College enriched by any important additions to its buildings, library, or ornaments, though 'many men drew £50,000 in salaries.' The apathy and indifference of the members of the society to anything but their personal interest is proved by the fact that the date of the bicentenary of the foundation passed unnoticed, and no festivities such as those which took place at the centenary and tercentenary were held. Under Baldwin, Andrews, and Hutchinson, Trinity College immensely extended her influence, increased her prestige, and added to the dignity of her establishment. She was now condemned for nearly half a century to minister to the greed and idleness of a generation of unworthy sons.

Before the death of Hutchinson, was passed, in 1793, the Act which admitted Roman Catholics to degrees in the University of Dublin. Before the passing of the Act many Roman Catholics had been members of the College, and it is a striking fact that, when the proposal to establish a separate College for Catholics was discussed in Grattan's Parliament, a strongly-worded peti-

* Dr. Mahaffy, *Book of Trinity College, Dublin*, p. 83.

tion against it was presented by the Roman Catholics of the kingdom.

'Having in common with the rest of their brethren, the Catholics of Ireland,' the petition ran, ' received as one of the most important and acceptable benefits bestowed on them by his Majesty and the Legislature, the permission of having their youth educated along with the Protestant youth of the kingdom in the University of Dublin, and experience having fully demonstrated the wisdom and utility of that permission, they see with deep concern the principle of separation and exclusion, they hoped removed for ever, now likely to be revived and re-enacted.' *

In 1788 a Relief Act dealing with the property in land of members of the oppressed Church had been carried, and from that date almost every year brought about a further measure of emancipation reform. In spite of the determined opposition of the Vice-Chancellor, Lord Clare, the statutable oath and declaration against Popery were for the first time omitted from the requirements for degrees,† and the University became free to the world. Not, however, till late in the nineteenth century‡ were the emoluments and honours of the College thrown open to adherents of any religious

* Irish Par. Deb. XV. 203. See also the *History of the University* by D. C. Heron, a Roman Catholic, for a similar line of argument.

† For an account of the action of Dr. Miller, Senior Master non-Regent, which secured the result aimed at by the Act in the year in which it was passed, see Stubbs' *History*, p. 284.

‡ Under the Fawcett Act in 1873, which abolished all tests and opened all offices and emoluments, except in the Divinity School, to all persons, irrespective of creed. Non-foundation scholarships open to all had been founded in 1854.

creed, and it is only within the last generation that there have been any Roman Catholic Fellows.

It ought to be added here that those Roman Catholics who have received their education in Trinity College have almost without exception cherished for it an affectionate regard equal to that of its Protestant alumni. A single instance must suffice. Thomas Wyse, M.P., a strenuous advocate of the rights of the Roman Catholic population of Ireland to a University of their own, made, in a speech delivered in 1844, the following generous acknowledgment of his own debt to Trinity College:

'I was educated in that University myself. I find its recollections in many instances twine around my heart with the dearest remembrances of my earliest years. I have never forgotten the friendships of its Fellows and of its students, nor can there ever be obliterated from my recollection the stimulus of honourable ambition that existed, and the feeling of generous rivalry that was inspired between student and student; and I feel here bound further to state, a Roman Catholic myself, that I never had to complain of any interference from the institution with respect to my religious opinions.'

I believe there are few among the Roman Catholic graduates of Dublin who would not be willing to make use of the same words.

CHAPTER VI

THE EIGHTEENTH CENTURY (*continued*)

IN 1789 the Deputies were assembling at Versailles, and the French Revolutionaries not far from the accomplishment of their dreams. England, serene behind her ramparts of wind-tossed sea, could not altogether escape the thrill communicated by great ideas in action, the tremor of a dissolving State. In Ireland, like France, a country far more susceptible to changes in the intellectual atmosphere, the leaven of democratic ideals worked with great rapidity. The soil of the national character was congenial, the facts of the national history favourable to a breach between the subject and the ruling race.

In the year 1791 Theobald Wolfe Tone,* a former

---

* Wolfe Tone was described by a contemporary as 'a slight, effeminate-looking man, with a hatchet face, a long aquiline nose, rather handsome and genteel looking, with lank, straight hair combed down on his sickly-red cheek, exhibiting a face the most insignificant and mindless that could be imagined. His mode of speaking was in correspondence with his face and person. It was polite and gentlemanly, but totally devoid of anything like energy or vigour. I set him down as a worthy, good-natured, flimsy man, in whom there was no harm, and as the least likely person in the world to do mischief in the State' (*Ireland Ninety Years Ago*, p. 136).

scholar of the College, founded a society with a pronounced political programme—that of Catholic emancipation and Parliamentary reform. His associates numbered some of the more eager spirits among the students, and one or two of the Fellows. As time went on, however, membership of the club seems to have involved acceptance of vastly larger and more ambitious designs—the separation of Ireland from England and the establishment of a Republican Government. The club became the famous society of the United Irishmen, whose programme was complete national independence. Before, however, its objects became known as unmistakably treasonable, and the patriotic feeling aroused by the events of the time had been split into widely separating channels, the general excitement and the establishment by the Government of a yeomanry force for the defence of the country set the youth of Dublin aflame with martial ardour. A College corps was formed, and divided into four companies, commanded by the four lay Fellows. It had its guard-room in the rooms of the Historical Society, and during the period of the Rebellion in 1798* took part in all the military movements around Dublin; but there is good reason to suppose that some among the volunteers would have preferred to turn their arms against the Government rather than its enemies, the rebels.

By 1795 the political excitement already ran so high that the Board forbade students to attend meetings

* It appears that the corps 'selected for their uniform scarlet faced with blue, without any lace, and plain gilt buttons, white Kerseymere waistcoat and breeches, with black leggings' (*Student Life in Trinity College, Dublin*, by H. A. Hinkson).

outside the College, and by 1798 it became evident that the disaffection within the walls was deep and far-spread. In February of that year the Fellows and scholars were summoned to attend at the Castle for the purpose of presenting an address from the Corporation to Lord Camden, the retiring Viceroy. One scholar refused to attend, and others were reported to have used seditious language in the College courts. A visitation was considered necessary, and Lord Clare and Dr. Duigenan proceeded to inquire ' whether the disaffection imputed to the College was founded in reality, or was a mere rumour or surmise.'

The visitation was held in April in the College Hall amid painful excitement, and occupied three days. All members of the College—even the inferior officials and porters—were required to attend. The roll was called, and an oath was tendered to each person, beginning with the Provost. One or two excuses for absence were admitted, but only after the most careful inquiry, and on the threshold of the proceedings Robert Emmet,[*] who failed to answer his name, was set down as contumacious. When sworn, each person was submitted to a strict cross-examination as to his knowledge of the

[*] Robert Emmet, the most prominent of the three brothers (Temple Emmet and Thomas Addis Emmet were also students of the College) of that distinguished family, is thus described in a letter of Provost Elrington:

'In 1798 Robert Emmet was twenty years of age; of an ugly, sour countenance; small eyes, but not near-sighted; at a distance looks as if somewhat marked with the small-pox; about five feet six inches high, rather thin than fat, but not of an emaciated figure, but, on the contrary, somewhat broad made; walks quick, but does not swing his arms.'

This does not read like the description of an orator, but probably Elrington saw nothing in Emmet but the rebel.

existence of any secret society in College, or seditious opinions among the members of the society.

'Those who have seen Lord Clare in his visitorial capacity,' wrote an eye-witness,* 'never will forget him—the hatchet sharpness of his countenance, the oblique glance of his eye, which seemed to read what was passing in the mind of him to whom it was directed.'

Whitley Stokes, a Junior Fellow, and a former member of the Society of United Irishmen, was early examined. It was believed that from him important and startling information would be obtained. When asked if he knew of the existence of secret societies within the College, he answered, 'Yes,' and the excitement grew in intensity. When further required to give an account of them, he said: 'The only societies of that description which I am aware of are Orange societies, and I know some members of them.' This totally unexpected reply brought Lord Clare to his feet in a spasm of surprise and anger, and it was not until a prolonged examination had satisfied most of those present that the probity of Stokes was beyond question that he was suffered to withdraw. As the inquiry proceeded, some of the students displayed considerable hesitation in taking the oath in the form in which it was first administered. Among the first who declined was Thomas Moore, the poet, then an undergraduate.† With those of his companions in the same position, he was set down for expulsion as contumacious. As the numbers of these

* *Ireland Ninety Years Ago*, p. 141.
† Moore (fourth volume of his collected works) gives an interesting account of the procedure of the Visitatorial Court. 'There were a few,' he writes, 'and among them poor Robert Emmet,

became very alarming, and it seemed probable that, unless the terms of the oath were modified, a large proportion of the members of the University would be implicated, a modification was introduced, and the recusants given another opportunity to clear themselves from suspicion. Many then came forward and gave information without adding the names of individuals. In the end it was found that four committees of United Irishmen existed in the College. The sentence of the court, afterwards confirmed by the Duke of Gloucester as Chancellor, was that the secretaries of these associations, together with a number of other students* found guilty of actual participation in treasonable conspiracy, or of contumacy in refusing to appear or be sworn, should be expelled from the College, and that Dr. Whitley Stokes, having confessed to intercourse with some of the members of the seditious societies, be ' precluded from acting as College Tutor, for three years be disqualified from sitting as a member of the Board, and from being co-opted to Senior Fellowship.'

The history of the University in the eighteenth

---

whose total absence from the whole scene, as well as the dead silence that, day after day, followed the calling out of their names, proclaimed how deep had been their share in the unlawful proceedings inquired into by this tribunal.'

* Robert Emmet, Thomas Flynn, Peter McLaughlin, William and Thomas Corbett, Dacre Hamilton, John Carroll, David Shea, Arthur Newport, John Browne, George Keough, John Penefather Lamphier, Michael Farrell, Edward Barry, Thomas Bennett, Bernard Killen, Martin John Ferrall, and Patrick Fitzgerald. Of these, the brothers Corbett both obtained commissions in the French Army, one of them rising to the rank of General and bearing a distinguished part in the Napoleonic wars. Emmet's career is well known; he was executed in Thomas Street in September, 1803.

century can show no more important movement than that which gave rise to the foundation of the earliest students' debating society in the United Kingdom, the famous 'Historical.' By many years senior to the Students' Unions at Oxford and Cambridge, the Historical Society has for a century and a half played the same important part in the education of its members for public life, and may fairly be described as the greatest of all the schools of the orators.

The Historical 'Club' founded in 1745 by Edmund Burke was the oldest debating society composed of students of the University of which we have any definite record. The first minute-book, a large part of which is in the handwriting of Burke, still exists in the library of the society. Another minute-book, known to have been in existence down to 1815, but unfortunately lost during the exile of the society from College (1815-1843), brought down the record of the debates to 1757. Between 1757 and 1770, the date from which the proceedings are known, all accounts fail, but it is clear from the speeches of the members in 1770 that the club founded by Burke was regarded as the parent of their association. Rooms were granted to it in that year, but the privilege was withdrawn for a time, owing to a dispute with the authorities in 1794, and again in 1815.* Meetings still continued to be held outside

* The expulsion of the society in 1794 created considerable public excitement. Madden, in his *Life of Emmet*, quotes one of the many pamphlets of the time which have reference to it, an amusingly ironical document.

'At a full meeting of the Vintners, Publicans, and Hetæræ in the City of Dublin, held the 1st of May, 1794—Mrs. Margaret Leeson in the chair—Resolved:

the walls, however, and in 1843, after its long exile, the society was received back again, and granted the accommodation which it still enjoys.

Of Burke's club the objects seem to have been comprehensive—'speaking, reading, writing, and arguing in Morality, History, Criticism, Politics, and all the useful

---

'1st. That the thanks of this meeting be presented to the Vice-Provost and Senior Fellows of Trinity College, Dublin, for their public-spirited suppression of the Historical Society.

'2nd. That the said Society has considerably injured our respective trades by employing the Gentlemen of the University (formerly their best customers) one whole evening in the week in Literary pursuits, and wasting many other evenings in preparation for it.

'3rd. That the kind interference of the College must cause the Custom of the College to return gradually to us, and the time of the young gentlemen to be more profitably employed than in the pursuits of the said Institution.

'That the Provost and Senior Fellows be made free of our Society, and that the freedom of the same be presented to them in a quicksilver box.

'Mrs. Leeson having left the chair, and Mrs. Simpson being called thereto, resolved—"That the thanks of this meeting be given o Mrs. Leeson for her very proper conduct in the chair."

'(Signed by order) CATHERINE GRANT,
'*Secretary.*'

Before its suspension in 1815 the society passed the following resolution:

'That a Committee of seven be appointed for the purpose of resigning into the custody of the Provost and Board the rooms hitherto appropriated to the use of the Historical Society, the late regulations of the Board being, in the opinion of the Society, inconsistent with the successful prosecution of the objects for which it was instituted; and that this Committee be empowered and directed to take such steps as to them may appear most effectual for the securing of the property of the Society until a favourable opportunity occurs for the renewal of the Institution, the utility of which the experience of 20 years has most satisfactorily evinced.'

branches of Philosophy.' He himself spoke frequently*
—in the character 'of Brutus on the death of Lucretia,'
'of a Roman Senator against Cæsar at the time he went
to command in Gaul,' 'of Ulysses on his embassy with
Menelaus to recover Helen.' During the early years of
its existence subjects appear to have been assigned to
each of the members, and a speech or dissertation
required. Some of the entries are amusing: 'Mr.
Ardesoif had not his speech off by heart. His paper
on Drunkenness was returned to him to correct, and he
was ordered on next Friday to produce one on Love.'
An entry of April 28, 1747, reads: 'Mr. Burke for an
essay on the Genoese was given thanks for the matter,
but not for the delivery.' At first consisting of but few
members, the Historical grew in popularity until, at
the period of the Irish Parliament, it had 600 names
on its roll, a number of whom were also members of
the House of Commons. Always famous for the freedom and vigour of its debates, and possessed in the days
of Grattan's Parliament of considerable political influence, it is hardly surprising that its existence within
the College walls became a source of uneasiness to the
Board, and that on the two occasions mentioned it was
driven into exile.

There have been few among the leaders of public

* For a full account of the club and its interesting proceedings from its foundation down to recent times, see the Addresses of the Auditors, Robert Walsh (1864) and John Edward Walsh (1901), an article by Mr. John Cooke in *Blackwood's Magazine*, and *Student Life in Trinity College, Dublin*, by H. A. Hinkson. Members of the Historical Society have since 1798 enjoyed the honorary membership of the Speculative Society of Edinburgh, founded in 1764, and of the Oxford and Cambridge Unions since 1843—a privilege which has been from the first reciprocal.

opinion in Ireland who did not pass through 'the Historical,' and gain there the experience in debate and in the arts of composition and rhetoric which contribute to success in public life. To the student of history its roll recalls the public life of Ireland for more than 100 years—the most crowded and eventful in the later story of that island. Besides that of its founder, Edmund Burke, many far-shining names appear in the records of the society. Grattan and Flood and Parsons;* Barry Yelverton;† Plunket, afterwards Lord Chancellor; Bushe,‡ who, in Grattan's words, 'spoke with the lips of an angel'; Lalor Sheil, Isaac Butt, and the two Magees, Archbishops of Dublin and of York, were perhaps the greatest of the speakers it has nursed; but its roll of fame contains other names no less illustrious—those of Tom Moore, the poet, and Sheridan Lefanu,§ Robert Emmet and Theobald Wolfe Tone, Charles Wolfe,|| Thomas Davis,¶ Archer Butler,** Thomas Lefroy,†† John Jebb,‡‡ Valentine Lawless,§§

* M.P. during his year of auditorship. Afterwards Earl of Rosse.

† Afterwards Lord Avonmore. Of a speech of Yelverton's on the Penal Code, Grattan thus spoke: 'It was detailed by the late Lord Avonmore—I heard him—his speech was the whole of the subject, and a concentrated and inspired argument not to be resisted; it was the march of an elephant, it was a wave of the Atlantic, a column of water three thousand miles deep. He began with the Catholic at his birth, he followed him to the grave; he showed that in every period he was harassed by the law—the law stood at his cradle, it stood at his bridal bed, it stood at his coffin.'

‡ Lord Chief Justice. § Poet and novelist.
|| Author of 'Burial of Sir John Moore.'
¶ The poet.
** The Professor of Moral Philosophy.
†† Lord Chief Justice.
‡‡ Bishop of Limerick.
§§ Afterwards Lord Cloncurry.

Robert Torrens,* Standish O'Grady (afterwards Lord Guillamore), Francis Blackburne,† Louis Perrin,‡ Maziere Brady,§ J. T. Ball,|| Edward Sullivan,¶ and many another ornament of the episcopal and judicial bench of Ireland, not to speak of those who in England or the greater colonies carved for themselves distinguished place or fame.**

At times the minutes are noteworthy as recording the interest taken by the members in matters outside the strict academic region. For example, in 1793 we read a resolution 'That 100 flannel waistcoats be granted by the Historical Society for the use of the British army in Flanders,' and on another occasion of a motion to confer a medal upon one of the members, Sir Richard Maguire, for 'his intrepid conduct' in making

---

* Justice of the Common Pleas. † Lord Chancellor.
‡ Justice of the Common Pleas. § Lord Chancellor.
|| Lord Chancellor. ¶ Lord Chancellor.
** Walsh, afterwards Master of the Rolls; Mr. Justice Fox; Mr. Justice Crampton; Corry, Chancellor of the Irish Exchequer; Lord Chief Justice Downes; John Wilson Croker; Lord Chancellor Walker; the two Pennefathers, afterwards respectively Baron of the Exchequer and Lord Chief Justice of Ireland; Saurin, the distinguished Attorney-General, are names of hardly secondary interest; while among living men, former members of the society, who have entered public life, may be mentioned those of Lord Ashbourne, Lord Chancellor; Lord Rathmore; Lord Justice Fitzgibbon; Mr. Justice Madden; Dr. Chadwick, Bishop of Derry; Mr. Justice Gibson; Mr. Justice Ross; Sir Ed. H. Carson, Solicitor-General for England; County Court Judges Snagge, Griffith, Bird, Webb; Mr. Freeman Wills; Dr. Robert Anderson, C.B.; A. J. Wrixon, K.C.M.G., Attorney-General for Victoria; Thomas Upington, K.C.M.G., formerly Premier of Cape Colony; and the Right Hon. W. E. H. Lecky, one of the present representatives of the University in Parliament. But injustice is done to the roll of the society by any such partial quotation of its register.

a balloon ascent. The auditorship, the highest office open to the student members of the society, is always, like that of presidency of the Oxford and Cambridge Unions, keenly contested, and is regarded as the highest distinction within the gift of the undergraduates of the University.

Tom Moore's *Journal* records many interesting experiences of the 'Historical'—his friendship with the Emmets, and admiration of Robert Emmet's oratory; the reception given to his own *Ode upon Nothing*, with notes by Dr. Trismagestus Rustifustius'; the subjects discussed by the society, and its political tendencies. His description of a fellow-member, Hugh George Macklin (afterwards Advocate-General at Bombay), is amusing:

'He was called, from his habits of boasting, Hugo Grotius Braggadocio, and had obtained a great deal of reputation both in his collegiate course and in the Historical Society, where he was one of the most showy speakers. Among the many stories relative to his boasting powers, it was told of him that, being asked on the eve of a great public examination whether he was well prepared in his conic sections, "Prepared!" he exclaimed, "I could whistle them." In a mock account of a night's proceedings in our Historical Society, one of the fines enforced for disorderliness was as follows: "Hugo Grotius Braggadocio fined one shilling for whistling conic sections."'

In that interesting little volume already referred to, *Ireland Ninety-Years Ago*, appears an account of the Irish House of Commons, and the privilege enjoyed by undergraduates of attending the debates:

UNDERGRADUATE PRIVILEGES

'The Irish House of Commons was a rotunda, the most ill-contrived in point of convenience that ever was built. Round it was a narrow circular gallery for spectators. . . . Admission to this place was obtained by a member's order only, except by students of the University, who were always admitted.

'The student's passport was his gown. He rapped at the wicket, and the porter looked through a grating; the applicant held up his gown, and the door was opened, admitted him, and again closed. This was a privilege often abused. The students' gowns were lent out indiscriminately to friends and acquaintances, and the gallery appeared sometimes half full of gownsmen, not half of whom were members of the University. When I first entered College, I was very fond of using this privilege. It was a proud thing for a " gib "* to present himself to a crowd round the door, hear many a cry, " Make way for the gentleman of the College !" pass the avenue made for him, find the door expand to the " open sesame " of his gown, and himself admitted alone to the great council of the nation, while the suppliant crowd were excluded. . . .

'After the fire the business of the house was adjourned to the Speaker's chamber, and the students of Trinity College were particularly favoured. At the end of the apartment, behind the Speaker's chair, there was a deep and convenient gallery, which was exclusively devoted to the gownsmen. They were instantly admitted here on

* The Trinity College term for a ' freshman.' The term ' skip ' corresponds to the Oxford ' scout ' and the Cambridge ' gyp '; ' skippery ' to ' scout-hole.' The term ' dunscope ' seems peculiar to Trinity, but explains itself, most of the rooms having been thoughtfully provided with a hole through which the occupant, himself unseen, can observe who stands and knocks at his outer door.

presenting themselves, and listened to the debate at their ease, while the public in general now found it difficult to obtain passes, and when they got admission were confined to a narrow strip of a gallery, from some parts of which they could neither see nor hear.

'This proud distinction the gownsmen, however, soon forfeited. Lord Fitzwilliam had been sent over as a popular Viceroy, and on his sudden recall a strong feeling of disappointment prevailed. On a night when the subject was brought before the House, our gallery was full, and I remember well the inexpressible excitement that seemed to actuate us all. At length it broke out. Grattan rose to deprecate the measure as one calculated to cause the greatest disturbance in Ireland, by what was considered the perfidy of the Government, first exciting the high hopes of the people by promised measures of liberal policy, and then dashing them by the sudden removal of the man who had been sent over expressly to accomplish them. At the conclusion of Grattan's inflammatory speech, the enthusiasm in the gallery was no longer capable of restraint. We rose as one man, shouting and cheering with the boisterous tumult of a popular meeting. When this subsided Foster's peculiar voice was heard through his nose, ordering the students' gallery to be cleared, and a serjeant-at-arms with a posse of messengers entered among us. We were pushed out in a heap, without the slightest ceremony, and were never again suffered to enter as privileged persons.

'The Speaker had counted on the loyalty and propriety of the students of the University, and this display of what he considered riot and sedition at once changed his estimate of their character. Many a penitent memorial was presented, and solemn promises were made of better manners in future, but Foster was inexorable. No student ever after found his gown a passport to the House, till the Union removed the Parliament, and extinguished the hope of recovering the lost privilege for ever. Groups of us were constantly seen in the passages, waiting to intercept the Speaker, or entreating, with uplifted hands, a passage to the gallery; but stern Charon passed in at the door, leaving us, like ghosts on the banks of the Styx, casting wistful and unavailing looks on the Elysium on the opposite side of the house.'

The Speaker here mentioned, Foster, afterwards Lord Oriel, was himself a graduate of Dublin, and one of the ablest opponents of the Act of Union. It is a significant commentary on Irish affairs that the Roman Catholic Bishops strenuously supported, and Trinity College opposed, that measure in 1799.

'Trinity College,' says Mr. Lecky, 'the great centre of Protestant learning, though divided, was on the whole not favourable to the Union; and it is remarkable that Magee, who was afterwards a very able and a very typical Archbishop, was one of its opponents. George Knox and Arthur Browne, who were the members for the University, both spoke and voted against the Union in 1799. In the following year Browne changed his side and supported it; but he acknowleged in the House of Commons that he was acting in opposition to the wishes of the majority of his constituents. He afterwards received some legal promotion, and he never again represented the University.'[*]

By the charter of Charles I. the number of Junior Fellowships had been fixed at nine. A tenth was added by royal letter in 1698, three more in 1723 out of Erasmus Smith lands, two more in 1761. As the

[*] Lecky, *History of Ireland in the Eighteenth Century*, vol. v., p. 325.

Senior Fellows acted as College tutors, and took pupils until at least the middle of the eighteenth century,* the income of the Junior Fellow of those days was extremely meagre—about £15 a year. This he might increase by £20 if he undertook the work of a lecturer, and was of course entitled to the fees paid by his pupils if he were fortunate enough to obtain any which had escaped the net spread by the Senior Fellows. The income of a Junior Fellow in the eighteenth century rarely rose to £100, while the Seniors enjoyed emoluments which, on an average, may be reckoned at £800 or £900 per annum.†

* No precise date can be given, but during the eighteenth century the value of the College estates rapidly increased, and thus the incomes of the Senior Fellows were pleasantly secured. Entrance fees and chamber rents also at this time went to the Provost and Senior Fellows.

† *The Conclave Dissected; or, The Character of the F——s of T——y C——t*, a poetical squib of about 1725, describes the Fellows of the time (Coll. Lib., Press A, 4, No. 66):

'When Baldwin will not with the Laws dispense,
Nor interest prefer to better sense—
When Gilbert misses Lecture, Club, or Prayers,
Acts partial or against the oath he swears—
When lazy Elwood, in his gown secure,
Reads, prays, drinks not, and is no Epicure—
When Helsham's more luxurious than he's wise,
And stoops to little acts and tricks to rise—
When in Delany learning wants a friend
Which modesty and morals recommend—
When Thompson's modest, humble, and beloved,
And scholars not for double fees approved—
When merit is preferred by Clayton's voice—
When Helen's left and Plato made his choice—
When Rogers does not by the statutes guide
His actions, but is hated for his pride—
When Rowan's not haughty, insolent and vain,
Stopford a pedant, impolitely plain—

THE RIGHTS OF THE CHANCELLOR 141

The second Duke of Ormonde, who in 1688 succeeded his grandfather as Chancellor of the Universities of Oxford and of Dublin, seems to have placed a generous interpretation upon his rights as Chancellor. In 1698 he recommended a former student, by name Hopkins, to the Board for the degree of Bachelor of Arts, and three years later sent to the Provost the names of several students whom he wished to have elected to scholarships. Although the former request was granted out of deference to the Chancellor, the Board declined to permit any further interference, and we find the following entry in the College Register, under June 15, 1701 :

'Whereas there were three letters to the Provost from his Grace the Duke of Ormonde, in the behalf of James Finglas, Lucas Greene, and Ossory Meddlycott, for scholars' places, they being persons not sufficiently qualified, according to the statutes, in their learning, standing, and otherwise, and therefore the House being under such obligation by the statutes that they cannot possibly comply with his

---

> When King's not hated, nor most learnedly slow,
> And Whitcombe willing proves a scholar's foe—
> When Stewart is no fop most vainly gay,
> Shaw studies and forgets to sip his tea—
> When Hughes is ungenteel, ill-bred, no wit,
> And Clarke shall publish what he never writ—
> When Cartwright reads much, is not a Bonfellow,
> And chooses tea before Margaux that's mellow—
> When Graffan is not proud, lavish of Tongue,
> And Berkeley can't discern 'twixt right and wrong—
> When Bacon's steady virtue can be bribed,
> And Dobb's knowledge by limits circumscribed—
> Then, and then only, shall my thoughts aspire
> To sit a Fellow of this learned Quire.'

Grace's recommendations, which otherwise they would with readiness obey, 'tis resolved that the House will forthwith represent their reasons to his Grace, and lay before him the great discouragement of such recommendations to learning in College.'

It does not appear that the Duke harboured any feelings of resentment against the College on account of this refusal to accept his nominations, for some years later he presented the chapel with an organ, the case of which is at present in the Examination Hall. Its history is of interest. In 1702 the English fleet, under the command of Rooke, entered Vigo Bay, where the French and Spanish fleets were at anchor. A landing party under the Duke of Ormonde silenced some of the shore batteries, captured forty pieces of cannon, and greatly contributed to the brilliant victory which followed. Many of the enemy's vessels were destroyed, and among the prizes containing immense treasure was found a ship which had on board an organ, built in the Spanish Netherlands for a church, perhaps, in Spain or South America. It became part of Ormonde's spoil, and was presented to the College during his viceroyalty.[*]

To Provost Murray, who presided over the College for four years, the Dublin School of Mathematics owes a debt of gratitude. Although he left behind him no original work of importance, his interest in the subject and encouragement of the young men of promise bore abundant fruit in the succeeding generation. Among

[*] It was repaired and enlarged by Cuvillie in 1705, and now contains the pipes built by Telford for the University Choral Society in 1839. See *Book of Trinity College*, p. 212.

his pupils was Matthew Young, afterwards the author of several scientific works, of which, perhaps, the best known is an essay on *Sounds and Musical Strings*. Murray died in 1799, and was the first Provost to be buried in the new chapel, then just consecrated. Kearney, who succeeded him, and died as Bishop of Ossory, is best remembered by his expulsion of John Walker, the classical scholar. Walker, who as Fellow was bound to read the services of the Book of Common Prayer in chapel, was troubled by religious difficulties, and offered to resign his Fellowship. The Provost, it is said, with tears in his eyes, declined to accept the resignation, but had no compunction in expelling him in the most public manner on the following day. Thus meanly ends the tale of the eighteenth-century rulers of the College.

There are few Irishmen to whom the name Erasmus Smith is not familiar. Associated as it is with splendid charitable endowments, it naturally falls upon the ear as that of a philanthropist and friend of education. But Erasmus Smith was an unwilling benefactor of Ireland. A wealthy citizen of London, and a member of the Merchant Taylors' Company, he purchased a number of the Irish estates which had been forfeited by rebellion, and granted by the Crown to adventurers who had assisted the armies of William of Orange. After some time it was discovered that the title to many of these estates was defective, and that the new owners might be dispossessed by the Crown. The negotiations which ensued confirmed the Erasmus Smith estates in the hands of their possessor on condition that out of them he should found and endow

144 THE EIGHTEENTH CENTURY

Grammar Schools in Galway, Ennis, Tipperary, and Drogheda, and certain exhibitions in the University of Dublin. By 1724 the estates so changed had greatly increased in value, and it was found possible to support out of the funds three new Fellowships and two professorships—Oratory and History, and Natural and Experimental Philosophy. In 1762 three other professorships were founded by the trustees of the fund—Mathematics, History (now separated from Oratory), and Oriental Languages.* It was directed by the Board of Trustees that the appointment to these posts should be by open competition among 'all such scholars and members of the said College as shall stand candidates.' It has to be confessed that this condition was frequently overlooked, no examination held, and a Fellow of the College appointed to any vacancy which occurred. Occasionally the right of the Provost and Senior Fellows to nominate was called in question,† and an examination held, but by far the greater number of appointments were made without notice to the members of the College, and in defiance of the original intention.

During the eighteenth century important developments took place in connection with the Medical School of the University. Before 1616, judging from extant records, only one medical degree was conferred by Trinity College. The Register for 1598 makes mention of a *concordatum* of £40 per annum, granted

---

* 'In 1834 the Erasmus Smith estates produced £7,584 10s., being the rental of 7,953 acres.'

† E.g., in 1799, when Dr. Elrington, and in 1814, when Dr. Crampton, was appointed to one of the Chairs. See Heron's *History*, p. 72.

THE MEDICAL SCHOOL 145

by Government to the University for a 'Physitian's pay.' This is generally understood to be the provision made for the Chair of Physic, but it is not impossible that the grant may have been made in return for medical services required by the troops stationed in the city. By Bedell's statutes (1628) it was ordered that one of the Fellows should be Professor of Medicine, and should deliver one lecture every term, and the offices of Medical Fellow and Professor of Physic were held by the same person down to the time of Dr. Stearne; but the Medical Fellows were so seldom found competent to discharge the duties of the Chair, that from 1662 only three persons combined these offices, viz., Dr. Stearne, Dr. Helsham, and Dr. Whitley Stokes.

Reference has already been made to Trinity Hall,* which in 1667 was recognised under the title of the 'Colledge of Physitians in Dublin.' This College was closely associated with the University; the Provost and Senior Fellows appointed the President, and stipulated that the medical students there should first become members of the College, conforming to its regulations with respect to attendance upon the chapel services, and in other matters. This College possessed the right of granting licenses,† and no one could practise physic in the city of Dublin or within a seven-miles radius without its permission; but after the death of Stearne,

* See p. 22.

† Bishops in Ireland, as in other countries, possessed the right of granting licenses to practise physic, surgery, and midwifery. This was probably a survival of the medieval practice of medicine by priests. The Council of Tours in 1163 forbade priests to leave their cloisters in order to practise medicine. The Archbishop of Canterbury still claims the right of conferring Medical as well as Divinity or Arts degrees.

as has been stated, his plan of a medical school dropped out of sight. In 1692 the first charter of the College of Physicians was surrendered for another, which incorporated the institution under the title of the King and Queen's College of Physicians in Ireland. A clause of this charter provided that every doctor of physic of the University of Dublin should be permitted to become a member of the College of Physicians without examination or payment of fees, and it was arranged that representatives of the College should be present at the examination for medical degrees in the University, an arrangement which was not discontinued until 1760.

In the meanwhile the necessity for organized instruction in medicine had become pressing, and in 1710 the Board of Trinity College proceeded to erect medical school buildings, including a laboratory and anatomical theatre, on the site of the present library. At the same time an agreement was come to with the College of Physicians, and at their desire it was ordered that—

'besides the usual acts required by the University regulations, every candidate Bachelor of Physic be examined in all parts of Anatomy relating to the *Œconomia Animalis*, and in all parts of Botany, Chemistry, and Pharmacy, and that every candidate Doctor in Physic be examined as to the aforesaid subjects, and likewise in the explanation of Hippocrates' Aphorisms, and in the theory and cure of external and internal diseases.'

By the charter of 1692 the College of Physicians obtained the right of receiving annually for 'anatomies' six bodies of malefactors who had been executed, that they might obtain 'further and better knowledge, instruction and experience, in the faculty and science of physic and surgery.' In spite of this provision, the arrangements for practical anatomy were necessarily very inadequate, and most of the teaching must have been done through diagrams. In 1716 Trinity College voted £60 to its anatomist, Surgeon Greene, for the purchase of illustrations of various parts of the human body. An account-book of the College of Physicians, beginning in 1672,

'mentions the items of expenditure incurred in connexion with the dissection of a body. The total is £2 4s. 10d., of which 9s. was given to the "souldiers who watched," and 3s. "to the said souldiers in drinke." Some years later Molyneux describes the dissection of a malefactor, and the conversion of his osseous remains into a skeleton. He says that the dissection lasted for a week, and that the chirurgeons and physicians present at it "spoke at random as the parts presented themselves." '[*]

During the eighteenth century body-snatching was a fairly lucrative employment, and many cases occurred in Dublin of the prosecution of these humble ministers of science.

In 1722 it was ordered by the Board of Trinity College 'that no person be admitted to take a degree in Physic or in Law unless he first commence as Bachelor of Arts.' It happened that some years later the University wished to confer a medical degree upon a distinguished practitioner in midwifery, Fielding

[*] Cameron's *History of the Royal College of Surgeons in Ireland*, p. 94.

Ould,* who had been a teacher in the Medical School, and, in order to meet the requirements of the regulation just mentioned, granted him the degree of Bachelor of Arts. The College of Physicians, however, when asked to examine him in 1759 for his medical degree, declined on the ground that Ould was a 'person who has no academical education, and whom you [Trinity College] know to be disqualified by his occupation for a license to practise in our profession.' The University in consequence renounced its connection with the College of Physicians, appointed its own examiners in medicine, and admitted Ould to the degree of M.D. in 1761.

The medical degrees of the University conferred a right to practise in Ireland, except in the city of Dublin, for which the license of the College of Physicians was required, and it was therefore fortunate that the dispute between the University and the College terminated before the end of the century. It appears, however, that very few students graduated in medicine at Trinity College during the latter part of the eighteenth and early part of the nineteenth century. Judging from the records, no medical degrees were granted between 1724 and 1740, and from the latter year to 1773 the average hardly works out as high as 1 per annum. In 1786, however, the medical school was constituted by an Act of the Irish Parliament,

* Afterwards knighted by the Duke of Bedford when Lord Lieutenant and Master of the Rotunda Lying-in Hospital. Ould's profession was not at the time regarded as particularly dignified, and a vulgar but amusing epigram records the general surprise on his attainment of the dignity of knighthood. It is quoted in Cameron's *History of the Royal College of Surgeons*, p. 27.

PARLIAMENT SQUARE AND CAMPANILE

the College of Physicians was associated with Trinity College in the management of the teaching, and by the end of the first quarter of the nineteenth century the average entry of students had risen to 66 per annum.

During the eighteenth century many Irish students studied medicine in Edinburgh, and of 800 degrees conferred in the last quarter of the century in that University, 237 were granted to Irish, 217 to English, 179 to Scotchmen, and the remainder to foreigners. As will be seen, however, under Provost Lloyd the Medical School of Trinity College was completely reorganized, and very few Irishmen now seek the degrees of English or Scottish Universities.

Between Trinity College, Dublin, and the Irish Parliament there existed during the eighteenth century a bond of the closest sympathy. Many members of both Houses of the Legislature had passed through the University, and bore with them into public life the memories of the triumphs and the friendships associated with its traditions and society. It was but natural, therefore, that they should continue to regard it with feelings of affection, delight in protecting its privileges, and in adding to its resources and dignity. The contributions of Parliament towards the erection of the library, and of the square which bears its name, amounting in all to nearly £50,000, form a magnificent memorial of its interest in the things of the mind, and may well be cited in defence of its acts and character. From 1662, when it was 'Ordered, upon question, that Trinity College, near Dublin, be exempted from paying any chimney or hearth tax, and that a clause to that effect be inserted in the Bill for raising such monies,' to 1787, when its last grant was made, the Irish Parliament placed the welfare and development of the national University in the forefront of its official duties.

By the Act of Union, Trinity College lost its most generous patron, and from 1798 owes nothing to the goodwill of Parliaments. The representation of the borough was reduced to one member in the English House of Commons,* and the era of its greatest local reputation and prestige, if not its most widespread influence or usefulness, came to an end. The prosperity of the College, bound up with that of Dublin and the wealthier and more aristocratic families of Ireland, now suffered a serious shock. A fresh tributary stream, one of the many by which London drains the best blood and brains, the wealth and resources, of the other great cities of the country, set towards the Thames, the sons of many men educated in Trinity College were sent to Oxford and Cambridge, and their fathers, in the vain attempt to vie with the idle expenditure of the upper classes of the society in which they now found themselves, impoverished their families while they neglected their estates. It was fortunate that the nineteenth century found the University of Dublin already well housed, and provided by the revenues from her estates for the growth and requirements of the coming time.

* The second member was restored to the University by the Reform Act of 1833, which enlarged the constituency from Provost, Fellows, and foundation scholars (always less than 100) to include ex-scholars, Masters of Arts, and Doctors in the several faculties. The constituency now consists of between 4,000 and 5,000 members.

CHAPTER VII

EIGHTEENTH CENTURY: LIFE IN THE COLLEGE—STUDIES

WITH the spirit and temper of the eighteenth century, 'the age of prose and reason,' the genius of Trinity College exhibited a peculiar affinity. Throughout its history the intellectual atmosphere of the University has been critical, the currents of its mental life keen and disillusionizing. Its most distinguished names are those of men who belonged to the great age of lucidity and precision, the classical age of English literature, and in Congreve and Swift, Berkeley and Burke and Goldsmith, its type of culture was most fully revealed.* As in her architecture, though she occupies the site of an ancient monastery, she betrays no traces of Gothic imagination or romance, so into the spirit of her

* 'The standard of taste prevailing in Ireland, or, at least, in Dublin, during the first three-quarters of the eighteenth century, appears to have been as far as possible removed from the exaggerated, overheated, and overornamented rhetoric which is so commonly associated with the term "Irish eloquence." The style of Swift, the style of Berkeley, and the style of Goldsmith are in their different ways among the most perfect in English literature, but they are simple sometimes to the verge of baldness, and they manifest a much greater distaste for ornamentation and rhetorical effect than the best contemporary writings in England.'—LECKY: *History of Ireland in the Eighteenth Century*, ii. 136.

dreams has been woven no magic light of mystery, no enchantments of a half-forgotten past. The medieval elements in the early curriculum gave way during the seventeenth century to courses and methods of study adapted to practical ends, determined by the requirements of the time, and in the middle of the eighteenth took on the character which they still preserve. Disputations in the old style seem to have held their ground until 1800, but the records of the term examinations* from 1740 show that the usual classical authors, Homer, Lucian, Sophocles, Demosthenes, Virgil, Horace, Cicero, Terence, and Longinus, were read, and that logic was still regarded as an important aid to the undergraduate's mental discipline. Through the influence of Molyneux, a friend of the author, Locke's *Essay on the Human Understanding*, as already noted, became a part of the curriculum, when it appeared in 1690, and still serves as an admirable prolegomenon to the philosophical works of a later day.

Although physics and astronomy were from the first taught in Dublin, these studies were associated with mental and moral philosophy under the common designation *science*, and it was not until 1815 that honour lectures in mathematics to advanced students were instituted, and soon after made the subject of a special Moderatorship examination.† Honour lectures in classics were introduced in 1800, and the Classical Moderatorship in 1816. It will be seen, therefore, that

* No records of the term examinations during the seventeenth century are preserved.

† The term in use at Dublin for a final honour school, corresponding to the Cambridge *Tripos*.

no final honour schools or honour lectures in preparation for them existed during the eighteenth century, and it does not appear that mathematics formed an important part of the work then done in the College. There is no record of the study of Euclid prior to 1758, and the scholarship examination took no note of any knowledge other than that of classics.*

* Science or mathematical scholarships were first founded in 1855.

Among the uncatalogued MSS. relating to the College is a poem which has been quoted by Dr. Stubbs (p. 331 of his *History*), descriptive of the Scholars' Table at Commons, *circa* 1780:

'COMMON CRANKS; OR, SALT FOR THE BACHELORS' TABLE.
BY A FRESHMAN.
'*Tota cantabitur urbe.*'—HOR.
'My Doggrel shall be chanted through the Courts.'

'McDonough, wilt thou ne'er be quiet,
 Maugre cuts and broken bones—
Wilt thou never cease to riot,
 Battering, bulging, pelting stones?

'From the Quays up to the Poddle,
 Every street has heard thy brawls;
On thy thick, ill-fated noddle
 Every ruffian's cudgel falls.

'When thou hear'st the bell's loud summons,
 Quickly hastening here from town,
Cicatriced thou sit'st at Commons,
 Shattered face and battered gown.

'Soon a shabby group surrounds thee,
 Politics on every tongue;
Gaping porters stand around thee—
 Haste, harangue the motly throng.

'Every mouth full crammed with mutton
 Swallows meat and swallows news;
Each an orator and glutton,
 Rav'ning speaks and ranting chews.

'Burdy, Whig, and John-a-Dory,
 Dive into the nation's state;
Sluttish Murray's fulsome story
 Swells the channel of debate.

'Deaf to decency and breeding,
 Cur Arbuthnot snarls and barks;
Sarcasm still his theme, or reading,
 Your *vix*.—or his own best marks.

'Apish Grier's broad Ulster cadence
 Joins with Johnston's grating tones;
Who, as soon as he has laid hands
 On the mass—meat turns to bones.

'Vulgar Boyton's bog-learned lingo
 Answers Farrell, blundering Teague.
Gunning, flushed with potent stingo,
 Staggers out opinions vague.

'Hear you from another quarter
 Marshall's puns and Ryder's jokes.
Hacket fiercely rates the porter;
 Laugh on slighly, Master Stokes.

'Hodgkinson, demurely seated,
 Views with scorn the babbling crowd.
Lysaght's waggish temper treated;
 Lysaght pert, and Lysaght proud.

'Like the many tongues of Babel,
 Thus the Bachelors are known;
Leave me, then, the Freshman's table,
 Where our knives are heard alone.'

A pencil note in another hand adds, 'Lysaght, who wrote this.'

In 1759 the schoolmasters of Dublin applied to the Board for some direction in regard to the classical authors suitable for boys at school. A list was drawn up and forwarded, together with the following extremely interesting letter, which goes far to explain the high encomium pronounced by Macaulay upon Congreve, who graduated in 1696, that his 'learning did great honour to his instructors':

'In reading these books,* they recommend to you that you forbid your scholars the use of literal translations.

'That you instruct your scholars early in quantity, and exercise them continually in Rhetorick, and in the Composition of Latin Verse; that you oblige your scholars constantly to translate from English into Latin, and from Latin into English, to write Themes, and to make use of the double translation as recommended by Ascham.

'That particular care be taken that they be well instructed in the Mythology and Fabulous History of the Ancients, in the Greek and Roman History and Antiquities.

'That Globes and Maps, such as those by Cellarius, be used in every school. It has been found of singular advantage to oblige the young gentlemen themselves to draw maps, and to trace out the boundaries of Countries

* The list was as follows—'In *Latin*: Castalio's Dialogues, select Colloquies of Erasmus, Cornelius Nepos, first twelve books of Justin's History, the Fables of Phædrus, Cæsar's *Gallic War*, select portions of Ovid's *Metamorphoses*, Sallust, Virgil (Eclogues and first six books of the *Æneid*), Cicero's Orations against Catiline, Terence, Horace, and Juvenal. In *Greek*: St. Luke's Gospel, first four books of Xenophon's *Cyropedia*, first eight books of the *Iliad* of Homer, first book of Hesiod, select Idyls of Theocritus, Bion and Moschus, Musæus, the Golden Verses, and Dugard's Lucian.'

and Provinces, and that you instruct them in the composition and proper pronunciation of English.

'There is another article, the care of which does not indeed so properly belong to you, but it is of great consequence, and yet much neglected; it is probable that your recommending it to the young gentlemen themselves and to their parents will gain it the attention which the importance of it deserves. It is that every young gentleman be completely instructed in the Common Rules of Arithmetic before he shall think of entering College; and they recommend to you to exercise your scholars in those Rules by Examples taken from the coins, weights, and measures of the Ancients.'

Burke, who entered College in 1744, and obtained his scholarship two years later, has left an account of both examinations. At his 'entrance' he was examined in Horace, Virgil, and Homer:

'He (Dr. Pellesir) made me construe "Scriberis Vario," etc., "Eheu fugaces Posthume," etc.; and in Virgil I began the 103rd line of the sixth Æneid, and in Homer with the 227th line of the third Iliad, and the 406th of the sixth. . . . I was examined very strictly by the Senior Lecturer in the Odes, Sermons and Epistles of Horace, and am admitted.'

Of the scholarship examination he says: 'We were examined for two days in all the Roman and Greek authors of note.'*

Goldsmith, who entered in the same year as Burke, mentions, as we have seen, in his life of Parnell the poet that the entrance examination at Dublin was more

* Letters to his schoolfellow, Richard Shackleton.

difficult than at Oxford or Cambridge, and Lord Chesterfield, in a private letter (1731), remarks: 'The Irish schools and universities are indisputably better than ours.'*

In 1731 prizes were first instituted in connection with the examinations. The proposal to establish such incentives to study was made by the Rev. Samuel Madden† in a pamphlet entitled *Plan of Premiums at the Term Examinations.*‡ The plan received very

* *Works*, iv. 237.

† Dr. Madden, one of the founders of the Royal Dublin Society, and the author of several pamphlets concerning Trinity College. He is to be distinguished from Samuel Molyneux Madden, the founder of the Madden premiums awarded to the best answerers among the unsuccessful candidates at Fellowship examinations. They were first awarded in 1798.

‡ A skit upon this proposal appears on a printed slip among the uncatalogued MSS. in the library, entitled *Articles to be Observed in Running for several Plates, to the value of £100, to be set up in Trinity College on the 1st of March*, 1731. Some of the clauses are of interest, as hinting at possible favouritism in the award of the premiums:

'*Imprimis*. That no Person shall presume to enter a Horse to run for any of the said Plates who cannot bring evident Proofs of his being lineally descended from *Pegasus*, or some of the Horses belonging to the Sun.

'*Item*. That a Horse's pouring forth Smoak instead of Fire at his Nostrils shall not be looked upon as a sufficient proof of his divine Origin.

'*Item*. That no Person shall hope to prejudice the Judges in his Horse's Favour by the number of Bells he hangs to his Ears, by adorning his Mane and Tail with gaudy Ribbons and Flowers, or cutting in his Forehead artificial Stars.

'*Item*. That no Person shall win any of the said Prizes, as Darius obtained the Kingdom of Persia, by making his Horse neigh at the Morning Sun!

'*Item*. That no Person by cutting the Ears and Tail of an Ass, and paring his Hooves into Shape, shall hope to impose him on his Judges for a Horse.

'*Item*. That no mealy-mouthed Horses are to be admitted.'

general support, one enthusiastic writer declaring that
'the catalogue of those that contribute to this design
will be the catalogue of our country's friends,' and that
'a fondness of glory was the great nurse of the *literati*.'
A premium fund was accordingly started; the Fellows
themselves contributed, and by 1740 a sum of £2,500
was already invested. Besides rewards for good answering at term examinations, prizes amounting to £40
were yearly offered for compositions in Latin and
in English,* which, however, were thrown open to
graduates.

It cannot be doubted that the distinguished
dramatists, poets, orators, and men of letters, who
were educated in the Dublin class-rooms owed much
to the careful training in rhetoric and composition,
both classical and English, which the University
afforded. In Provost Hutchinson's time it appears
that '£200 a year was voted by the Board of Erasmus
Smith for Prizes in Composition alone,' and it is certain
that to this subject a larger share of attention was
formerly given in Trinity College than at the English
Universities. Instructive, too, is the reference that
Burke, in acknowledging the honorary degree granted
him in 1790, makes of his own debt to the University
in this respect, when he speaks of the 'taste for Com-

* Some of the subjects proposed have been preserved. A few
are appended:

>   1733. On Queen Elizabeth.
>   1736. On the Linen Manufacture.
>   1738. On Horse-running.
>   1739. On the Battle of the Boyne.
>   1740. On the British Fleet.
>   1747. On the Public Examinations.
>   1748. On Commerce.

position' which (with the principles of liberty and morality) 'are infused, and have always been infused, into the minds of those who have the happiness to be instructed by it.'*

Early in the eighteenth century sizars were first admitted by competitive examination. Up to the year 1709 it had been customary to admit them on the nomination of the Provost and Senior Fellows at various periods of the year. After receiving the Bachelor's degree, such students as remained (as a rule only scholars) attended the lectures of the Professor of Divinity, as well as those of some other of the Professors.

The Erasmus Smith's Chair of Natural Philosophy was founded in 1724, and the Chair of Modern History, founded at the same time, was in 1762 separated from that of Oratory, to which it was originally attached. These, together with the professorships of Greek, Civil Law, and Divinity, continued for long after their foundation to be filled by Senior Fellows, a system which in many cases led to a singularly low estimate of the requirements of the subject. An anonymous letter of the early part of the nineteenth century, preserved among the uncatalogued MSS. in the College library, calls the attention of the Vice-Chancellor to the pass to which matters at that time had come. It affords amusing reading. There is something unusually piquant in the idea of an assistant to a Professor who does not lecture.

* The Professor of Oratory (founded 1724) delivered four public lectures annually, and in addition gave special instruction to his class in the principles of English composition.

'My Lord,

'If the subject of the following lines will not excuse the liberty taken in addressing you, the writer of these must plead guilty of a very impertinent intrusion. There are several professorships in your Lordship's University shamefully mismanaged, and calling loudly for authoritative interference. The Professor of History gives no lectures, neither does his assistant. This has been the case for at least a dozen years. The Professor of Oratory does his duty most inadequately. His assistant is in England on a three-years' leave of absence. These sinecure places are all in the hands of Fellows of the College. The situation of the present Professor of Natural Philosophy[*] certainly calls for the regret of every humane mind. But public considerations should be the more important of the two. His senior fellowship, independent of all accidental advantages, is twelve hundred pounds a year, and he has no family or immediate connexions. There is no provision whatsoever for the supplementary discharge of his duties, and the professorship produces eight hundred pounds annually, paid principally by the students, who receive nothing in return. There is a professorship of Natural History similarly charged on the students, and similarly unprofitable to them.'

It appears from the papers accompanying this letter that the Professor of Modern History, when appointed, '*did attempt*, at the suggestion of the Provost, *to prepare himself for reading a prælection, in doing which he contracted a disorder in the eyes, which put a stop to further exertion.*' The assistant, Dr. Sadler, ' to whom the Provost did express a wish that he would enter into an arrangement with the Professor so as to read

[*] His illness.

Prælections,' never did so, and it seemed that 'no precise duty had ever been prescribed so as to make him liable to be called to an account.'

'The disorder of the eyes,' which for a dozen years interfered with the performance of his duties by the Professor of Modern History, probably in no respect limited his enjoyment of life or of the emoluments of his office. The Fellows of those days were in many cases no more careful of their own reputation than that of the University which they did not adorn.

In the year 1704 there were 472 students on the College books. The number then decreased for some years, until in 1715 it was 413. It rose again to 525 in 1731, but fell once more, until at Provost Baldwin's death it stood at 313. The influence of Andrews was soon felt, however, and in 1774, the year of his death, the numbers had increased to 583. The improvement continued during the rule of Hutchinson, and in 1792 there were 933 names on the student register. The highest number yet reached was in 1886, when there were over 1,300 students on the roll under the standing of M.A.*

* Stubbs gives the following table of admissions for the last ten years of the eighteenth century:

Year.	Noblemen and Fellow Commoners.	Pensioners.	Sizars.	Total.	Year.	Noblemen and Fellow Commoners.	Pensioners.	Sizars.	Total.
1791	34	168	11	213	1796	29	73	15	117
1792	39	145	13	197	1797	30	101	8	139
1793	42	128	9	179	1798	20	71	11	102
1794	30	126	6	162	1799	32	90	8	130
1795	25	90	7	122	1800	27	67	14	108

TURBULENCE AND DISORDER

Turbulence and insubordination were very prevalent in the College during the early part of the century and gave rise to the publication of a large number of pamphlets, the authors of whom upbraided and reprimanded the unheeding undergraduate, and offered him much sage advice.

'Such Wars and Tumults,' writes one,* 'as are never heard of even at the Barracks, the very Court of *Mars*, must be monstrous in the very Seat of the Muses, and make Foreigners who hear of them think us a nation of wild *Tartars*.'

Another declares the 'unhappy convulsions' to have reduced the University to a low ebb in the opinion of the world. Owing to the national spirit displayed by some noblemen and gentlemen in sending their sons, its condition had been one of growing prosperity:

'The youth of Fortune began to crowd into you, most of whom formerly used to be banished their own country for education. . . . Thus was there rising among you a sort of Augustan Age,' when there followed 'the tumultuous proceedings for two months . . . of which this last affair has been the bloody catastrophe.'†

Another writer‡ remarks, 'As to this College it was never secure from Riots, and I have some apprehension it never will be,' and proceeds to explain the 'universally lamented' fact by the lack of civil power resident in

* *Letter to the Young Gentlemen of the University of Dublin on occasion of their late Disturbances*, 1734.
† The murder of Ford; see page 102.
‡ *A Letter to G—— W——, Esq., concerning the present condition of the College of Dublin*, 1734.

the governors. There are no stocks for the offenders, no prison, no Proctors as in the English Universities. A second letter from the same hand calls attention to the abuse of privileges accorded the undergraduates. 'Night Rolls and Tickets are the Guard of the Boys from Evil,' but these are controlled by the porter, who can excuse those who are absent without leave, and can be prevailed upon for 'half a dozen of ale or half a crown.'

In some of these publications the Fellows are attacked, and the disorders ascribed to their lack of zeal in the discharge of their duties, and, with a somewhat inconsequent indignation, to their preference for good wine.

'That they are luxurious, particularly in the Article of Wine; drinking it much in their Room, having Cellars to keep it in, and that it is better, and of a higher Price, and a more delicious Flavour than it ought, to such a Degree as to give Offence to many.'

The Fellows were not without their champions, however, and various excuses are offered for their alleged idleness, intellectual and physical. They write no books,[*] but they have multifarious duties. 'The truth is the Fellows are no better than Schoolmasters ... and from twenty Schoolmasters what mighty matter can the world expect?' They are frequently absent from Commons, no doubt, but

'In Winter Time, a Man who is in a warm Room, with a Book in his Hand, had need of a very good Appetite to

---

[*] *Sir Tegue O'Regan's Address to the Fellows of T——y C——e* begins, 'Gentlemen, the extraordinary taciturnity for which you are so remarkable has been complained of both at home and abroad.'

make him quit his Situation, for the Pleasure of passing an Hour at Dinner or Supper in a large and spacious Hall, flagged under Foot, open in a manner at both Ends, never aired by Fire, and which (if not grown warmer since I knew it) is, I believe, the coldest Room in *Europe.*'

'For the Allowance at Dinner, that of the Fellows is said to be very well, it being their great Meal, there is appointed them five Pence Half-penny per head. Tho' I must own, I have often heard it complained of, that the Servants are neither so careful, nor so cleanly in preparation, as in all Reason they ought.'

'For the Supper there is allowed the Fellows two Pence Farthing each, in the same comfortable Place and Manner; the same airy Hall to sit in.'

The dinner-hour at this time was 2.40, which was changed to three o'clock in 1791, and, following the fashion of polite society, moved on to six o'clock in the next century.* Much of the College work seems to have

* At Oxford 'twelve during the earlier part of the eighteenth century was the dinner hour,' says J. R. Green. He continues: 'The Rebellion of 1688 brought with its other "glorious" consequences a march of the dinner hour to two; the Rebellion of 1745 marks its progress to four. But at the beginning of this century, Oxford was on this point in the rear of the Metropolis. . . . Each advance was made amidst grumblings from the older and more conservative members. "University disputations," growls Hearne in his diary, "began on Ash Wednesday, at two and after, instead of at one, occasioned by several colleges altering the hour of dinner from eleven to twelve, from people lying in bed longer than they used to do." "It hath been an old custom," he writes in 1723, "for the scholars of all houses on Shrove Tuesday to go to dinner at ten o'clock, at which time the little bell, called pancake-bell, rings, or at least should ring, at St. Maries, and at four in the afternoon; and it was always followed in Edmund Hall as long as I have been at Oxford till yesterday, when they went to dinner at twelve and to supper at six. Nor were there any fritters

been done after evening service in the chapel, which was held at four. Dr. Kyle, speaking of his life as a Junior Fellow, complains of the inconvenience of these arrangements. 'Often I have been obliged to remain at work in College until seven o'clock in the evening, for there we had evening lectures which obliged me to dine at commons.'*

It ought to be borne in mind that the disturbances in the College were due rather to the spirit of the times than to undue relaxation of the proper academic discipline. Readers of Addison will call to mind the excesses of the Mohocks, and the insecurity of life, limb, and property in the streets of London during their excursions. The Dublin 'Bucks,' a similar tribe of 'gentlemanly' assassins, with like amiable eccentricities, were no less dreaded by respectable persons. Many of these were University men, and the catalogue of their atrocities can now hardly fail to awaken an incredulous surprise. The case of a printer named Mills, who had published in his paper, the *Hibernian Journal*, some reflections on the College students, may be cited as fairly representative of a period marked by extraordinary social disorganization.†

'On the 11th of February, 1775, some scholars drove in a coach to his door, and called him out on pretence of bargaining for some books. He was suddenly seized,

---

at dinner, as there used to be. When laudable old customs alter, 'tis a sign learning dwindles." How horrorstruck would he have been had he seen the great move in 1804, 1805, when those colleges that had dined at three advanced to four, those that had dined at four, to five!'—*Oxford Studies*, by J. R. Green, pp. 34, 35.

* Stubbs' *History*, p. 256.
† *Ireland Ninety Years Ago*, p. 12

thrust into the coach, and held down by the party within with pistols to his head, and threats of being shot if he made any noise. In this way he was conveyed to the pump, and after being nearly trampled to death, he was held there till he was almost suffocated—indeed, he would have expired under the discipline but for the prompt interference of some of the fellows. . . . The form of admonition actually excused the act. It was drawn up by the celebrated Dr. Leland, the historian of Ireland. It commenced in these words: " Cum constet scholarium ignotorum cœtum injuriam admisisse in typographum quendam nomine Mills, qui nefariis flagitiis nobiliora quæque collegii membra in chartis suis lacessivit." '*

The classic story of the College pump is associated with the name of Dr. Wilder,† an eccentric Fellow of the society:

'The interior of the College was considered a sanctuary for debtors; and woe to the unfortunate bailiff who violated its precincts. . . . He was going through the College courts on one occasion when a bailiff was under discipline; he pretended to interfere for the man, and called out: "Gentlemen, gentlemen, for the love of God, don't be so

* 'Since it appears that a body of unknown scholars committed an assault against a certain printer, named Mills, who wickedly attacked in his paper certain noble members of the College,' etc.

† Theaker Wilder, elected Fellow in 1740, was Goldsmith's College tutor. Of Wilder another story is told in the same volume (*Ireland Ninety Years Ago*): 'He once met a young lady in one of the crossings where she could not pass him without walking in the mud. He stopped opposite her, and, gazing for a moment on her face, he laid his hands on each side and kissed her. He then nodded familiarly at the astonished and offended girl, and saying, "Take that, miss, for being so handsome," stepped out of the way and let her pass.'

cruel as to *nail his ears* to the pump." The hint was immediately taken; a hammer and nails were sent for, and an ear was fastened with a tenpenny nail: the lads dispersed, and the wretched man remained for a considerable time bleeding, and shrieking with pain, before he was released.'

The same author, probably the Right Hon. J. E. Walsh, afterwards Master of the Rolls, says:

'The theatre was the scene of many outrages of the College students. One of them is on legal record, and presents a striking picture of the then state of society.'

A student named Kelly climbed upon the stage, interrupted the progress of the play, and insulted in the grossest fashion the manager and members of the company. He was, however, permitted to retire with impunity.

'Unsatisfied by this attack, he returned a few nights after with fifty of his associates, gownsmen and others. They rushed towards the stage, to which they made their way through the orchestra and across the lights. Here they drew their swords, and then marched into the dressing-rooms in search of Mr. Sheridan (the manager) to sacrifice him to their resentment. Not finding him they thrust the points of their weapons through chests and clothes-presses, and every place where a man might be concealed—and this they facetiously called *feeling* for him. He had fortunately escaped, but the party proceeded in a body to his house in Dorset Street, with the murderous determination of stabbing him, declaring, with the conspirator in *Venice Preserved*, " each man might kill his share." For several nights they assembled at the theatre, exciting riots, and acting scenes of the same kind, till the patience of the manager and public was exhausted. He then, with spirit and determination, proceeded legally against them. Such was the ascendancy of rank, and the terror these "Bucks" inspired, that the general opinion was, it would be impossible that any jury could find a *gentleman* guilty of an assault upon a *player*. A barrister in court had remarked with a sneer that he had never seen a "gentleman player." "Then, sir," said Sheridan, "I hope you see one now." Kelly was found guilty of a violent assault, sentenced to pay a fine of five hundred pounds, and, to the surprise and dismay of all his gentlemen associates, sent to Newgate.'*

The story told of the first Lord Rosse, whose profligacy was only equalled by his wit, illustrates another side of the life of Ireland at the time. On his death-bed he received from the Dean of Kilmore a letter, reminding him of his wicked life, and urging him ere he left this world to repent of the countless immoralities of which he had been guilty. Rosse cast round in his mind for the man of most blameless and religious life in his acquaintance, and fixed on the then Earl of Kildare, to whom he despatched the Dean's letter, as if it had originally been directed to him. Kildare, in a fury of indignation at the aspersion cast upon his character by the Dean, wrote an angry note to the Archbishop, and it was not until after Rosse's death that his jest was discovered.

Probably the conditions in Ireland favoured the reign of brutality and license, but Mr. Lecky, in his *History of the Eighteenth Century*, draws a picture of

* This occurred in 1746.

the social life of London which is, if anything, more startling. The excessive drinking habits of the upper classes, the character of their pleasures—the beargarden, bull-baiting, and cock-fighting—and the entire absence of literary or artistic taste among the great mass of the people, mark an era which had all the features of an irruption of medieval barbarism.

One of the most amusing of the many pamphlets of the eighteenth century referring to Trinity College is an ironical paper entitled *Advice to the University of Dublin*, published in 1791. In the section dedicated to students we read:

'If you have chambers on the ground-floor . . . get screws to one of the bars of the window, so as to remove it occasionally, and make a passage to get out. . . .'*

'I once, when an inexperienced Freshman, knew a Scholar of the House, who among other things diverted himself by flinging an odd stone at the Chapel windows. I asked him with astonishment how he could so wantonly break through his oaths. "'Tis quite the contrary," says he, with great deliberation; "I swore I would consult the good of the College; and, pray, is not opening a passage to let in the fresh air doing a material service to those who might otherwise be suffocated in the ardour of their devotion?"'

In *Walker's Hibernian Magazine* for September, 1793, appeared a letter describing Trinity College, which reads like the sarcastic work of a student who

---

* 'Then the secret screw-bar was unscrewed, and the "townhaunter," after his revels, frequently managed to get into his own or some friend's chambers without being discovered.'—TAYLOR: *History*, p. 337.

knew the place well, but assumed the air of a casual visitor:

'Up a pretty flight of stairs on our left hand as we came out of the dining-hall, I was highly pleased with a noble room elegantly fitted up in the most modern stile, with a taste and expence I had not observed since I entered the College walls till then:* this I find is a room ceded about 23 years ago by the board to a society of the young gentlemen who since that time to the present day have had the exclusive care of it, and who are well known through the three kingdoms by the name of the historical society.

'The rooms in which the gentlemen students reside are in general small, but being elegantly fitted up by the youths themselves are with few exceptions vastly neat, and like stars shine in the dark expanse they are fixed in.

'On hearing the word "boy" often vociferated from different windows, I observed a kind of old, wretched, ragged, half-starved beings immediately commence a progressive totter to that quarter from whence the noise issued; these I understand are the academic messengers out of livery, or, if you please, gentlemen in waiting. Old women (if I dare use such an expression), indisputably, however, elderly ones, supply the place of housekeepers, chamber-maids, etc., etc., all of the filthiest sort you have ever seen. The academic dress is pretty enough; it consists of a square cap resembling what you may see painted over grocers' shops on the head of the Chinese emperor, their long black gowns differing according to the rank or standing of the wearer, some as full of tassels as a livery servant's, and some as plain as a parish sexton's; add to these a small ornament projecting out from under the

* Probably the writer was a member of the Historical Society.

chin like gills, and called a band, and I believe you know the whole.'

The wearing of bands with academic dress has not been continued save on grave official occasions, and, to judge from the description of a 'fopling' of the period,* the most precise of modern University men have fallen terribly away from the standard of 150 years ago.

'I have seen a prim young Fellow with a cue or *Adonis*, as they call the effeminate Wigs of the present Vogue, *plaistered* rather than *powdered*, and appearing like the Twigs of a *Gooseberry-Bush* in a *deep Snow*; his Shoulders also crusted or iced over with a White, as thick as a *Twelf-Cake*; with a plaited Shirt, ruffled at Hands and Bosom; a Coat with a Cape, reaching like an Old Wife's Tippet, halfway down his Back; Stockens, milk-white; and perhaps Velvet-Breeches, with Silver Buckles at the Knees, Tassels hanging halfway down his Legs; Spanish Leather Pumps (without Heels), and the burnish'd peeked Toes, seeming to stare the Wearer in the Face; fine-wrought Buckles, near as big as those of a Coach-Horse, covering his Instep and half his Foot, and on his head a diminutive Hat, hardly bigger than we have seen of Ginger-bread at a Country Fair, gallantly cocked and adorned with a Silver Button and Loop: In this manner, with white Gloves upon his Hands, if he has no Rings, and a Staff nearly as tall as himself.'

Such a gilded youth, 'versed in the mysteries of Bacchus and Venus,' must frequently have been seen sallying forth through the College gates to the diver-

* *The Apprentice's Vade-Mecum, or Young Man's Pocket Companion;* Dublin, 1734.

sions of the city, and it is not difficult to imagine that the official duties of the Junior Dean demanded an earnest attention.

'I was not two days in office,' wrote Magee,* 'when I was obliged to sally out at eleven at night, from a warm room, and under a heavy cold, to put a stop to a battle between a body of our sanctified youths and a body of the police. After plunging through the dirty streets on a very wet night for more than an hour, I raked them all into the College; some out of the watch-house, and some out of the kennel.'

In 1794 a certain Theophilus Swift had a son in College who was 'cautioned' at one of his term examinations owing to his inadequate attainments in mathematics and logic. The blow to the family pride was avenged by the father in a pamphlet entitled *Animadversions on the Fellows of Trinity College*, from which some amusing censures may here be extracted. 'In Dublin College,' declares Swift, 'the Muses blush to be seen; and the only Graces that appear there are Silence, Stupidity, and Sorrow.' The Fellows provide a wisdom that none can use. 'Barbara celarent has both more music and more meaning than the hymns of Callimachus, or the luminous and instructive pages of Thucydides.' 'They sup on syllogisms,' he cries out in another euphuistic passage, 'are enamoured of their cobwebs, and bigoted to their bye-laws.' 'Why,' he asks, as some at the present day also unwisely ask, 'should a physician or a lawyer necessarily spend four years in poring over majors and minors, cycloids and cylinders?'

* Fellow in 1788, afterwards Archbishop of Dublin.

Swift found, he says, 'with very few exceptions the whole library of the different youths to consist of a Locke and a Murray, with an Elrington's Euclid thumbed into importance.' 'I would turn,' is his poetical conclusion, 'the streams of Helicon through the College, and teach them to flow unceasingly till they should visit the oracles of Jupiter, till they should bathe the vocal groves of Dodona, and murmur without end through the happy and unfading vales of Tempe.'

The College library contains a pamphlet entitled *The College Examination, a Poem*, 1731.* It brings the scene, familiar to all old Trinity men, vividly before us:

'Conscious of studious Pains, with Joy elate
Some wish the Dawn, and chide the lingering hours;
While others, who (less provident) postponed
Their painful Task, now with a rapid Course,
And nimble Eye, scan o'er the knotty Page
Of Burgerdiscius . . .
But when at Seven resounds the warning Peal
The Freshmen shudder at the dire Alarm . . .
Again at Eight they hear the boding Sound
Din dreadful in their Ears; from every Dome,
In wild Amaze, confus'd the Scholars haste,
Justling along, and with a mingl'd noise
Crowd to the Hall. As when a thousand Rills
Trickling from Hills around, at once unite
And down the Vale a roaring Torrent drives.
Behold! the Senior Lect'rer now appears;
Quick all are seated, and the spacious Hall,

* Quoted in part by Dr. Stubbs, p. 202.

Where many a mingl'd voice humm'd indistinct,
Falls into Silence. Gently down each Form
The stern *Roll-Gerent* walks, and in his hand
His faithful nomenclator dreadful waves.
Now, one by one, some solemn Fellows come
With gravity affected. Arm in arm
Some walk less serious, chatting up the Hall.
While in the midst the Senior Lect'rer stands,
Divides his *Rolls*, and gives to each a part.
They talk facetious, or in circling jests
Inhuman laugh: ah, little they regard
What ceaseless panics throb in Freshmen's hearts! . . .
Lo! Baldwin comes,* how dreadfully serene!
How grand his looks! while at his itching cheek
His nimble finger faithful to its trust
Incessant labours. As he walks along,
The scholars moving thick on either hand,
Respectful rise. He passes stately on,
While awful majesty around him shines.
Now on the upper aisle the Fellows stand;
With heads uncovered, and submissive bow,
They own their monarch. Hence they all disperse,
And down each crowded form, in order ranged
Begin th' important business of the day.
Through Logick's crabbed Rules some steer their Course,
When wonderful Invention nicely shows
How syllogistic well-formed Arguments
Strike Opposition dumb.'

Others, the poem continues to tell, roam through 'Physic's pleasing scene,' pass through 'motion's wondrous laws,' and 'explore the nature of the liquid world.' This done, they proceed to where the aspiring

* 'Gentlemen, the Provost!'

mind 'Views all the motions of the heavenly orbs,' and 'discerns the Eclipse's course.' 'Again they wander through the moral world,' and 'Now with the elegance of Greece and Rome facetious they converse.'

> 'In these while posing Fellows are employ'd
> The awful Provost saunters o'er the Hall.
> Attentive here and there he listening stands
> And turns important Ears. . . .
>   'Twice two long Hours
> Two days successive thus the Youth attend.'

And when all is over, some

>   'sunk in dishonour
> Haste to the refuge of the fumy bowl;'

others, more fortunate, tell

> 'what perils they have safely passed.'

The names of some of the eighteenth-century Fellows still linger in the College. John Walker, the classical scholar and editor of Livy; Berkeley, the good and great, of whom a word must be said in another place; Leland, the author of the *History of Ireland;* Hugh Hamilton, of whose work, *The Analysis of Infinites*, Euler said, 'There are but three perfect mathematical works: these are by Archimedes, Newton, and Hamilton'; Patrick Duigenan, the enemy of Hutchinson and author of *Lachrymæ Academicæ;* Whitley Stokes, *Medicus;** Magee, afterwards Archbishop of Dublin;

---

* *Medicus.* From the time of Charles I. two of the Fellows were exempted from taking Orders; one was obliged to study Medicine, the other Law. The Caroline charter runs: 'Finally, we will that each of the Fellows (excepting those two who have given their names to jurisprudence and medicine), within three years after

Hales, the author of the famous *Chronology* and *Analysis of Equations*; John Barrett, Vice-Provost and Professor of Oriental Languages, who for learning and eccentricity bears off the palm among Dons, and of whom full many a tale is told. But with the exception of Berkeley, no Fellow of the time can be said to have made for himself a deathless name. It is to those who entered the wider arena of public life that the far-shining names upon the roll of fame belong. Yet for Jacky Barrett, 'the extraordinary Doctor,' a niche in any chronicle of Trinity College must be found.

'He was a man of low stature, with a huge head, disproportioned to the size of his body, and a large hooked nose disproportioned to the size of his head. He wore the skirts of his coat very wide, and always walked with his hands buried in his pockets, and his arms fixed close to his sides. His feet were small, and he stood with them close together, so that, at a distance, he looked like an equilateral triangle standing on its vertex. . . . He was a man of great acquirements, and his memory was so tenacious that, like Pascal, he could recollect almost everything he had ever seen or read. . . . Though acquainted with the abstrusest things of science, he was so ignorant of the things of common life, that he literally did not know a live duck from a partridge; and though he had dined at commons on mutton for forty years did not know a live sheep when he saw one.'

Parsimonious to the extremest degree, and, like Charon, *terribili squalore*, he lived in rooms uninhabit-

---

taking the degree of Master, take upon himself the holy order of priesthood.' The two lay Fellows were expected to deliver prælections once a term each *in sua facultate*, but the conditions of the tenure of these offices were rarely observed.

able for ordinary mortals, and, save on one or two celebrated occasions during a long life, never ventured on a journey beyond the College gates. One of them was to Clontarf, on the sea, an hour's walk from Dublin. 'It was then that passing by Lord Charlemont's beautiful demesne, and seeing the sheep grazing, he asked what extraordinary animals they were, and when told expressed the greatest delight at seeing for the first time *live mutton*.' As he passed along the shore, the sea attracted his particular admiration. He described it as 'a broad flat superficies, like Euclid's definition of a line expanding itself into a surface, and blue like Xenophon's plain covered with wormwood.' The great College bell can be heard at Clontarf, and that evening at dinner Barrett, a confirmed misogynist, was asked, as usual at that time, to propose the name of a lady as a toast. 'I'll give you,' said he, 'the College belle, for I'm told she's finer than big Tom of Lincoln.'

Though a profound scholar, best remembered by his discovery and reproduction of the celebrated palimpsest Codex, known to all Biblical critics as Z, 'if the conversation turned on moral or political topics, or on the commerce of the world, the part he took, and the notions he expressed, were often such as can be truly compared to the talk of a child of ten.'

With Barrett, and not with Newton, originated the anecdote of the cat and the kitten :

'A friend, seeing two holes in the bottom of his door, asked him for what purpose he made them there. Barrett said it was for his cats to go in and out.

'"Why," replied his friend, "would not one do for both ?"'

OLD ROW IN LIBRARY SQUARE, REMOVED TO MAKE ROOM
FOR GRADUATES' MEMORIAL.

DR. BARRETT.

' "You silly man!" answered the Doctor, "how could the big cat get into the little hole?"

'"But," said his friend, "could not the little one go through the big hole?"

'"Egad!" said Barrett, "and so she could, but I never thought of that."

'Equally ingenious was the plan he proposed at the board for removing the rubbish after some buildings had been pulled down in the College courts. He considered it a very unnecessary expense to have it drawn away in carts, and said it would be a more expeditious way of getting rid of it, to dig a hole and bury it. When asked what was to be done with the clay taken out of the hole—"D'ye see me now," replied the philosophic Doctor, "can't you dig another hole and bury that?"'*

* *Dublin University Magazine*, vol. xviii., p. 350. See also Wills' *Lives of Illustrious and Distinguished Irishmen*, vol. vi., p. 441.

CHAPTER VIII

THE NINETEENTH CENTURY

THE task imposed upon Trinity College, Dublin, during the first two centuries of its existence was, we have seen, one of infinite difficulty. Founded at a period when Ireland was a good country to hunt and to fight rather than to dwell in, a country throughout whose length and breadth nothing at all resembling a tolerable road was to be found, the greater part of which was covered by treacherous bog or pathless forest, where the dispossessed native prowled by day and the less fierce wolf by night, it is a matter of surprise that the University should have survived the generation that planted it. That having survived it advanced in strength and resources, though for long harassed by lack of funds and supported by a population continually distracted by the fire and sword of rebellion and war is scarcely less remarkable. *Inter Martis strepitus silent Musæ.* Unlike the Scottish and the English Universities, which could count upon the loyalty and affection of a nation, Trinity College, like Dublin Castle, was the stronghold of an alien faith and a victorious minority, towards both of which the great mass of the people preserved a bitter and inflexible hostility.

During the eighteenth century, though it ended in years of gloom and disaffection, the prospects of Ireland brightened, and Trinity College under its great Provosts reflected in its new buildings and the increased number of its undergraduates the more hopeful conditions. Officered as the University was at the close of that and the opening of the next century with men of low ideals and mediocre abilities, little was added to her reputation, except, indeed, as a school of mathematics, until the accession to the provostship of Bartholomew Lloyd. It was in those years she incurred the deserved reproach in the designation of 'the silent sister,'* but it can hardly be forgotten that of the English Universities also harsh sayings were then abroad. Oxford was once described with epigrammatic bitterness as *la vedova di buone lettere*—' the widow of sound learning ' —and few indeed are the human institutions which have not had their periods of hibernation, their listless and lethargic moods. Nor can it have been altogether without effect upon the moral tone of the University that the upper classes in Irish society became during the eighteenth century increasingly indifferent to their duties in the country, and spent more and more of their time and money in England.

'Prior in 1730 calculated the rental spent by absentees in England at about £620,000. Another list drawn up in 1769 put the value at no less than £1,200,000. Hutchinson

* 'Among all Irish institutions, probably the only one ever accused of silence is the University of Dublin.'—Dr. MAHAFFY (*in Macmillan's Magazine*, 1869).

in his *Commercial Restraints,* which was published in 1779, stated that " the sums remitted from Ireland to Great Britain for rents, interest of money, pensions, salaries, and profit of offices amounted, on the lowest computation, from 1668 to 1773, to £1,110,000 yearly." Arthur Young in 1779 estimated the rents alone of the absentees at about £732,000.'*

Dr. George Hall, who succeeded to the provostship on Kearney's elevation to the Episcopal Bench in 1806, held office for five years only, and died seven days after his consecration in the College chapel as Bishop of Dromore. No University events of importance mark the reign of his successor, Dr. Thomas Elrington,† a man who made up in piety what he lacked in distinction of mind and character, and presided with rigour and inefficiency over the College until 1820; but the visit of

* Lecky, *History of Ireland,* vol. i., p. 213.

† The Elrington Theological Prize was established in his memory, 1837. Elrington was described by one of his pupils (Lawless, afterwards Lord Cloncurry) as 'A learned man, but stupid and blockish, and thoroughly imbued with the narrowest views of his class and profession.' The breadth of Elrington's intelligence may be gauged from the following jejune remarks which he addressed to the Historical Society in reproof of their debates on the well-worn subjects 'Execution of Charles I.' and 'The Assassination of Cæsar':

'To admit a defence to be made for assassination must be injurious to morality; to discuss the right of a subject to put a monarch to death, who by the Constitution was exempted from personal responsibility, unquestionably tends to weaken those principles of loyalty which at a time like the present should be cultivated with peculiar care. The example of Brutus can no longer be considered as harmless, for we have seen its effects in stimulating in a Christian country to the murder of a lawful King. The splendour of a voluntary devotement has thrown a false lustre around the assassin Marat, and increased the temptation to the crime by diminishing its deformity.'

George IV.* gave some distinction to the provostship of Dr. Samuel Kyle, who held the reins of government until 1831. King George, who landed in Ireland on August 12, 1821, received the usual address with its protestations of loyalty from the University, and signified his gracious intention of dining at the College on the evening of the 27th. The preparations for the banquet and the proceedings are described in Taylor's *History* with so overflowing an appreciation of the sacred character of the occasion that no other words need be employed:

'His Majesty . . . was received by the Provost, Fellows and Scholars at the entrance of an octagonal vestibule, surmounted by the royal crown. The entire of this vestibule and of the covered galleries connected with it were beautifully arranged: one of them, leading to the entrance of the library, was used as a reception-room, the other to the dining-room: the vestibule and galleries were temporary, being fitted up for this occasion.

'His Majesty, on entering the library, was evidently struck with its chaste and simple grandeur, and having stopped some moments to enjoy its effects, he was addressed by Dr. J. Barrett, the Vice-Provost, in an elegant Latin speech, to which his Majesty paid very marked attention. . . . His Majesty entered into a gracious and free conversation with the members of the University until dinner was announced, when the King, with a captivating politeness, bowed to the ladies who exclusively occupied the fine gallery of the library, no gentlemen being allowed admission there. When we add this splendid assembly to

* On the occasion of this visit the University asserted and secured the right of precedence next after the Corporation of the city, among all the Corporations of Ireland.

what has been already described, and fancy the floor of the superb hall filled with nobility and gentry, clergy and military men, in the various costumes of the church, the law, the university, and the profession of arms, with the monarch enthroned in the centre, a more brilliant assemblage or interesting picture can hardly be presented to the imagination. . . .

'It is difficult to conceive the splendid effect of the theatre on first entering it. This noble hall was fitted up with that classical purity of taste which presided over all the arrangements and decorations belonging to this interesting and magnificent festival. The throne, of crimson velvet of considerable* richness, was placed in the centre of the circular space which terminates the room. A platform, elevated two feet, filled the semicircle, and the royal table was adapted to the curvature of the place. In the centre of the room on one side was erected a splendid Bacchanalian altar of chaste and classic design, upon which stood five bronze figures supporting lights; the summit was crowned with a marble vase filled with flowers, and the whole backed by a very rich drapery of crimson velvet suspended from a wreath of flowers. The room was splendidly lighted, and the *coup d'œil*, on entering the room, inconceivably grand. The gallery at the end of the room was occupied by ladies of distinction, and its effect from the other end, where the throne stood, was peculiarly beautiful.

'The choir occupied the two first rows of this gallery, and immediately on the King's entrance an ode, composed for the occasion by a student of the university, was performed, accompanied by the ancient organ. . . . The table was furnished with a magnificent gold plateau, a fine

---

* An adjective hardly worthy of Taylor.

service of silver plate and beautiful cut glass. The provost helped his Majesty to soup, and the King then invited the provost to occupy a chair next on the right of the royal seat.'

After dinner the King's health was proposed by the Provost, and drunk with appropriate enthusiasm. Other toasts followed, and the proceedings were diversified with music. Then—

' His Majesty rose to depart; as he walked down the centre of the hall to the great door he bowed with great affability, yet with much dignity of manner, to the company at each side of the hall, who had all risen: he recognised and saluted particularly several persons as he passed along.'

' The great cordiality of feeling which characterized the acts and expressions of the monarch on this memorable occasion . . . *were excited and called forth by the favourable and correct opinion which his Majesty had then an opportunity of forming of the course of education carried on in this College*, and of the means by which this system had been made so extensively useful.'

The favourable and correct opinion of so perspicacious a monarch should, one would think, have rendered unnecessary the Royal Commission appointed later in the century.

Dr. Kyle was created Bishop of Cork and Ross in 1831, and was succeeded by Bartholomew Lloyd, described by Dr. Waller as 'the most devoted, the most enlightened, and the most energetic governor the University ever possessed.' Before his appointment to the provostship, Lloyd, as Professor of Mathematics, had been engaged upon work of the highest value and interest. The mathematicians of the Continent, following in the wake of Descartes, were pursuing studies destined to revolutionize the methods of modern science. While Cambridge slept, unconscious of the dawn of a new day, Dublin was awake. Lloyd, in a series of lectures, introduced the new principles to the College, and not long after published his treatise on *Analytic Geometry* (1819), which was followed when he had exchanged the Chair of Mathematics for that of Natural Philosophy by his *Treatise on Mechanical Philosophy* (1826). In these works Lloyd showed the way to the English mathematicians, and laid the foundation of the school of which McCullagh, Humphrey Lloyd, Sir William Hamilton, Roberts, Townsend, Haughton, Jellett, Dr. Salmon, the present Provost, and the late George Fitzgerald, are the great outstanding names.[*]

But Lloyd's labours as a pioneer of science constitute but a small part of his claim to the gratitude of his University. During his brief six years' tenure of the provostship,[†] he achieved more reforms justified by their results than can be ascribed to any other head of the College at any period of its history. The Mathematical Chairs, hitherto held by Senior Fellows only,[‡] were now confined to Junior Fellows, and

[*] Lloyd's influence is also seen in the alteration made at this time in the courses laid down in mathematics and physics for the degree examination; *e.g.*, Poisson's *Mechanics* was added to the course.

[†] It is to be observed that Lloyd died as Provost, not as Bishop, like so many of his predecessors.

[‡] All the important Chairs were held by Senior Fellows up to 1831.

charged with more responsible duties. To these James McCullagh and Humphrey Lloyd were first appointed. In 1833 the undergraduate courses were wholly reconstituted, honour courses and prizes at term examinations introduced, and to the distinctions hitherto obtainable only in mathematics and classics were added those of a final school in mental and moral science.* From 1815 it had been customary to award a gold medal to the best answerer at the degree examination in mathematics and classics respectively; the term *moderatorship* was now introduced to distinguish the honour examination in the final schools, and gold and silver medals awarded to candidates who obtained first or second classes (senior or junior moderatorships) in one of the three subjects above mentioned.† A few years after (1837) Lloyd induced the Board to emphasize still further the importance of philosophical studies by the establishment of a Professorship of the Moral Sciences. To this Chair Archer Butler, the first Senior Moderator in Logics and Ethics, was elected, and an impetus given to the pursuit of metaphysics in the University, whose effect is not yet exhausted.

'It may be well to remark,' says Dr. Stubbs in the *Book of Trinity College*, 'that the University of Dublin was really in advance of Cambridge in encouraging new studies at the B.A. Degree examination. In 1816 the

---

* Hitherto the term *science* covered logics and ethics, but these studies fared badly while associated with mathematics and physics.

† Moderatorships in *Experimental and Natural Science* were instituted in 1850—altered to two moderatorships, *Experimental Science* and *Natural Science*, in 1871. Moderatorships in *History, Political Science and English Literature* in 1856, separated in 1873 into two, moderatorships in *History and Political Science* and *Modern Literature*.

examination for gold medals in Classics was established in Dublin; eight years afterwards Cambridge instituted the Classical Tripos. In 1834 the examination for Moderatorships in Ethics and Logics was founded in Dublin; seventeen years after that date the Moral Science Tripos was instituted at Cambridge. In 1833 Theological Examinations, as they are at present, were first established in Dublin; this example was followed by Cambridge in 1856. In the latter year the Provost and Senior Fellows founded a Moderatorship in Law and History. Cambridge did the same twelve years after. In one case the two Universities acted simultaneously, in founding in 1851 the Honour Degree Examination in the Natural Sciences.'

The year 1833 was also marked by an alteration and extension of the classical courses, a reconstruction of the Divinity School, and the establishment of a systematic course of two years' study for all students of theology.* But the most far-reaching of the reforms of this period was the change made in the terms, and the system of undergraduate lectures and examinations. The terms had hitherto been *four* of variable length, because dependent upon movable Church feasts. A royal

* Until late in the eighteenth century there was no Divinity School and no special lectures for Divinity students. The religious instruction of undergraduates was in the hands of the Catechist, while all resident Bachelors were obliged to attend lectures either with the Regius Professor of Divinity or Archbishop King's Lecturer. In 1790 the Irish Bishops decided to admit to Orders only such candidates as had graduated in Arts and attended one year's theological lectures. In 1879 Lord Belmore introduced into the House of Lords a Bill to transfer the control of the Divinity School from the University to the Synod of the Irish Episcopal Church. It was strongly opposed both in and out of College, and eventually withdrawn.

statute was obtained which reduced the number of terms to *three*—Michaelmas, Hilary, and Trinity—and gave them equal length. At the same time the hours of examination were altered from 8 a.m. to 9.30 a.m. on the first day. In 1835 the tutors agreed, on the suggestion of the Provost, to a new system of lectures and emoluments. These latter were now arranged to depend, not upon the number of pupils under the charge of a tutor, but upon his seniority, thus assuring to him a certain and improving income. The lectures formerly given by each tutor to his own pupils only were also redistributed, the range of subjects which he was required to teach considerably reduced,* and the work required of him fixed at two hours a day.

Until early in the nineteenth century the scholars of Trinity College were of two classes—'natives,' and those who were not natives. Their salaries, as fixed in 1758, were £20 and £4 respectively. A royal letter raised the emoluments of the latter scholarship to £20 in 1827, and in 1846 the Board improved the position of the scholar by granting him rooms in College at half rent and exemption from tutorial fees.

While in 1793 the degrees of the University were thrown open to members of any religious community, scholarships and Fellowships were still confined to Protestants. In 1843 Denis Caulfield Heron,† a Roman Catholic student, competed for a scholarship, and on

* A tutor's fees had depended upon his 'chamber,' as it was called; but if he were popular and had many pupils his work was correspondingly heavy, as he was supposed to give at least an hour's instruction per day to the members of each of his three junior classes.

† Author of *The Constitutional History of the University of Dublin*.

the results of the examination was declared entitled to election. He declined to take the usual oath, and appealed to the Visitors. It was held, however, that the Act of 1793 did not confer upon Roman Catholics the right to become members of the corporation, and it was not until 1854 that the Board founded non-foundation scholarships of equal value to those on the foundation for such students as declined to submit to the necessary test. The Fawcett Act of 1873, however, abolished tests, and, with the exception of the professorships in the Divinity School, opened all the appointments in Trinity College, including scholarships and Fellowships, to the world.

Many voices have in the past railed against the University of Dublin for its supposed narrow sectarianism, and called for the reforms which have made it an 'open University.' Her Roman Catholic historian[*] in 1847 urged with great ability and eloquence that Trinity College should become 'the noble instrument of advancing the intellect of the whole nation,' and, commenting upon the intentions of the Queen, its foundress, added:

'A Queen now rules the Western Islands. No boon could be granted by her more welcome to her loyal Irish Catholic subjects than that Royal Letter would be which should open more fully to them the University of their country, and the blessings of the highest order of education; and that statesman shall earn our lasting gratitude who shall grant this most important aid towards making us a prosperous and united people.'

[*] D. C. Heron.

How strange is the sound of these words to-day! The statesman to whom lasting gratitude is due has arisen, the ardently desired boon has been granted, but the 'narrow sectarianism' of Trinity College, once so passionately denounced, is, now that it has been abandoned, declared the only sound and acceptable basis for all education. Gone, it seems, are the old ideals of intellectual freedom, of the extinction in youth of sectarian prejudice, gone the hope that the religions 'which were intended to unite men in eternity would not separate them in time,' gone the splendid conviction that

'Truth, like a torch, the more it's shook it shines.'

The reorganization of medical studies in the University also claimed Provost Lloyd's attention. Although medical degrees had been conferred almost from its foundation,[*] and some provision for teaching the subject existed, the number of students in the faculty until late in the nineteenth century was but small. This may have been partly owing to the fact that the social position of members of the medical profession was not high, and that Trinity College insisted, as she still insists, upon the acquisition of an Arts degree by all candidates for a degree in physic. So late as 1864, out of 18,000 medical practitioners on the Register of the United Kingdom, only 541 possessed the degrees of Oxford, Cambridge, or Dublin;[†] that is to say, about 3 per cent. were men of University education. Between 1830 and 1850 the

[*] For the early history of the Medical School, see pp. 144-149.
[†] '71 for Oxford, 126 for Cambridge, and 344 for Dublin.' See Professor Stokes' *Medical Education in the University of Dublin*, 1864.

number of medical degrees conferred by the University of Dublin varied from ten to twenty annually; between 1870 and 1880 it rose to nearly forty, and has since continued to increase. Before Provost Lloyd's reforms, although all candidates for medical degrees were required to be graduates in Arts of seven years' standing, only a single year's systematic course of study was provided for them in the College. The *annus medicus* was now extended to four sessions, suitable exercises provided, and the degree conferred without the vexatious interval.

It ought to be mentioned that surgery formed part of the work required from medical students in Trinity College from 1711, in which year the joint Professorship of Anatomy and Surgery was established, and that Dublin was the first University to establish a separate degree in surgery (1858), an example which was followed by the Universities of England and of Scotland in later years.*

---

* 'The change of opinion with respect to the status of the profession of surgery is well illustrated by a correspondence which has been preserved in the College Register. . . . On June 30, 1804, a letter was received from the Vice-Chancellor of Cambridge, in which it was stated that that University had declined to consider any student who had, subsequently to his admission, practised any trade or profession whatsoever as qualified for a degree, and consequently had refused this to Frederick Thackeray, who, since the time of his admission as an undergraduate, had been constantly engaged in the practice of surgery. The Provost and Senior Fellows, in reply, informed the Vice-Chancellor of Cambridge that, after consideration of his letter, they had agreed to adopt the same regulation.'—*Book of Trinity College, Dublin*, p. 111.

The barber's pole still bears witness to the ancient association between the arts of hair-dressing and surgery. The Guild of Barber-Surgeons were in the habit of placing a staff in the hands of the

LATIN OR ENGLISH

Before Lloyd's time all the examinations in the University, except those for the medals given at the degree, were conducted orally. The Fellowship examination was entirely *vivâ voce* and in Latin until 1853.* A curious correspondence exists which passed between the College of Physicians and the University in 1814. The former body informed the Board that they had

'ordered the King's Professor not to be present at any examination for medical degrees in the University in which any question was put or answer received in the English language. The Registrar was directed to write to the Regius Professor to enquire whether these examinations were conducted in Latin. In reply he assured the Board that he would not under any circumstances examine in English.'†

In 1835 the British Association paid its first visit to Dublin. Its meetings were held under the presidency of Dr. Lloyd. Many of the members were entertained in College, and a banquet was given in the Examination Hall. Among the distinguished foreigners who were present may be mentioned Agassiz, De Toqueville, Montalembert, and Barclay de Tolly. The honour of knighthood was upon this occasion conferred by the

---

patient about to be bled. The red stripes on the barber's pole represent the blood, the white stripes the tape with which the wounds were bound. The brass basin occasionally seen suspended from the pole represents the vessel which received the blood.

* It may be surmised that in the case of mathematical candidates the Latin was occasionally post-Augustan. It is related of an Oxford Moderator that, his faithful dog having followed him into the Schools, he exclaimed, ' Verte canem ex !'

† *Book of Trinity College, Dublin*, p. 113.

Viceroy, the Earl of Mulgrave, upon William Rowan Hamilton, the greatest mathematician ever produced by the College.

During the provostship of Franc Sadleir, who succeeded Lloyd in 1837, an important Royal Commission* which made rigorous inquiry into the constitution and methods of the University was held, and reported

'that numerous improvements of an important character have been from time to time introduced by the authorities of the College, and that the general state of the College is satisfactory. There is great activity and efficiency in the different departments, and the spirit of improvement has been specially shown in the changes which have been introduced into the course of education, to adapt it to the requirements of the age.'

Trinity College had set her house in order before the visit of the Commissioners, and was on the whole in a better position to meet investigation than Oxford and Cambridge had been in the previous year when subjected to a similar ordeal. 'The studies of the University,' said the Commissioners of 1850, speaking of Oxford, 'were first raised from their abject state by a statute passed in 1800.'

Whatever tests may be applied to bring to a test the efficiency at any period of Dublin compared with that of Oxford and Cambridge, whether it be the test of results in relation to the money expended, or that of the standard of scholarship preserved at examinations,

* 1851. The Commissioners were Archbishop Whately, Lord Chancellor Brady, the Earl of Rosse, the Bishop of Cork, Dr. Mountiford Longfield, and E. J. Cooper, Esq.

or that of the number of graduates distinguished in science, in letters, or the public service of the State, Trinity College need not shrink from the comparison. In Ireland, at least, where tongues wag with speed and old-time grievances taint the air of controversy, inhabited by a people quick to quarrel and slow to find content, alive to every weakness in institutions and in men—in Ireland, at least, none has yet been found hardy enough to challenge the academic awards of Trinity College, to cavil at her standards of scholarship, or decry the methods of her teachers as outworn. The Commissioners of 1857 recommended some minor alterations in the constitution and curriculum, most of which were subsequently adopted. Senior Fellows have ceased to hold professorships, the obligation upon Junior Fellows to take orders has been removed, and the distinction between pensioners, Fellow Commoners, and noblemen as to the course required for the Arts degree discontinued.* College officers are now paid regular salaries in lieu of the fees which they formerly received, the whole financial system has been revised, and an auditor of the accounts is appointed yearly by the Visitors.

The nineteenth century saw the establishment of a number of new Chairs in the University,† and letters patent in 1874 transferred the nomination of most of the Professors from the Board to a new body, the Academic

* A *nobilis, filius nobilis*, or *eques* was formerly entitled to graduate B.A. in two years after admission on keeping two term examinations in each year. From Fellow Commoners two terms less were required than from pensioners.

† Among others, Engineering (1842), Geology (1843), Sanskrit and Comparative Philology (1858), Ancient History, Zoology (1871), Comparative Anatomy (1871).

Council.* The statutes have from time to time undergone revision, and various Acts of Parliament have altered or modified the University system. In 1851 an Act which extended the leasing powers of the College came into operation, and the renewal fines which swelled the incomes of the Senior Fellows, among whom they had been divided, were exchanged for an annual payment of £800 a year in each case. The loss to each of the Fellows amounted to nearly £400 annually, and the amounts thus accruing to the College are now expended upon studentships and exhibitions. A later Act (18 and 19 Victoria) 'dispossessed the College of its earliest and only subvention from the State, which was granted by Queen Elizabeth—an annual charge of £358 16s. on the revenues of Ireland.'†

The Law School of the University of Dublin, though under the control of the Provost and Fellows, is conducted with the advice and concurrence of the Benchers of the King's Inns. During the seventeenth and eighteenth centuries the Professorship of Civil Law‡ was always held by a Senior Fellow, who was often a clergyman, and the duties were merely nominal. In 1850 the curriculum was revised, the professorship confined to barristers of six years' standing, and the

* The Council consists of the Provost and sixteen members—*four* elected by the Senior Fellows, *four* by the Junior Fellows, *four* by the Professors who are not Fellows, and *four* by the Senate. The Board still nominates to professorships in the Divinity School, to Medical Chairs founded by Act of Parliament, and certain Chairs of private foundation.

† *Book of Trinity College, Dublin*, p. 96. The grounds assigned for the deprivation was the removal of the stamp duties on degrees, imposed thirteen years previously.

‡ Sometimes styled Regius Professor of Laws.

number of lectures fixed at twelve each term. Besides the Professor of Civil Law, there are in the University Professors of Feudal and English Law* and of Constitutional and Criminal Law,† all of whom lecture to candidates for either branch of the legal profession in Ireland.

It is of no little interest that the University of Dublin was the first to establish a School of Engineering, and to grant degrees in that subject. The proposal to establish such a school originated with Dr. Humphrey Lloyd when Professor of Natural Philosophy, and the Chair of Civil Engineering was founded in 1842, its first occupant being Mr. (afterwards Sir John) McNeill. It was hoped that the curriculum laid down might prove of special service to men engaged in the construction of Irish railways, planned and projected about that time, and the growing importance of the work led in 1845 to an extension of the original curriculum to one of three years. Diplomas and licenses were awarded to successful candidates, and in 1872 the degrees of Bachelor and Master in Civil Engineering for the first time created.‡ The degree, as in the case of medicine, is only obtainable by graduates in Arts of the University.

Provost Sadleir died in December, 1851, and letters patent admitted Richard McDonnell as Provost in January of the following year. The new Provost while a Fellow had displayed considerable administrative and financial abilities, and had in 1828 published an

---

* Founded in 1761, as was also the Regius Professorship of Greek.

† Founded in 1888, entitled the Reid Professorship.

‡ Between 1860 and 1891 352 students obtained degrees and licenses in engineering.

examination of the curriculum and methods of examination which proved of assistance to Bartholomew Lloyd in carrying out his extensive reforms. In 1855, therefore, when opportunity offered, Provost McDonnell urged the necessity of further improvements in the University system. Appointments to the Civil Service of India and to the Army and Navy Medical Service were in that year thrown open to public competition, a new career was offered to men of talent and scholarship, and a number of subjects—such as modern languages, literature, and modern history—were brought into academic prominence. To meet the requirements of candidates for these Government posts, a number of modifications were introduced into the organization of University teaching. The Chair of Oratory was associated with the teaching of English Literature; Hindustani, Arabic, and soon after Sanskrit, were provided for among professorships, and more responsible duties laid upon the Professors of Greek, Geology, and Experimental Physics. The results were gratifying. During the first seven years over eighty candidates entered these Government services from Trinity College, and the stimulus and variety of interest given to the intellectual life of the place was found altogether beneficial. From 1856 until the present time 150 members of Trinity College have passed into the Civil Service of India.

While the history of Trinity College in the nineteenth century ran more smoothly than in the eighteenth, and offers fewer picturesque incidents, it must not be supposed that the student population declined into habits of uninterrupted study. Every generation of undergraduates produced its 'lords of misrule,' and probably no member of the College ever looked back upon his University career and found it unstarred by days and nights of undisciplined hilarity. Commencements or the election of the Parliamentary representatives usually afford scope to original minds, and rarely fail to provide matter for the attention of the Junior Dean. But bonfires in the Bay, squibs at elections, or pigeons at meetings in theatre or hall, rarely lead to serious mischief, and on one occasion only during the past 100 years has student mirth been productive of more than passing annoyance. In 1858 Lord Eglinton returned as Viceroy to Dublin amid considerable popular enthusiasm. Some hundreds of students assembled around the College gates, and whiled the time away by the usual discharges of flour, orange-peel, and crackers. The Superintendent of Police, Colonel Browne, lost his temper, and asked Colonel Griffiths, in command of the Scots Greys, keeping the route of the procession, to charge the undergraduates. Colonel Griffiths contemptuously declined to use steel against squibs and oranges, and Colonel Browne ordered the mounted police to charge. They did so, sabring the luckless undergraduates, and even cutting pieces out of the great gate through which the enemy retreated. The charge of the mounted men was followed by that of the foot police with batons, and as the students were absolutely unarmed, having given up their sticks to the Junior Dean, they suffered severe maltreatment. The scandalous character of this attack led to the prosecution of Colonel Browne by the authorities for his assault, and, though acquitted, he had to resign his post.

Since this, the last serious conflict between students and police, a College row has fortunately never produced a scene of such thrilling interest.

In 1867 Humphrey Lloyd succeeded McDonnell in the provostship. As Professor of Natural Philosophy he had already contributed to the advancement of physical science by important original researches, and in his new office worthily sustained the traditions of his name. John Hewitt Jellett, who followed in his steps as a mathematical physicist and held the same Chair, brought to the provostship on Lloyd's death in 1881 an impressive personality and some of the gifts of an orator. But to his successor, George Salmon, theologian and mathematician, the academic world has conceded a reputation which challenges that of his most distinguished predecessors. It is pleasant to think that, when in 1892 the Universities of the world offered to the old Irish College their congratulations on her three hundredth birthday, in her official head they were able to recognise one whom many of them had already delighted to honour, and to whose services in the advancement of knowledge all were indebted. Nor will the dignity, the humour, the oratorical felicity with which the Provost presided over the hospitality of the College during the brilliant week of festivity easily be forgotten by any, either of the guests or members of the University, who had the fortune to be present.

THE PROVOST DR. SALMON

CHAPTER IX

COLLEGE BUILDINGS, PICTURES, PLATE

THE Irish sister of the great English Universities possesses none of that subtile charm which cloister and tower and tracery give to their ancient Colleges. Stern and cold she seems, as one who neither shares the enthusiasm of buoyant youth nor claims the world-worn dignity of age; gray and cold as the granite of Ireland's Atlantic walls, and as unmoved by the ocean of human turmoil and passion, which through the centuries has surged at her feet, there in College Green where Grattan stands. But if the medieval touch of human sympathy is wanting, a noble prospect waits for him who enters beneath the groined and vaulted roof of the West Gate, guarded by Foley's great bronzes of Burke and Goldsmith.* 'It is the College of magnificent distances; for a space of over twenty-eight acres is enclosed by the outermost walls—twenty-eight acres of granite and of green sward, of park and plantation.'† And if

---

* Erected by public subscription—Goldsmith in 1864, Burke in 1868.

† Ulick R. Burke in *Book of Trinity College, Dublin*, p. 190.

no comparison with the Colleges of Oxford and Cambridge is possible, it is not by reason of inferiority, but because upon 'a site unsurpassed in any modern city, and needing nothing but running water to make it unrivalled in the world,'* stands a group of buildings so varied, so stately, and so magnificently disposed, that Trinity College, Dublin, as Johnson said of the oratory of Burke, resembles nothing but itself. Beautiful as it all is, perhaps most beautiful when the moonlight veils the stern edges of the granite and lends a touch of softness to the massive columns, the position of the College in the very heart of a great city adds to the contrast which it offers to Oxford or to Cambridge. Around this temple of learning and the arts pour the ceaseless currents of the national life, and from within the peaceful seclusion of its quadrangles the attentive ear can catch the sound of the far-off surge, the noises of the human sea.

There is nothing in the architecture of Trinity College suggestive of the country to which it belongs. It was unfortunate for the civilization of the Celt that the arts in which he was a master did not include architecture, the most enduring of them all. Hence, save in its round towers, the remains of that civilization offer nothing so impressive to the view of succeeding generations as those of Egypt, of Greece, or of Rome. The skill of hand and eye which produced the delicate jewel-work of Tara, the genius and affectionate industry which achieved the marvellous intricacies of illumination in the Book of Kells, fail to impress the imagination or attract even the cultivated eye, by comparison

* Ulick R. Burke in *Book of Trinity College, Dublin*, p. 190.

THE EARLY BUILDINGS

with the Pyramids, the Parthenon, or the Colosseum, those warders of the memory of antiquity, and Ireland's golden age is half forgotten.

With the splendid exception of the Schools,* the chief buildings in Trinity College, as in Dublin itself, were the work of foreign architects, and belong to the period of classical revival in the eighteenth century. Founded by Danes, inhabited by English colonists, both at war with the native inhabitants of the country, probably security from attack alone was thought of in connection with early Dublin architecture, and, save the cathedrals, there exist in the city to-day no memorials in stone even of medieval times.

Between the sea and the walled city of Dublin lay in the sixteenth century a tract of marsh and sand, in the midst of which on slightly more elevated ground stood the ruined walls and steeple of the All Hallows Monastery, surrounded by 'the sub-prior's orchard and the common orchard, a field called the Ashe-park, wherein the Prior and the Monks had their haggard and cistern.' In all the monastic lands consisted of about twenty-eight acres, which towards the river ran into bogs and pools, while towards the city lay Hoggin Green, one of the three public commons. The earliest College buildings seem to have been almost entirely independent of those of the ruined monastery, and lay towards the east side of the present campanile, in the direction of what is now called Library Square. The old priory steeple was, however, utilized, the College bell was hung in it, and the lower part served as a porter's lodge.

* Often erroneously styled the Engineering School, which occupies part of the building.

'As the visitor approached from Hoggin Green he crossed an outer enclosed court, which formed an entrance to the College; he then entered through the great gate, and found himself in a small square surrounded by buildings constructed of thin red Dutch brick, bedded in well-tempered mortar, with probably a good deal of wooden framework inserted.'[*]

On one side—the east—lay the hall, the library and the Regent House, a gallery belonging to which looked into the chapel. On the south were rooms for the Fellows, on the west and east for the students. 'The three sides comprised in all seven buildings for residence —three on the south side, and two on each of the east and west sides. The windows of the upper story were of the dormer kind, and mostly formed for leaden sashes.'

The College pump stood in the middle of the quadrangle, the courts were laid out in grass, and the whole of the precincts were surrounded by a wall, with two gates, one opening towards the city, the other towards the river.[†] 'The old buildings,' says Dr. Madden (1734), 'were extravagantly timbered after the old fashion,' and

---

[*] Stubbs' *History*, pp. 11, 12. 'Stubbs is wrong,' says Dr. Mahaffy, 'the gate was under the steeple, and faced north' (see p. 204).

[†] Part of the meadow and orchards were leased for ten years to Peter Vanhey, shoemaker, in 1594, 'to the end and purpose that he may frame the same and make thereof three fair gardens, planted with good and profitable herbs, and also fruit-trees of several sorts as shall conveniently be requisite for the said grounds to be good and pleasant orchards, at a rent of two pence a-year, he binding himself to have his doors and free ingress and egress to the said ground, without molestation or any trouble by any of the said house, except that the Fellows shall have free liberties at their pleasure to have their key and door to walk therein for their recreation, and they are to contribute twenty shillings to make a partition wall of mud between the orchard lying on the east and the said ground.'

no doubt the Elizabethan College, though far from impressive, had picturesque features of its own. Fine as the existing architecture is, most Trinity men would have been glad to see part of the old, however incongruous the effect, in existence to-day; but the Elizabethan quadrangle was removed in the eighteenth century, and no relic of sixteenth-century architecture, no gable or gallery, remains. The steeple of the Aroasian priory* disappeared in 1733 to make room for a new one; the first chapel had gone much earlier in the time of Provost Marsh. An entry in the Register of the Dublin Diocese records the consecration of the second:

'1684, 5 October.—The ABp. consecrated ye New Chapel of ye College of ye H. Trinity, extending from E. to West 82 feet, and from N. to South 38 feet, reserving to himself and his successors ye right of visiting ye same manner as by the Statutes he has a right to visit ye College at large. Provost Robert Huntingdon, and ye Fellows and Scholars, in their petition for this consecration, set forth that ye old Chapel built in proportion to the Model and Fabrick of Q. Elizabeth's College was too small to contain ye Students, and was also much decayed. Therefore, Dr. Narc. Marsh, ye late Provost, and Fellows were encouraged by Benefactions to proceed in rebuilding and enlarging their Chapel, which was now completed.'

In this chapel, then consecrated, the services were held for more than a hundred years. It possessed neither architectural grace nor dignity. 'The Chapel is as mean a structure as you can conceive,' remarks a visitor of 1775, 'destitute of monumental decoration within; it

* Restored by Provost Seele. See p. 54.

is no better than a Welsh Church without."* The present chapel,† corresponds externally in style to the theatre that stands opposite, and contains some oak wainscotting and carved woodwork. Of the windows, that in memory of Bishop Berkeley is the most interesting, but the visitor will find in the little cemetery which lies to the east of the chapel the earliest as well as the most neglected of College monuments, the tomb and effigy of Challoner. Within the Communion-rail of the chapel itself lie many of the undistinguished Provosts;‡ without the walls the recumbent figure of the great founder of the College, desolate and ruined and forgotten. ΚΑΤΑΡΑ ΕΣΤΙ ΜΗ ΑΠΟΘΑΝΕΙΝ—'It is an accursed thing not to die'—says the epitaph of another of the Fellows, Dr. Stearne, and to survive in the memory of men is perhaps the least desirable, though the most desired, of blessings. With Challoner it is well, and his works do follow him, though the undergraduate knows him not, and the rain has beaten on his marble face this hundred years.

There seems to have been no entrance into the Elizabethan College from Hoggin Green. In 1629 a certain Mr. Arthur attempted to erect a building which would have blocked a possible entrance, which, though not then in use, might at any time have been reopened. Arthur's action was resented by the students, and their pro-

* *Philosophical Survey of the South of Ireland*, by Dr. Campbell. The author adds in the above passage: 'The old Hall, where College exercises are performed, is in the same range and built in the same style.'

† Finished in 1798. Designed by Sir William Chambers. It cost £22,000. The theatre was designed by the same architect in 1777.

‡ The chapel was closed as a burying-place in 1867.

ceedings are recorded in a letter of Provost Bedell's:

'In the meanwhile the Scholars, upon St. Matthew's day, at night, between Supper and prayer-time, have pulled it all down, every stick, and brought it away into the College to several chambers. Yet upon warning that night given at prayers that every man should bring into the quadrangle what he had taken away, there was a great pile reared up in the night, which we sent Mr. Arthur word he might fetch away if he would; and he did accordingly.'*

John Dunton, who visited Dublin in 1698, tells us something of the Trinity College of that day, and of the sights he saw there.†

'We went,' he says, 'to see the Library, which is over the Scholars' lodgings, the length of one of the quadrangles, and contains a great many choice Books of great value, particularly one, the largest I ever saw for breadth; it was an Herbal, containing the lively portraitures of all sorts of Trees, Plants, Herbs and Flowers.... At the East end of this Library, on the right hand, is a chamber called the Countess of Bath's library, filled with very handsome folios and other books in Dutch bindings, gilt with the Earl's arms impressed upon them, for he had been some time of this house ... the Hall and Butteries run the same range with the Library, and separate the two inner squares. It is an old building, as is also the Regent House, which from a gallery looks into the Chapel....

* The matter was settled by the purchase of Mr. Arthur's plot of ground.
† *Life and Errors of John Dunton.*

'We were next shewed ... the skin of one Ridley, a notorious Tory, which had been long ago executed; he had been bagged for an anatomy, and being flayed, his skin was tanned and stuffed with straw. In this passive state he was assaulted by some mice and rats, not sneakingly behind his back, but boldly before his face, which they so much mortified, even after death, as to eat it up; which has since been supplied by tanning the face of one Geoghan, a Popish Priest, executed about six years ago for stealing: which said face is put in the place of Ridley's. . . .

'After this Theophilus showed us the gardens belonging to the College, which were very pleasant and entertaining. Here was a sun-dial on which might be seen what o'clock it was in most parts of the World. This Dial was placed upon the top of a stone, representing a pile of Books. And not far from this was another sun-dial, set in Box, of a very large compass, the gnomon of it being very near as big as a Barber's pole. Leaving this pleasant Garden, we ascended several steps, which brought us into a curious walk, where we had a prospect to the West of the City, and to the East of the Sea and Harbour; on the South we could see the mountains of Wicklow, and on the North the river Liffey, which runs by the side of the College.'

Dunton describes the College as consisting

'of three squares, the outward being as large as both the inner, one of which, of modern building, has not chambers on every side; the other has, on the south side of which stands the Library, the whole length of the square ... the Hall and Butteries run the same range with the Library and separate the two inner squares. It is an old building, as is also the Regent House, which from a gallery looks into the Chapel, which has been of late years enlarged, being before too little for the number of scholars, which are now, with the Fellows, etc., reckoned about 340. They have a garden for the Fellows, and another for the Provost, both neatly kept, as also a bowling green and large parks for the students to walk and exercise in.'

Dunton mentions a larger library as contemplated, and a new house for the Provost as a-building. About the time of his visit the Irish Parliament petitioned King William for a grant of £3,000 to enable the College to increase its accommodation for students. By private benefactions for the same purpose £2,500 more was secured, and the library square was begun, the foundation-stone of the present magnificent library building being laid in 1712. The remaining three sides of the quadrangle in which it stood provided the additional rooms required for students, and were built of red brick. Of these, one side still stands, another has just gone to make room for the Graduates' Memorial, while the third, or west side which was cut in two by the end of the chapel erected in 1683, was removed in 1839.*

On the east side, and on the site of the present new square, was a walled-in quadrangle, to which access was obtained through two arches under numbers 23 and 25. This was the only recreation-ground provided for the students until, in 1722, the College Park was walled in and planted, and a porter's lodge placed at the north-east end.†

The old hall and chapel occupied the ground from the present campanile halfway to the College gate, towards

* It was in this row of buildings that Goldsmith's rooms were situated.
† The oldest wall was built in 1688, and was of brick. The existing granite wall and railing were erected in 1842.

which it presented a blank and ugly wall. Cassels, a German and a prominent architect, was commissioned to mask the unsightly end of the building, and designed a new front with a bell-tower surmounted by a dome and lantern.* In this was hung the great bell cast by the famous Rudhall, of Gloucester, which weighs nearly 37 cwt., and on which the import duty was £20.

'The aspect of the Court, therefore, upon entering the gate was that of a small square, closed towards the east with a building much nearer than the present belfry. The centre of this east range had the ornamental front and belfry of Cassels' design, which, according to the extant plan,† must always have been ugly, and looks very top-heavy. The north and south sides of this Front Square (built 1685) were of inferior character, while the small quadrangle beyond was still the original structure of Queen Elizabeth's time.'‡

Between 1700 and 1800 the College began to put on the appearance by which it is familiar to us to-day. The early part of the eighteenth century was a period of great building activity in Dublin. The Irish Parliament was itself splendidly housed by 1739, and interested in the adornment of the capital.§

* Completed 1746. 'On the north side of this tower was an arched passage to the interior of the Library Square. The upper portion of the building was removed in 1791, having been considered to be unsafe, and the entire of the front was taken down, along with the Hall, before 1800' (Stubbs' *History*, p. 187).

† For this plan, see Stubbs' *History*, p. 187.

‡ *Book of Trinity College*, p. 61.

§ 'In the reigns of Elizabeth and of the early Stuarts the Irish Parliament met in the Castle under the eyes of the Chief Governor. It afterwards assembled at the Tholsel, in Chichester House, and

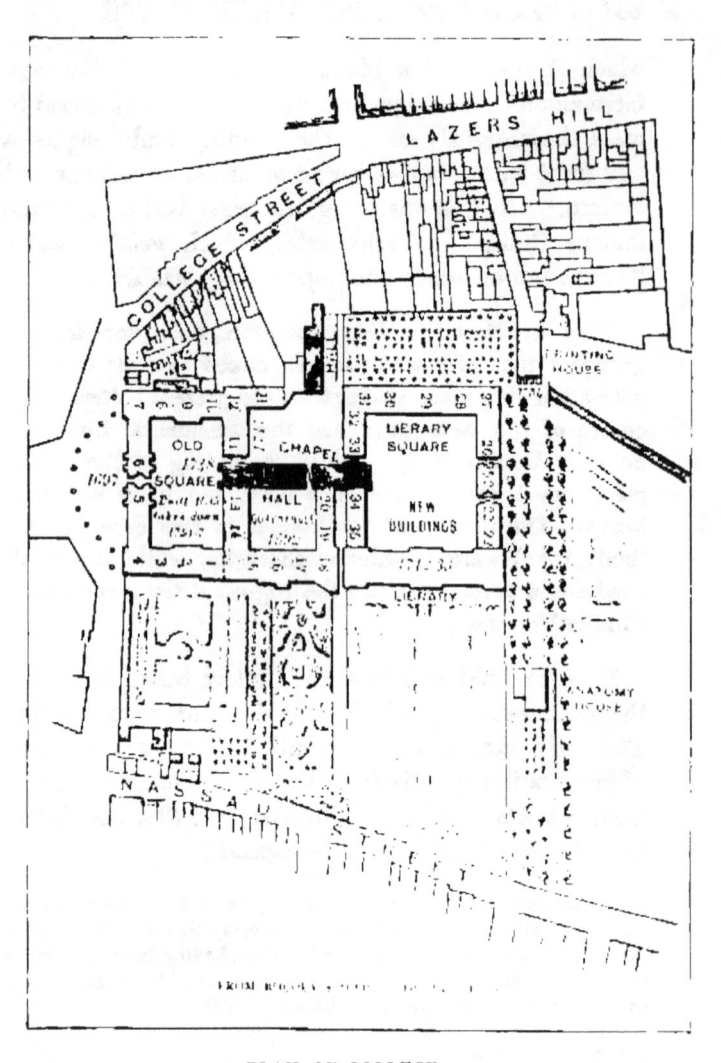

PLAN OF COLLEGE, 1750

■ Old Front Square, 1685.   ■ Quadrangle, 1592.   ■ Library Square, 1722.   ■ Printing House, 1734.   ■ Chapel, 1683.   ■ Bell Tower, 1748.   ■ Hall, 1697   ■ Dining Hall, 1745.

In 1740 the dining-hall was commenced to replace that which, with the chapel, occupied the middle of the College. The new hall proved to be so badly constructed that in 1758 it was taken down, 'Mr. Plummer, the bricklayer,' dismissed for his incompetence, and the present hall built without serious alteration in its plan. The clock in the pediment is famous as that which kept the College time, giving fifteen minutes of grace to all students who resided outside the walls.* In the hall is the wooden pulpit of the old chapel, which now serves for the scholar who says grace.†

The front square, built in 1685, which occupied the site of two still older quadrangles, was removed in 1751. Like the library square, it was built of brick, and in less than a hundred years from the time of its erection was seriously dilapidated. A petition presented by

---

during the erection of the Parliament House in two great rooms of the Foundling Hospital.'—LECKY: *History of Ireland*, vol. i., p. 320.

* For an Herodotean version of how 'it came to pass that the clock was so arranged as to correspond with the course of the sun,' see *Kottabos*, vol. i., p. 267.

† The graces are as follows:
Before meat: 'Oculi omnium in te sperant Domine. Tu das iis escam eorum in tempore opportuno. Aperis tu manum tuam et imples omne animal benedictione tua. Miserere nostri te quæsumus Domine tuisque donis quæ de tua benignitate sumus percepturi. Benedicite per Christum Dominum nostrum.'

After meat: 'Tibi laus, tibi honor, tibi gloria, O beata et gloriosa Trinitas. Sit nomen Domini benedictum et nunc et in perpetuum. Laudamus Te benignissime Pater pro serenissimis, Regina Elizabetha hujus Collegii conditrice, Jacobo ejusdem munificentissimo auctore, Carolo conservatore, ceterisque benefactoribus nostris; rogantes Te ut his tuis donis recte ad tuam gloriam utentes in hoc secolo, Te una cum fidelibus in futurum feliciter perfruamur, per Christum Dominum nostrum.'

the College to the House of Commons resulted in an immediate grant in 1752, and the present west front was at once proceeded with. The original design included a dome over the central gateway* and two cupolas over the pavilions at the north and south ends. One of these, the south cupola, was erected, but in 1757 the plans were changed, the completed cupola taken down, and the palladian façade, as it stands at present, finished in 1759. Further grants from the Commons and the Board of Erasmus Smith enabled the Board some years later to complete Parliament Square, so called in gratitude to the legislature which provided the necessary funds, by the addition of the existing wings. The theatre was begun in 1777, and the chapel facing it in 1787.† The theatre contains, as all undergraduates know, Baldwin's monument, the Spanish organ, the gilt chandelier, which once hung in the Irish Parliament House, and, among

---

* The construction of the gateway shows that it was intended to support a dome.

† 'It was intended to complete the Front Square by an ornamental range, with a bell-tower, and arches dividing it from the Library Square.'—STUBBS: *History*, p. 192. 'This design may be seen in Pool and Cash's *Views of Dublin*.' A letter (1779) from Sir William Chambers the architect (No. 153, MSS. of Earl of Charlemont) is of interest. He writes: 'A couple of years ago I was requested to make designs for some very considerable additions to the buildings of Trinity College, which I readily agreed to ... but the great difficulty attending the vast work I am now about [Somerset House] and the perplexed measures sent me from Dublin at different times obliged me to desist, and all I could do was to give a general disposition of what I intended, from which, as I have since learnt, the buildings are now executing. If there be any merit in the general intention I may claim some little share in it, but the whole detail on which the perfection of these works must greatly depend is none of mine, and whatever merit that has is Mr. Meyer's, who, I understand, is the operator.'

others, portraits of Elizabeth—*hujusce Collegii fundatrix*—under which, says College superstition, it is unlucky, if not fatal, to sit at examinations—Archbishops Ussher and King, Bishop Berkeley,* Fitzgibbon, Earl of Clare, Edmund Burke (by Hoppner), and Jonathan Swift.

Of the minor College buildings, the little Doric temple which looks out upon New Square and harbours the University Press† is perhaps the most interesting; but the Magnetical Observatory,‡ standing in the centre of the Fellows' garden, has something of a similar charm, with its simple portico, also of Doric type, partly copied from an Athenian model. A few years after the completion of the University Press an edition of seven select dialogues of Plato was printed there, and in 1745 an edition of Horace. These were the first books printed in the College.

Of 'Botany Bay,' begun about 1795, it is unnecessary either to appraise the architecture or the character usually assigned to its undergraduate population. The famous Junior Dean, described by Lever, numbered among his accomplishments the art of 'smelling out the devil in Botany Bay,' and it is not improbable that the quadrangle acquired its name and fame at an early stage in its history. The antipodean 'Botany Bay' was discovered by Captain Cook in 1770, and became

* It seems extremely doubtful whether this picture really represents Berkeley. It may be a portrait of Provost Peter Brown.

† Built on Cassel's design in 1734. The funds were provided by Bishop Stearne, Vice-Chancellor of the University.

‡ Built in 1837 on the suggestion of Dr. Humphrey Lloyd. At the time it was built it was the only magnetical observatory, except that at Greenwich, in the United Kingdom.

a penal settlement about twenty years later.* It may be conjectured that the gloomy, prison-like character of the new buildings, and their remoteness from the rest of the College, are sufficient to account for the sarcastic designation they received, which, perhaps, gained a subtle propriety from the fact that the name 'Paradise' was frequently given to quadrangles in medieval times. The 'Bay,' at least, has never been sacred to the loftier moods of poetry or romance, and it is better to seek for inspiration or an hour of peaceful dreams among the daisies in the park or the hawthorn-bloom of the New Square than beneath its forbidding tiers of blank and ghostly windows.

Of the buildings due to the nineteenth century, the new square, completed in 1844, the campanile, erected in 1853,† the Schools and the Medical School buildings, it may be said in general that they conform to the genius of the College, and harmonize with their surroundings. The campanile, in which hangs the great bell once in the earlier belfry, is a singularly attractive work of unique design, while in the Schools,‡ Trinity College possesses a building which is, perhaps, the most

* The name had become a familiar one in Ireland, for great numbers of Irish political prisoners were sent there after the '98 rebellion. An insurrection, raised by five or six hundred United Irishmen, was discovered in the colony in 1801, and for some years a very turbulent spirit prevailed there. In 1804 a rebellion in New South Wales was only suppressed after bloodshed. See Lecky's *History of Ireland*, vol. v., 101, 102.

† Erected by Lord John Beresford, Primate of Ireland and Chancellor of the University.

‡ This building, praised by Mr. Ruskin, was designed by Messrs. Deane and Woodward, who afterwards designed the University Museum at Oxford. The Sheas, journeymen stonecutters, who did the carving, were subsequently employed on the Oxford Museum.

successful piece of modern architecture in the British Isles. Designed by an Irish firm, its rich stone carvings, copied from groups of natural flowers, were the work of two Cork artisans of extraordinary native talent, and it may therefore be regarded as the only College building which is wholly due to Irish brain and hand.

'The style has been described as Byzantine Renaissance of a Venetian type; but the building is in truth a highly original and beautiful conception, worked out into a harmonious and satisfactory whole. . . . The exterior may suggest Venice, and the interior certainly suggests Cordova; and yet there is nothing incongruous with the very different surroundings, nor is there in the work any of that patchiness so often apparent in adaptations of foreign styles. It is something in itself complete, dignified, and appropriate.'[*]

To a student of architecture this building alone would warrant a visit to the Irish capital, while to those who suffer when they walk the streets of our modern cities it affords a respite to their pain.

In the College park, sacred to physical culture, and the scene of all University athletic contests, stand the fine blocks of building that make up the Medical School.[†] Remote from the residential quadrangles, and peacefully disposed among the trees, they possess a character of their own, though their severity of design and cut granite masonry are in keeping with the distinctive architecture of the rest of the University. The south-

---

[*] Ulick R. Burke in the *Book of Trinity College, Dublin*, p. 221.
[†] The museum was completed in 1876, the Medical School laboratories and theatre in 1887.

east entrance to the College, once familiarly known as the 'Hole in the Wall,' has since 1855 lost all claim to such a title, and with its granite lodge and iron gateway completes the general design in harmonious fashion.

No visitor should leave the park and Fellows' garden without a passing glance at the once famous Holy Well of St. Patrick, one of the most celebrated in Ireland, to which many thousand devotees have made pilgrimage. The old lane which led to this well is mentioned in 1592 as the south boundary of All Hallowes—*venella quæ ducit ad fontem S. P.*—and a quaint account of the rush thither every 17th of March is given by an English writer of the same period.[*] A pamphlet of 1612 records the advice given by a Catholic priest to a student of the College, in which the virtues of the well are expounded,[†] and contrasted with those of the new drug, tobacco.

'But let me draw somewhat near to your College itself: are you not eyewitness how every 17th March what flocking there is of men and women and children to that holy, sanctified pool, Saint Patrick's Well. I hope you do not think the whole multitude that do so yearly frequent the place be stark mad to come running there so thick if they did not find some sanctity in the water. I warrant you they are not so arrant fools as a number of those that do use to take tobacco, that will be still stuffing themselves with smoke, but upon a vain conceit.'

[*] See Gilbert's *History of Dublin*, p. 245.
[†] *A Catholycke Conference betweene Syr Tady MacMarrall, a Popish Priest of Waterforde and Patrick Playne, a young Student of Trinitie Colledge by Dublyne in Ireland*, 1612.

THE SCHOOLS—INTERIOR

The Provost's house, a noble mansion designed in 1759,* contains the most interesting and valuable pictures in the College collection. In it are hung portraits of all the Provosts from Adam Loftus downwards, besides those of many other distinguished members of the University. To the ordinary visitor the famous half-length portrait of Queen Elizabeth by Zucchero, and the magnificent Gainsborough representing the Duke of Bedford as Chancellor, will probably prove most attractive; but to anyone acquainted with the history of the College many of the inferior paintings must prove of equal or greater interest. Here is the great seventeenth century scholar Anthony Dopping, and here Sir Hans Sloane, M.D., of the University, the great physician and virtual founder of the British Museum. Here also are two portraits of Archbishop Ussher, and two which are generally regarded as portraits of Challoner. Besides these and many other worthies, are pictures of George, Prince of Wales, Chancellor of the University in 1715; of George I., by Sir Godfrey Kneller; and of George III., by Allan Ramsay.

On the walls of the dining-hall of the College hang chiefly pictures of Chancellors or Vice-Chancellors of the University, but the most interesting are perhaps those of Grattan and of Flood.† In the Fellows' common-rooms are portraits of the Earl of Mornington,

---

* This house is said to be a copy of General Wade's House, designed by Lord Burlington, and now part of the Burlington Hotel in Cork Street, London.

† Among the others are portraits of Earl Cairns, Primate Lord John Beresford, and the late Earl of Rosse, sometime Chancellor of the University.

Bishop Berkeley, Archbishop Palliser, Archbishop Magee, and others of more recently distinguished members of the University. In 1897 the College collection was enriched by the presentation of the portraits of the two Dukes of Ormonde, who were Chancellors in 1645 and 1688,* and in 1898 by an additional portrait of Adam Loftus, presented by an old graduate of the College, Lord Iveagh.

But for the vicissitudes of fortune, Trinity College would have been to-day in possession of a collection of plate not to be rivalled by any academic foundation. In the diary of Lord Cork, dated 1630, we find the following: 'I give my chaplain 50s. to pay the ffees to the officers of Trinitie Colledge, near Dublin, for the admittance of my two sons, Lewis and Hodge, into that house, and must also present plate.' It is evident from this that the custom of presenting plate dates from the earliest years of the College, and it continued until the eighteenth century, when the tax for *argent* seems to have been discontinued. For over 200 years, however, the custom yearly added something to the wealth and dignity of the foundation, and but for the crisis already noted,† during which it became necessary to draw upon its last resources, would by this have resulted in a collection of silver of the highest intrinsic and historical value.‡

The earliest mace belonging to the Corporation was

* These were given by the Marquis of Ormonde.
† The periods of the Irish Rebellion and of the Civil War in Ireland.
‡ 'In eight years from 1758 a sum of close upon £1,250 was expended in purchases of this description.'—DR. MAHAFFY: *Book of Trinity College, Dublin*, p. 273.

purchased in 1600 at a cost of £12. It was extant in the time of Provost Humphrey Lloyd, but has unfortunately disappeared, since the mace at present in use, dating from 1707, came to be regularly employed.

Of the existing silver, the oldest pieces are those which compose the Communion plate, bearing the date 1632, but very little more survives from the early seventeenth century. There are, however, a number of fine almsplates, salvers, candlesticks, and flagons which came into the possession of the College between 1660 and 1708. Of these some are of exquisite design and workmanship, especially fine being a pair of salvers given by the Marquis of Abercorn on the occasion of the entrance of his two sons. 'But the number of these beautiful gifts and their variety is such that it would require a volume to produce them, and a specialist to describe them.'* Despite the losses, therefore, when the College produces its treasure on occasions of State, it can make a magnificent display, and those who have dined in Hall on a great guest night, or attended the banquets which took place during the Tercentenary celebrations, are not likely to think of the corporation as beggared by the tribulations of its evil days.

The first Lecturer in Botany in the University, Dr. Nicholson, published in 1712 a pamphlet entitled *Methodus plantarum in horto medico collegii Dublinensis jam jam disponendarum Dublini*. This 'Physic Garden' appears to have lain in the College park between the Anatomy House and the Nassau Street wall. The necessities of the Medical School transferred it to

* Dr. Mahaffy in *Book of Trinity College, Dublin*, p. 272.

Harold's Cross about 1800, and in 1806 the College leased the present Botanic Garden at Ball's Bridge for 175 years. The laying out of the grounds, which now form a delightful and secluded lounge, was undertaken by the curator, James Townsend Mackay,* who was successful in introducing and naturalizing a number of foreign plants.

'He gives a list of thirty-seven plants, chiefly natives of Chili, China, New South Wales, and the South of Europe, planted in the open air, and among them, "*Veronica decussata*, a native of the Falkland Islands, the only shrubby species of the genus. *Olea europea*, which was unprotected for the last seven years. *Ligustrum lucidum;* one plant in the open border was now six feet high [it is now twenty feet]. *Pittosporum tobira*, lately introduced, stood without protection. *Solanum bonariense* stood planted near a wall. *Cassia stipulacea* stood out by a wall, in a south-east exposure, for the last eight years, and produced copiously its showy blossoms in April and May, but required some mat protection in severe weather. *Aristotelia Macqui:* one specimen is now fourteen feet high; it retains its leaves in mild winters, but drops them in spring before another set is produced. *Mespilus japonica* (Loquat) grows to a large size, retains its leaves throughout the winter, but never flowers; and *Melaleuca alba* stood out on a south-east wall for the last five years, and blossomed last summer." '†

To-day the garden, with its high, creeper-covered walls, its luxuriant hollies and flowering shrubs, its

* Author of *Flora Hibernica*, Dublin, 1836.
† See *Book of Trinity College, Dublin*, p. 279.

trees and pond, orchid and fern houses, attracts many an undergraduate, for whom the flowers are nameless and the genera indistinguishable. In spring the walks are lanes of crocus and daffodil; while many a shady nook in summer invites to old-world memories and scorn of bustling crowds.

CHAPTER X

THE LIBRARY

THE beginning of the vast collection in the library of Trinity College, which takes rank with the great libraries of the world, marks a momentous period in the troubled history of Ireland. In 1601 the rebellion in Munster had been put down, and the Spaniards driven from Kinsale. As a memorial of their victory, the English army subscribed £700 for the purchase of books to be presented to the College,* and the old plan of the Battle of Kinsale, which hangs in the gallery outside the present great room, fitly calls attention to the unique origin of this among University libraries. Luke Challoner and James Ussher, afterwards the great prelate and friend of Charles I., were entrusted with the money, and sent as the College representatives to England to procure suitable books. Their choice was a wide one, for no more than forty books, of which ten were MSS., seem before 1600 to have been in the possession of the Provost and Fellows.† By singular

* 'These souldiers,' says Dr. Nicholas Bernard, 'were for the advancement of learning.'
† Among others, editions of Plato, Aristotle, Euripides, and Cicero.

chance Ussher and Challoner met during their visit to London Sir Thomas Bodley, engaged upon a similar errand—the purchase of books for the Oxford Library which bears his name—'and there was a commerce in supplying each other with rarities.' On the whole, however, the money was spent upon books valuable to the student rather than to the antiquarian, and we find that a Hebrew Bible and copies of Homer and Virgil were among the first purchases. By 1610 the forty books in the library had grown to 4,000, and already contained a number of rare and interesting works. The earliest account of the collection was given by Brereton, the Parliamentary general, who records a visit to Trinity College in 1635: 'They glory much in their library, whereof I took a full view, and there were showed unto me many manuscripts; one they highly esteem, which they call Friar Bacon's work.'*

In 1661 the officers and soldiers of the army in Ireland again laid the University under a debt of gratitude. Archbishop Ussher's library, brought together by the greatest scholar of his day, and originally intended for presentation to the College, was confiscated by Parliament on the Primate's refusal to admit the authority of the Westminster Assembly of Divines. Although the greater part was eventually restored to Ussher through the exertions of his friend, John Selden, the Primate, having fallen upon evil days, was forced to alter his original intention and leave the books to his daughter (Lady Tyrrel), for whom he could make no other provision. On Ussher's death various offers were

* The MS. from which Jebb published Bacon's *Opus Majus*.

made for so famous a collection, and it is said that 'the King of Denmark and Cardinal Mazarin endeavoured to obtain it'; but Cromwell, by an Order in Council, refused to permit the sale, and it was purchased by the Parliamentary army in Ireland at a cost of £2,200. The generosity, spontaneous and magnanimous, on the part of the English soldiery, thus twice displayed, is unique in the history of any country. Not unnaturally does Williamson* exclaim of this army in his panegyric on the Lord Deputy, Henry Cromwell, who proposed the purchase, 'Quos Deputatus docuit primum armorum usum deinde librorum'; and again, comparing the Trinity College library with that of Ptolemy Philadelphus in Alexandria, 'numero librorum cedimus, virtute superamus.' It was Cromwell's intention to place Ussher's books in the library of the new College in the University for which he had at that time prepared the plans, and they were accordingly sent over to Dublin to await the completion of the design. In 1659

'the Commissioners of Parliament for the Government of Ireland referred to "certain persons named" to take a view of the gallery at Cork House and the armoury-room near the Castle, and to consider with workmen which place may be most convenient for placing Dr. Ussher's Library, and to present an estimate of the charge for making Presses and Chains for the Books in order to their use and security.'

The confusion of the times led, however, to neglect of books and MSS. Many were stolen or destroyed before

* Caesar Williamson, Fellow of Trinity College, 1660.

GROWTH OF THE LIBRARY

the Restoration, when an order of the Irish House of Commons transferred them to Trinity College, Cromwell's idea of another College in the University having dropped out of sight on his departure from Ireland.

By the acquisition of Ussher's books the library of Trinity College was at once raised to high rank. Grants from the Irish House of Commons and the benefactions of many private persons added to its treasures in the seventeenth and eighteenth centuries. To Dr. Claudius Gilbert it owes nearly 13,000 volumes; to Archbishop Palliser 4,000; to Dr. John Stearne many important MSS.; to Sir John Sebright a great part of its magnificent Celtic collection,* which includes the *Book of Leinster*; to the Board of Erasmus Smith 20,000 volumes, which formed the splendid library of M. Greffir Fagel, and were removed for sale to England in 1794, when the armies of France invaded Holland; and to Henry George Quin many of its choicest treasures among *editiones principes* and costly bindings. During the nineteenth century the chief increase in the number of volumes has been due to the Act of Parliament which, in 1801, gave to Trinity College Library the right to a copy of every book published in the United Kingdom.†

At the end of the eighteenth century there were less than 50,000 books in the possession of the College, by the middle of the nineteenth the number had grown to 100,000, and it may now be set down as over 250,000, and 2,000 MSS. If pamphlets were counted separately,

---

* From the library of that great scholar, Edward Lhuyd.

† A privilege at present shared by four other libraries—the British Museum, the Cambridge University, the Bodleian, and the Advocates' Library, Edinburgh.

and not bound volumes only, this number would, of course, be greatly increased. To the bibliophile and antiquary the interest of Trinity College Library is practically inexhaustible, and it would be difficult to imagine its treasures more nobly housed. Although the British Museum and the Bodleian Library at Oxford contain a larger number of volumes, and each in its own way must impress the visitor, neither possesses so stately a grace, so simple and immediate an effect, as the long room in the University of Dublin. The length, including the Fagel Library, is just short of 240 feet, and the breadth and height so proportioned as to give to the eye the impression of distance without narrowness, while the galleries and curved ceiling suggest space, and about 100 magnificent windows flood the whole with light. Down both sides are ranged between the stalls, on their carved oak pedestals, the busts of men whom the College is proud to number among her sons, together with some copies of antiques. By the main entrance on the ground-floor is the MS. room, where the reading-room is also now located. Until a few years ago a fine cloister extended on both sides of the building almost from end to end, but it has been built up to find the additional accommodation necessary for both books and readers—an unfortunate sacrifice of beauty to utility.

Among the Greek and Latin MSS. in the library* is the celebrated palimpsest codex known to Biblical students as Z, a tenth-century cursive of the Gospels, a palimpsest fragment of Isaiah, the well-known *Codex*

* For a complete account of the contents of the library, see Dr. Abbot's chapter in the *Book of Trinity College, Dublin*.

THE LIBRARY—INTERIOR

THE IRISH MANUSCRIPTS

Montfortianus, the sixth-century *Codex Usserianus*, and a number of less important works.* These, with the Egyptian papyri presented by Lord Kingsborough in 1838, are the most ancient of the College treasures. But probably they are of less value than the splendid books from the hands of Irish scribes who worked in the monasteries of the ancient Celtic Church: the *Book of Armagh*, whose date is 807, formerly regarded as the work of St. Patrick himself, in a finely embossed leather satchel; the *Book of Dimma*, in an exquisite shrine of silver; the *Book of Mulling*, with its satchel embroidered with crystal;† the *Book of Leinster*, a twelfth-century folio of the highest interest; the *Book of Durrow*, with its characteristic Celtic ornament; and the incomparable *Book of Kells*, 'the most beautiful book in the world.' The extraordinary accuracy of the minute spiral patterns, the exquisite beauty and harmony of the colouring, and the variety of the designs, have given to this book its world-wide celebrity.

'If you look closely,' said Giraldus Cambrensis, 'and penetrate to the secrets of the art, you will discover such

* Among printed Bibles is a copy of the first German Bible (1466), and a leaf (vellum) of the famous Mazarin Bible.

† 'The case or shrine of the *Book of Mulling* appears to have been originally plain, except for some small pieces of crystal and lapis lazuli inserted on one side. In 1402, however, a very large crystal, set in fine niello work, was inserted in the same side. In 1891, thinking I saw trace of a letter under this crystal, I raised it, and thereby revealed a brass plate, hitherto concealed by dust, and bearing the inscription: "Artturus | rex domin | us 3 lageniæ | elnsdabe | tilia 3 baroni | anno 3 dni | millio | quadrin | gentesi | mo sedo | ." This Arthur was Arthur or Art MacMurrough Kavanagh, who opposed Richard II.'—Dr. Abbott: *Book of Trinity College, Dublin*, p. 166.

delicate and subtile lines, so closely wrought, so twisted
and interwoven, and adorned with colours still so fresh,
that you will acknowledge all this is the work rather of
angelic than of human skill. The more frequently and
carefully I examine it, I am always amazed with fresh
beauties, and always discover things more and more admirable.'

The *Book of Kells* was probably written in the eighth
century in Columba's monastery at Kells. It was
originally protected by a golden cover, and remained in
Kells until the dissolution of the monasteries, when it
was given by the last Abbot, Richard Plunket, to a
certain Gerald Plunket, from whom Ussher received it.

The oldest MSS. of Irish origin which the library
possesses are copies of the Gospels—the *Book of Dimma*,
the *Book of Durrow*, the *Book of Mulling*, and the
Book of Kells. These are Latin MSS., with here and
there a gloss in Irish, and belong to the eighth and
ninth centuries. The *Book of Armagh*, which is of
about the same age, is by its contents the most interesting of this class; for, besides Biblical and hagiological
documents in Latin, it contains documents, partly in
Latin, partly in Irish, which are our oldest authority
for the life of St. Patrick.*

From the literary point of view, the MSS. which are
Irish in language and matter are still more interesting.
The chief of these is the *Book of Leinster* (twelfth
century), the most important collection of Irish literature now extant.† Like other such MSS., it is a kind

* It will shortly be published in facsimile by the Royal Iri
Academy.
† Edited in facsimile by Dr. Atkinson.

THE IRISH MANUSCRIPTS

of bibliotheca in which are to be found mingled the various elements that go to make up the medieval literature of Ireland. No book so well represents the blending of the indigenous and the imported—the old legends which had lived, who knows how long, on the lips of the people, mixed with the late inventions of erudite pedants and the lore of Churchmen. Here is the *Cattle Foray of Cualnge*, most famous of the ancient stories; here is many another tale of Cuchulinn and Conchobar, of Ailell and Medb; here is the collection of folk-lore known as the *Dindsenchas* (the Irish *Fasti*); here is the history of the world as seen by the scholarly monks of the ninth and tenth centuries; here is the story of Troy, strangely unfamiliar in its Irish dress; here are lives of saints, legal documents, Rabelaisian anecdotes, etymologies, pedigrees. Part is prose, part metre; but the latter is, with few exceptions, nothing more than mnemonic verse and rhymed chronicle—very little deserves the name of poetry.

The *Yellow Book of Lecan* is a compilation similar in character, but later in date. Of the later MSS., the larger number is ecclesiastical, and devoid of literary value; there are tracts on law and medicine, and there are late romances of the Ossianic cycle in which Finn, Macpherson's Fingal, is the central figure. These are less primitive, more diffuse, more penetrated by foreign influences than those earlier legends which preponderate in the older MSS., and whose principal heroes are Cuchulinn and Conchobar.

With the library of the Royal Irish Academy, the library of Trinity College is of prime importance for the student of Irish history and literature. Much has been done since the days of O'Donovan and O'Curry (1840-60) to advance the scientific study of the language, and import some kind of order into the chaos of documents. Much, indeed, remains to be done, yet it is already possible for a student who consults the works of specialists to attain a just conception of the characteristics of ancient Irish society. As to the æsthetic value of the literature, very different opinions have been maintained. It is unfortunate that partisan feeling should have intruded on the tranquil sphere of art, but it need not cloud the scholar's vision.

No one will deny the epical simplicity of the earlier sagas, the picturesqueness of the later romances, nor can there be a doubt that this literature has both a style and a spirit of its own—a special *Weltanschauung*. Critically examined, it will be found to express the individuality of the Celtic race, and suggest what elements it has contributed to European civilization.

Of the Celtic MSS. of the Gospels it is interesting to note that they were believed to possess medicinal virtues, and in some cases they bear the marks of water which was poured upon them and then drunk by anxious invalids. In MacGeoghan's MS. *Annals of Ireland*,[*] it is told of St. Columba that

'Hee wrote 300 bookes with his one hand, they were all new testaments, left a book to each of his churches in the Kingdome w[ch] Bookes sunck to the bottom of the Deepest waters, they would not lose one letter signe or character of them, w[ch] I have seen partly my selfe of that book of them w[ch] is at Dorow in the K[s] County, for I did see the

[*] Trinity College, Dublin, Library. Quoted by Dr. Abbott, *Book of Trinity College, Dublin*, p. 160.

Ignorant man that had the same in his custody, when sickness came upon cattle, for their Remedi putt water on the booke and suffered it to rest there a while and saw alsoe cattle returne thereby to their former or pristinate and the book to receave noe loss.'

Among other interesting Irish MSS. may be mentioned the *Psalter of Ricemarch*, formerly in the possession of the Bishop of St. David's, who died in 1099, and the *Book of Hymns*, both excellent examples of the best Celtic work; the latter of the highest importance for linguist and liturgiologist.* Besides these there are many important series of MSS. dealing with Irish affairs, among which are thirty-two volumes of the much-canvassed *Depositions relative to the Rising of* 1641, and other State papers of consequence—*Letters of Queen Elizabeth on Public Affairs in Ireland*, 1565-1570; *Lord Deputy Chichester's Correspondence with the English Government*, 1612-1614; *Major Sirr's Papers chiefly connected with the Rebellion of* 1798 (12 vols.), and many more.

Of MSS. not already mentioned, the twenty-five volumes of *Memoirs of the Foreign and Financial Affairs of France in the Reign of Louis XV.* should repay perusal by a student of history, as should also the volumes of Waldensian literature catalogued by Todd. *The Chronicle of Florence of Worcester* and the *Life of St. Alban* in Norman-French, probably in the handwriting of Matthew Paris, both of which are now published, are among the most interesting of the medieval manuscripts in the collection. Trinity College

* Published by the Henry Bradshaw Society.

Library is rich in Wyclif literature, and possesses one of the two known copies of the first complete *English Prose Psalter*. Among early English books, the most interesting are two MSS. of *Piers Plowman*, five of Rolle's *Pricke of Conscience*, and one volume which came from the Caxton press, a second edition of the *Dictes and Sayings of the Philosophers*.*

The Oriental MSS. are of great interest and value. Besides a splendid Koran from the library of Tippoo, presented by the East India Company, there are many books from the Royal Library of Shiraz, and a number of other MSS., Persian and Syriac.

'A book of some interest exhibited in the glass case is *Theseus Ambrosius: Introductio in Chaldaicam Linguam* (1539). It is of interest as being the first book in which Syriac types were used, and next as containing a specimen of spirit-writing dating from the sixteenth century. It seems that a question having arisen about some property of a deceased lady which was supposed to be concealed, it was resolved to evoke a demon to answer the question. A sheet of paper and a pen were placed on the table, and the proper incantation being gone through, the pen rose up without anyone seeing the hand that held it, and wrote the characters of which Ambrosius gives a facsimile, and which, unfortunately, no one has been able to decipher. I am informed that in the copy of this book in the Bodleian Library this particular leaf is pasted down, the "devil's autograph" no doubt being deemed uncanny.'†

---

* There are a number of modern MSS. of interest—*e.g.*, Berkeley's *Principles of Human Knowledge*, and Spottiswoode's *History of the Church of Scotland*.

† Dr. Abbott, in the *Book of Trinity College, Dublin*, p. 171.

In the Quin collection are some of the most valuable early editions—the *editio princeps* of Petrarch's *Sonetti e Trionfi* (1470), of Dante's *Divina Commedia* (1472), of Boccaccio's *Theseide* (1475), a very rare volume; the second edition of Virgil on vellum (1470), the only known vellum Elzevir (*De Contemptu Mortis*, 1621), and *editiones principes* of Aristophanes, Euripides, Sophocles, and Plato. The Quin collection also contains the best examples of elaborate binding—Grollier, Maioli, Monnier—most of which are exhibited under glass in the long room, where may also be seen a number of interesting coins, medals, and seals. The attention of most visitors is, however, chiefly attracted by the Irish harp, which tradition assigns to Brian Boroimhe (1014). The story goes that it

'had been taken to Rome, and remained there until Innocent XI. sent it as a token of goodwill to Charles II., who deposited it in the Tower. Soon afterwards the Earl of Clanricarde, seeing it, assured the King that he knew an Irish nobleman (meaning O'Brien, Earl of Thomond) who would probably give a limb of his estate for this relic of his great ancestor; on which his Majesty made him a present of it. Lord Clanricarde brought the instrument to Ireland; but Lord Thomond, being abroad, never became possessed of it. Some years after a Lady Henley purchased it by barter, in exchange for twenty rams and as many ewes of English breed, in order to give it to her son-in-law, Henry McMahon, Esq., of Clunagh, Co. Clare, from whom it passed through other hands to an accomplished gentleman, the Right Hon. William Conyngham,'

by whom it was given to the College. It appears, however, that the Chevalier O'Gorman, from whom

Conyngham obtained the harp, gave a different version of the tale, which declared that it was taken to Rome by Donogh, son of Brian Boroimhe, and that a later Pope gave the harp to Henry VIII., who in turn presented it to the first Earl Clanricarde.* Be this as it may, the harp is of considerable antiquity, and the singular recovery of the silver badge with the O'Neill arms which belonged to it, and had for some time disappeared,† adds additional interest to a national relic. Besides the harp, the library contains some other pieces of Celtic work, including the largest gold ornament yet found in Ireland, which weighs 33 ounces, and was dug up in the neighbourhood of Clones.

The earliest printed catalogue of books in the College library is without date, but is believed to have been published about 1707. The present catalogue is one in nine folio volumes, which cost nearly £5,000 in printing and paper. The supplementary MS. catalogue contains the names of books added since 1872. Of the MSS., the earliest catalogue extant is one prepared in 1688. Another, the work of Dr. John Lyon, was made in 1745, but is incomplete. In 1814 Dr. Henry Monck Mason undertook the preparation of a complete catalogue. He was assisted in the department of Oriental MSS. by that great scholar, Edward Hincks, then sub-librarian; in the department of Icelandic MSS. by George Cash, and in that of Irish by Edward O'Reilly. This work has never been published, but a summary catalogue of MSS. is now in print, which serves most

* See Dr. Abbott's account in *Book of Trinity College, Dublin*, p. 172.
† It was attached to a piece of armour dug up in Phoenix Park.

purposes. There are two other catalogues of Irish MSS in the library, one the work of Dr. Donovan, another consisting of about 20,000 cards, prepared under the direction of the late Dr. Benjamin Dickson when assistant-librarian.

The marble busts, which add so much to the dignity of the great room, vary considerably in merit, but many of them are striking and effective works of art. In 1743, when Dr. Claudius Gilbert bequeathed a sum of £500 for the purchase of busts for the library, the College requested Sir Edward Walpole to recommend the name of a competent sculptor. He suggested Roubiliac, at that time a young and unknown artist. To Roubiliac, consequently, a commission was given, and fifteen of the busts in the library are from his chisel, including that of Swift, presented to the College by the Senior Sophister Class in 1745. It is not improbable that the admirable bust of Delany, Swift's lifelong friend, is by the same sculptor. The bust of Provost Humphrey Lloyd was executed by Bruce Joy.

The Tercentenary Festival made an important addition to the treasures of the library. In a large oak chest in the *Bibliotheca Quiniana* are placed the addresses presented to the College by the representatives of the various universities of the world. Many of these are of great beauty. 'Some are superbly bound in the shape of folios, but the majority are encased in morocco, or plush, or velvet rolls of elaborate and costly design.'* The collection forms a permanent memorial of a brilliant and impressive episode in the history of the University.

* *Tercentenary Records*, p. 234.

CHAPTER XI

DISTINGUISHED GRADUATES

To ask what Newton would have been without Cambridge or Berkeley without Dublin were no doubt an idle inquiry, nor would it be just to give the preference to that University upon whose rolls appear the best-remembered names. Yet it must be admitted that here and not there in history is found the quickening power, that here and not there is virtue, and the man is born. To soil and clime no plant can be indifferent, the seed may fall on good or stony ground, and with good reason, therefore, do the Universities claim a share in the intellectual victories of their children.

Her position, which condemned Trinity College to share in the misfortunes of Ireland, conferred upon her the compensating advantage that she drew her students from the blood of mixed and brilliant races.

> 'Here came the brown Phœnician,
> The man of trade and toil—
> Here came the proud Milesian,
> A-hungering for spoil;

> And the Firbolg and the Cymry,
> And the hard enduring Dane,
> And the iron Lords of Normandy,
> With the Saxons in their train.'

The men of these races, the colonists who settled in Ireland, the fathers and grandfathers and ancestors of the men who have been educated in the University of Dublin, were necessarily possessed of vigorous initiative, hardy, keen-witted, energetic, and transmitted to their sons their own fine qualities. Thwarted in its natural development, the Irish race fell short indeed of any national achievement; its very capacities embittered its unhappy fortune, and often assisted to degrade its social and political life.

> 'Lilies that fester smell far worse than weeds.'

Yet the careers carved by Irishmen abroad, the brilliance of single names, and the flashes of indisputable genius that illuminate Irish history, prove that beneath its troubled surface were powerful depths and currents of incontestable strength.

When the tale is told of the distinguished graduates of the University of Dublin, the proportion they bear to the actual population of Ireland must not be forgotten, and that this, at no period comparable to that of England, has continually suffered depletion. Not Roman Catholics only, but hundreds of thousands of Protestants—in blood and brain at least the equals of those who remained—were during the seventeenth and eighteenth centuries driven from the country. The population in 1700 was probably about two millions, which increased during the next fifty years to about two and a quarter millions, of whom probably one-fourth or one-fifth were Protestants. Mr. Lecky tells us that the religious convulsions of the sixteenth century and the disasters which followed sent many of the ablest and most energetic Irishmen abroad.

'Thus Luke Wadding, the one great scholar of the Irish Franciscans, and the historian of the Order, lived chiefly in Rome, where he founded an Irish College, and died in 1657. Colgan, one of the most remarkable of early Irish antiquaries, and the collector of the Lives of the Irish Saints, though a native of Donegal, was Professor at Louvain, where he died in 1658. O'Daly, an Irish monk, born in Kerry, founded an Irish convent at Lisbon, represented Portugal at the Court of Lewis XIV., refused two bishoprics, and died Vicar-General of Portugal in 1662.'*

Before the Revolution the number of Irishmen who had left Ireland to serve foreign States as soldiers or ecclesiastics could not have been less than 100,000. These men were no doubt almost all Roman Catholics, but the condition of affairs in Ireland after 1688 gave rise to a Protestant exodus hardly less remarkable. The persecution of Dissenters, the policy of filling all appointments with Englishmen, the destruction of the wool trade, and the other devices by which the ruin of Ireland was compassed, left a very restricted sphere for native enterprise.

* See Lecky, *History of Ireland in the Eighteenth Century*, vol. i., p. 243, where the whole subject is treated at length. See also in the *Proceedings* of the University Philosophical Society, 1899, an essay by J. J. Nunan.

'The manufacturers and the large class of energetic labourers who lived upon manufacturing industry were scattered far and wide. Some of them passed to England and Scotland. Great numbers found a home in Virginia and Pennsylvania, and they were the founders of the linen manufacture in New England. Others, again, went to strengthen the enemies of England. Lewis XIV. was in general bitterly intolerant to Protestants, but he warmly welcomed, encouraged, and protected in their worship, Protestant manufacturers from Ireland, who brought their industry to Rouen and other cities of France. Many others took refuge in the Protestant States of Germany. . . . The famine of 1740 and 1741 gave an immense impulse to the movement, and it is said that for several years the Protestant emigrants from Ulster annually amounted to about 12,000. More than thirty years later, Arthur Young found the stream still flowing, and he mentioned that in 1773, 4,000 emigrants had sailed from Belfast alone.'*

* Lecky, vol. i., pp. 245-247. The number of Roman Catholics who left Ireland was, of course, far greater. The Abbé MacGeoghan, in his *History of Ireland*, asserts that 450,000 Irish soldiers died in the service of France, and it is at least certain that many rose to the highest positions on the Continent.

'Lord Clare became Marshal of France. Browne, who was one of the very ablest Austrian Generals, and who took a leading part in the first period of the Seven Years' War, was the son of Irish parents; and Maguire, Lacy, Nugent, and O'Donnell were all prominent Generals in the Austrian service during the same war. Another Browne, a cousin of the Austrian Commander, was Field-Marshal in the Russian service and Governor of Riga. Peter Lacy, who also became a Russian Field-Marshal, and who earned the reputation of one of the first soldiers of the time, was of Irish birth. . . . He sprang from an Irish family which had the rare fortune of counting Generals in the services of Austria, Russia, and Spain. Of the Dillons, more than one obtained high rank in the French army, and one became Archbishop of Toulouse. The brave,

It is hardly necessary to comment upon the immeasurable loss to the intellect and vigour of the country which these facts represent. And when the roll of honourable names associated with Trinity College is read, it must be with an inextinguishable regret that beside them cannot be placed those of many men of their kindred equal in honour, but whose lives enriched the history of countries not their own.

The first scholar who entered the newly-founded College came of the best colonial stock. His name was James Ussher, and his ancestors had settled in Ireland at the beginning of the thirteenth century. His grandfather had been Speaker of the Irish House of

---

the impetuous Lally, who served with such distinction at Dettingen and Fontenoy, and who for a time seriously threatened the English power in Hindostan, was son of a Galway gentleman, and member of an old Milesian family. It is a curious fact that Sir Eyre Coote, his opponent and conqueror in India, was an Irish Protestant. Among Spanish Generals the names of O'Mahoney, O'Donnell, O'Gara, O'Reilly, and O'Neill sufficiently attest their nationality, and an Irish Jacobite named Cammock was conspicuous among the Admirals of Alberoni. Wall, who directed the Government of Spain with singular ability from 1754 to 1763, was an Irishman, if not by birth, at least by parentage. MacGeoghan, the first considerable historian of Ireland, was chaplain of the Irish Brigade in the service of France. The physician of Sobieski, King of Poland, and the physician of Philip V. of Spain, were both Irish; and an Irish naturalist named Bowles was active in reviving the mining industry of Spain in 1752. In the diplomacy of the Continent Irish names are not unknown. Tyrconnel was French Ambassador at the Court of Berlin. Wall, before he became chief Minister of Spain, had represented that country at the Court of London. Lacy was Spanish Ambassador at Stockholm, and O'Mahoney at Vienna.

'These examples might easily be increased; but these are quite sufficient to show how large a proportion of the energy and ability of Ireland was employed in foreign lands, and how ruinous must have been the consequences at home.'—LECKY, vol. i., pp. 250-252.

Commons, and his uncle, Henry Ussher, preceded James in the primacy of Ireland. With Ussher the opening years of the history of Trinity College are intimately interwoven. He graduated at the first Commencements held in Dublin, and was soon after a Fellow. As already recorded, Ussher's earliest visit to England was made on behalf of the College library. His extraordinary attainments and sweetness of disposition soon made for him friends among the most eminent Englishmen of his time, like Selden* and Bodley, while his European reputation in scholarship attracted the attention and homage of Cardinal Richelieu. Ussher's public acts, and the part he bore in ecclesiastical affairs, are too well known to need repetition; but it is significant of the impression made by the gifts and character of this 'Cape merchant of all learning,' as Fuller affectionately styles him, that, despite his unswerving loyalty to the Crown, Cromwell not only ordered that his tomb should be in Westminster Abbey, but for Ussher's obsequies alone permitted the Church of England service to be read at the grave.

As Ussher was the greatest prelate of his day, so he was the first and greatest of the remarkable series of eminent Churchmen and scholars who, as its graduates, early gave distinction to Trinity College. Dudley Loftus, the grandson of the first Provost, whose acquirements give him a place beside Ussher as an Orientalist, and Henry Dodwell, who was a Fellow

* Upon the debate in the House of Commons whether Ussher should be admitted to the Westminster Assembly of Divines, Selden remarked: 'They had as good inquire whether they had best admit Inigo Jones, the King's architect, to the company of mouse-trap-makers.'

in 1602, and afterwards Camden Professor in the University of Oxford, must always take rank with the highest names in the world of scholarship. To them may be added, as worthy of their company, Thomas Lydiate, James Ware, to whom Irish antiquarians owe an immense debt, and William Daniel (or O'Donnell), one of the earliest Fellows, and afterwards Archbishop of Tuam, who translated the New Testament out of Greek into Irish in 1602, and a few years later translated also into the same language the Book of Common Prayer.

It is not a little surprising that the first generation of undergraduates in the little Irish College should have produced men of such calibre in the domain of learning. That the greatest scholar of his day, and that by universal consent, should have been able to lay in the newly-established University the foundation of that profound erudition which is the wonder of ours, as it was of his own times, argues well for the methods and acquirements of his masters.*

It would be tedious to recount the names of those who during the seventeenth century passed through the College to the work of the Irish Church, and obtained in it the highest preferments, nor will it be possible here to enumerate all the men who, like Chandler, afterwards Bishop of Durham, or Lucius Cary, Lord Falkland, the generous young poet and philosopher who fell at the Battle of Newbury in 1643, won for themselves distinction in a wider sphere. Yet men-

---

* Bishop Lightfoot speaks of Usher's work on Ignatius as 'showing not only marvellous erudition, but also the highest critical genius.'

tion must be made of a few noteworthy names. Leslie, one of the leaders of the Non-Jurors, who accompanied the Pretender to Italy after 1715, was educated here, as was also Sheridan, who was deprived of the See of Kilmore for similar sympathies. Here, too, were educated Vesey, Archbishop of Tuam, on three occasions appointed one of the Lords Justices of Ireland; Palliser, Archbishop of Cashel, the munificent benefactor of the library; and Wilson, Bishop of Sodor and Man, the well-known author of *Sacra Privata* and *The Principles and Duties of Christianity*, the first book published in the Manx language (1707). An interesting circumstance connects in the Commonwealth period the newly-founded University of Harvard with that of Dublin. Two brothers, Samuel and Increase Mather, who had graduated in the Cambridge of New England, came to Dublin during the provostship of Winter. Samuel was for a short time a Fellow of Trinity College, and Increase Mather entered and proceeded to the degree of M.A. in 1658. Several other eminent Nonconformist divines were educated in the Irish College during the vice-chancellorship of Henry Cromwell.

In the seventeenth century there graduated in Dublin two men inseparably united in the public memory, Nahum Tate and Nicholas Brady, the authors of the *New National Version of the Psalms*. Although Tate attained the coveted appointment of Poet Laureate, the verdict of posterity is not in his favour as a poet. But his work has still currency, and the lines 'While shepherds watched their flocks by night' are more widely known throughout the world to-day than any poem by Chaucer or by Dryden.

Among the statesmen-ecclesiastics of the time Archbishop King ranks next to Usher. In the days of confusion preceding the Battle of the Boyne, King, assisted by Bishop Anthony Dopping, an ex-Fellow of Trinity, administered the affairs of the Church in Ireland, and was twice imprisoned during the Jacobite term of power. His *State of the Protestants in Ireland* is, as Burnet says, 'a copious history of the government of Ireland during the reign'; his great work, *De Origine Mali*, proves him no mean philosopher, and King's private character and public services called forth the admiration of all who knew him. 'He spends his time,' said Swift, 'in the practice of all the virtues that can become public or private life. So excellent a person may justly be reckoned among the greatest and most learned prelates of this age.'

With Swift himself, who entered College in 1682, opens the line of dramatists, orators and men of letters who, in the second century of its existence, added to the reputation of the University laid by scholars and ecclesiastics. Among his contemporaries were Southerne, whose tragedies *Oronooko* and *The Fatal Marriage* were high favourites in their day; Congreve,* who, springing at one bound to fame, led the great world of fashion and of literature; and Farquhar, who in the *Beaux' Stratagem* and *The Recruiting Officer* anticipated the genial humour of Goldsmith. It is intelligible that to such a genius as Swift the logic and grammar of the seventeenth century curriculum, Burgerdiscius, Smiglecius, Kekermannus, seemed monstrous intellectual diet,

---

* Swift and Congreve were schoolfellows at Kilkenny. Berkeley received his early education at the same school.

but the marks obtained by him in Easter Term, 1685, show at least attention to his classical studies. They were *male* for physics, *bene* for Greek and Latin, and for theme *negligenter*. Of Congreve, Macaulay says:

'His learning does great honour to his instructors. From his writings, it appears not only that he was well acquainted with Latin literature, but that his knowledge of the Greek poets was such as was not in his time common, even in a College.'

Parnell, the author of *The Hermit*, was also, as is attested by Goldsmith, one of the most elegant classical scholars of his time,* and, indeed, few men who were not scholars attained celebrity as writers in the Augustan age. Parnell, like Congreve, is now little read except by students, yet the latter's position in the history of literature is of the first importance, and the former must always be remembered as an interesting figure in the early Romantic movement. The very title of Parnell's chief poem, *The Hermit*, suggests the coming medieval revival, while his *Hymn to Contentment* and *Night Piece on Death*, display the vein of reflection, the inward spiritual touch, which marks the decay of the influence of Pope. In polish of versification, says Dr. Johnson, 'his poetry surpasses that of Pope himself.' Another graduate of Dublin and prolific writer who was a friend of Pope, and made for himself a literary reputation in England, was Henry Brooke, the first editor of *The Freeman's Journal*, and author of *The Fool of Quality*. This singular work was re-

* He contributed the translation of the *Battle of the Frogs and Mice* to Pope's *Odyssey*.

published in 1859, with an introduction by Kingsley, who praises it in terms almost extravagant, but Brooke's fame in his own day rested perhaps as much upon his play *Gustavus Vasa* and his poem *Universal Beauty*, which gave the model to Darwin's *Loves of the Plants*, as upon his essay in fiction.

It must be claimed for the University of Dublin that in her class-rooms were educated the men who were the chief makers of eighteenth-century English prose. Swift and Berkeley were at work from the beginning of the century until 1745, Burke and Goldsmith during its second half. These names can be placed second to none, and, paradoxical as it may sound, it is none the less certain that what Mr. Matthew Arnold called the victory of the prose style, 'clear, plain, and short,' over what Burnet calls 'the old style, long and heavy,' owes more to Irish than to English writers.

Before the advent of Berkeley, probably the best metaphysicians produced by Trinity College were Provost Peter Browne, and William Molyneux. Browne bore a great reputation in his own day, and published several ponderous philosophical works, written, however, with great acumen and in an austere but dignified style.* Molyneux, who graduated in 1674, represented his University in Parliament, and was a man of various accomplishments. A friend of John Locke, he was an

* *The Procedure, Extent, and Limits of the Human Understanding*—a work, says Mr. Lecky, 'which is remarkable as anticipating the doctrine of a modern school about the generic difference of Divine and human morality, and the impossibility of human faculties conceiving either the nature or the attributes of God'; *Answer to Toland's Christianity not Mysterious; Things Divine and Supernatural conceived by Analogy with Things Natural and Human.*

ardent student of philosophy, and carried on a controversy with Hobbes. He was author, too, of many important scientific papers, and the first secretary of a Dublin society formed on the plan of the Royal Society of London. Molyneux is now, perhaps, best remembered in connection with a powerful political pamphlet entitled *Case of Ireland's being bound by Acts of Parliament made in England*, so admirable an argument for self-government that it was condemned by the English House of Commons. But with Berkeley the University of Dublin achieved its great philosophical triumph. A Fellow of the house when he published his metaphysical theory, like Ussher he owed nothing to any other influence than that of his College, and like him shares with it his enduring fame.[*] Berkeley's important works were all composed within a few years. He became a Fellow in 1707, his *New Theory of Vision* was published in 1709, his *Principles of Human Knowledge* in 1710, his *Dialogues between Hylas and Philonous* in 1713. The theories here expounded were the direct outcome of the studies pursued by the author in the University, where Locke and Descartes and Newton were read and discussed. At first little understood, the young philosopher's speculations soon began to make their way, and the waters of European thought were troubled. They remain troubled, though 200 years have come and gone, for the book of questions opened by Berkeley has not yet been closed, and 'the new principle' which he expounded still lies at the root of most modern speculation.

[*] Before he left Ireland, in 1752, Berkeley instituted in his old College the two medals which bear his name, for proficiency in Greek.

But Berkeley the metaphysician was by no means the whole man. He is, wrote Swift to Lord Carteret,

'an absolute philosopher with regard to money, titles, and power, who for three years past has been struck with the romantic notion of founding, by a charter from the Crown, a College at the Bermudas for the Christian civilization of America, where he exorbitantly proposes a whole hundred pounds a year for himself as its head, and whose heart will break if his deanery be not for this purpose taken from him.'

The grant voted by the House of Commons for the College in the Bermudas was afterwards withdrawn, and Berkeley's project failed, but its conception and the noble simplicity of mind and heart which it revealed, have surrounded his name with a halo of affectionate regard. In temperament a poet, by conviction a Christian, in philosophy a genius, there is no more winning figure than that of Berkeley in the whole range of British history. No writer since Plato has discussed the deepest things of mind in so lucid, so luminous, and so sweet a style. Ireland lost in him, perhaps, the most sagacious counsellor she ever bred,* and the intellectual world one

* Of Berkeley's *Querist*, Mr. Lecky remarks that it is 'a work which is in itself sufficient to give him a place among the greatest economists of his age. Probably no other book published in the first half of the eighteenth century contains so many pregnant hints on the laws of industrial development, or anticipates so many of the conclusions of Adam Smith and of his followers. Two points in this admirable work may be especially noticed as evincing both the sagacity and the rare liberality of this Protestant Bishop. He clearly perceived the disastrous folly of the system which was divorcing the Catholics from all ownership of the soil, and suggested that they should be permitted to purchase forfeited land as tending to unite their interest with that of the Government. He also advocated their admission

of its most daring explorers. *Si Christianus fueris* reads his epitaph in Christ Church, Oxford:

> 'Si Christianus fueris
> Si amans patriæ
> Utroque nomine gloriari potes
> Berkleium vixisse.'

Among the contemporaries of Berkeley who were educated in Trinity College, none save Swift approached him in genius. The place taken by the author of *Gulliver's Travels* in literature is too high, his services to Ireland too well known, to claim here more than passing notice. Nor need the tragedy of his life be retold.

> 'I lay like chain'd Prometheus, bosom-bared
> To torment, on the cold Caucasian peak,
> With dreadful pause at times, wherein I heard
> The vulture whet his beak.'*

Unapproachable as a satirist, as a publicist unrivalled save perhaps by Defoe, there are many sides of his character which his fame has tended to obscure. 'To Jonathan Swift,' wrote Addison in a copy of his *Travels in Italy*, '*the most agreeable companion, the truest friend*, and the greatest genius of his age, this work is presented by his most humble servant, the author.' No man more frequently encouraged a young and struggling author, no man served his friends with more disinterested fervour,

---

into the national University, in order that they might attain the highest available education without any interference with their religion' (*History of Ireland*, vol. i., p. 301)

* Vice-Chancellor's Prize Poem, 1892: *The Tercentenary of Trinity College, Dublin*, by Robert Ashe.

than Swift, and when the accounts are finally rendered it may be found, if justification be by works, that the greatest misanthrope of his age has reached through acts of kindness a place beside the greatest saints.

If Ussher laid in the University of Dublin the foundations of his learning and Berkeley of his philosophy, the eighteenth century group of writers and orators found it a no less excellent school of rhetoric and composition. Oliver Goldsmith and Edmund Burke entered in the same year, 1744, and in 1747 the latter founded the Historical Club, which, as already mentioned, became the parent of the Historical Society.* Here Burke made his first essays in rhetoric and composition, betraying the bent of mind and character which were to distinguish him. While Burke, however, thus early saw and resolutely drove towards his goal,† Goldsmith worked by fits and starts, but found protracted study little attractive. Tradition tells that he was censured for participation in a town riot, and his career in the College brought him no glory. The Senior Lecturer's books record him 'on two occasions as remarkably diligent at Morning Lecture; again as cautioned for bad answering at Morning and Greek Lectures; and finally as put down into the next class for neglect of his studies.'‡ Thus inauspiciously opened the public career of this 'very great man,' as Dr. Johnson, 'the most beloved of English writers,' as Thackeray, calls him.

* See Chapter VI.
† Burke mentions in one of his letters the books he is reading in College—'nine first chapters of Burgerdiscius, the six last Æneids of Virgil, the Enchiridion of Epictetus, with the Tabula Cebetis, which my tutor recommends me as a very fine picture of human life.'
‡ Stubbs' *History*, p. 201, note.

Dissimilar as were Burke and Goldsmith in character, gifts, and career, both retain their place in the public memory by the talisman of style. And if the style of Burke, the greater man, lack any quality to make him indisputably the first of English prose writers, as Arnold indeed called him, it is a quality which he might have borrowed from his friend and contemporary—that lightness of touch, that winning charm, which the personality of Goldsmith infused into his work. The eighteenth century was the great age of English prose; it produced no greater masters in the art than the scholar and the sizar of Trinity.

Among the contemporaries of Burke and Goldsmith at Trinity College, Malone, Garrett Wesley (afterwards Earl of Mornington, father of the Duke of Wellington), and Augustus Toplady, are among the best-known names. Malone, beside his valuable Shakespearian work, found time for the preparation of an edition of his friend Sir Joshua Reynolds' lectures and papers.* Garrett Wesley graduated in Arts in 1754, and took his doctorate in Music ten years later. His appointment as Professor of Music in the University gives the date to the practical foundation of the School of Music. Choral services were

* Anthony Malone, the uncle of the Shakespearian scholar, received his early education in Trinity College, and afterwards migrated to Christ Church, Oxford. Malone was a man of extraordinary talent. 'Mr. Malone,' says Mr. Lecky (*History of Ireland*, p. 463), 'one of the characters of 1753, was a man of the finest intellect that any country ever produced. "The three ablest men I have ever heard were Mr. Pitt (the father), Mr. Murray, and Mr. Malone. For a popular assembly I would choose Mr. Pitt; for a Privy Council, Murray; for twelve wise men, Malone." This was the opinion which Lord Sackville, the Secretary of 1753, gave of Mr. Malone to a gentleman from whom I heard it.'

about this time regularly established in the chapel, and from this and other evidences it appears that Mornington's influence was at work, and to him may be ascribed the early encouragement of that interest in music which has since distinguished the University, and in 1837 led to the foundation in the University of the Choral Society. Toplady graduated in the same year as Foster, afterwards Speaker of the Irish House of Commons, and Lord Oriel. In his own time Toplady's influence as a leader of evangelical opinion, though not, of course, comparable to that of Wesley, was considerable; but it is as the author of 'Rock of Ages,' and not that of a religious leader, that his fame survives.

The most brilliant names among the later eighteenth-century graduates of Dublin are those of the patriotic group, the friends and allies of Grattan. It may well be conceded that no such assemblage of orators as that which gathered in the Irish House of Commons before the Act of Union has ever appeared in any Parliament. All had been members of the Historical Society, and it is said that their maturest achievements hardly exceeded in brilliance some of their early speeches within the University. As an orator, though Grattan must be assigned the first place, it is his rather by right of the eminence of his works and character than because he easily surpassed Bushe or Flood or Plunket. The two latter were students in the school of Demosthenes, and it may at once be said that in their extant speeches nothing florid, nothing merely ornamental, appears. The great exponents of Irish oratory display a severity of style singularly at variance with that which is commonly supposed to characterize them. Grattan's, indeed, was 'an oracular loftiness of words which certainly came nearer the utterance of inspiration than any eloquence ancient or modern,' but Flood's* strength lay in measured, incisive, almost dispassionate argument, and the texture of Plunket's speeches was so strictly logical, that, says Mr. Lecky, 'his popularity was somewhat limited by the extreme severity of a taste which rarely stooped to ornament, or indulged in anything that was merely rhetorical or declamatory.'

Perhaps next to Grattan, Flood, and Plunket, Bushe, afterwards Chief Justice of Ireland, was the greatest speaker of the day. In grace, in imagination, in sustained power, in distinction of matter and manner, he was almost unrivalled. Kemble declared him 'the greatest actor off the stage,' and it was said of him as an advocate that 'he charmed the verdict from the jury by the fascination of his eye.' In sheer intellectual quality the orators of this age, like those of all others, must give place to Burke; but in the arts of rhetoric, partly no doubt owing to their forensic training, they were all his superiors. The triumph of the great speaker is a personal triumph;

* Of Flood, Burrowes said that he was 'perhaps the ablest man Ireland ever produced, indisputably the ablest man of his own times.'

'One of the ablest of his contemporary admirers said of him that, on whatever subject he spoke, "he spoke with such knowledge, accuracy, and perspicuity, that one would imagine that subject had been the chief object of his inquiry"; and in the most brilliant period of the career of Grattan there were always some good judges who maintained that, in the more solid intellectual qualities, Flood was his superior.'—LECKY: *History of Ireland*, vol. ii., p. 139.

Flood left an estate of £5,000 to Trinity College for the purchase of Irish MSS. and the encouragement of the study of the Irish language.

his hour is that in which he faces his audience, and few are the orations that can move the reader a hundred years after their delivery. Yet it is difficult, if not impossible, to read to-day a speech by Bushe or Flood or Plunket or Grattan without exclamations of admiration and astonishment. Theirs was a force and cunning in words rarely equalled, never surpassed.

Of the prominent members of that Irish Parliament, none who were educated in Trinity College, except Fitzgibbon, Earl of Clare, viewed the Act of Union with any feelings but those of the bitterest hostility. Foster, the Speaker,* was one of its most vehement opponents, and in 1799 the Fellows and scholars of the College, then the electors, presented an address to their members against the measure. A passage from a speech made by Plunket in the House will serve to represent the attitude towards it of intellectual Ireland. A member who had insinuated that corruption was being employed for the purpose of carrying the measure was interrupted by a Ministerialist who threatened to have his words taken down. Plunket rose and said:

'It has, sir, been intimated, from high authority, that an honourable friend of mine has been guilty of a grave offence, in venturing to insinuate against the Government the charge of corruption; and the defender of His Majesty's Ministers threatened that, if the charge was repeated, he would call upon you to take down his words. Now, sir, I do not insinuate, but I boldly assert, that base and wicked as is the measure proposed, the means used to accomplish it are still more flagitious and abominable. Do you choose to take down my words? I had thought we had for a

* Afterwards Lord Oriel.

Viceroy in this country a plain honest soldier [Cornwallis]—one unaccustomed to and disdaining the intrigues of politics—who had chosen as his secretary a simple and a modest youth, *puer ingenui vultus, ingenuique pudoris,* whose inexperience was the voucher for his integrity; and yet I will be bold to affirm that, during the viceroyalty of this unspotted veteran, and during the administration of this unassuming stripling, a system of black corruption has been carried on within the walls of the Castle which would disgrace the worst period of the history of either country. *Do you choose to take down my words?* Dare me to the proof, and I will prove the truth of them at your bar.'

It has already been mentioned that in the Irish Parliament Trinity College had an unwavering friend and benefactor. Of the services of the English Parliament to that University it will be sufficient to say that it withdrew in 1858 the only State grants ever enjoyed by Dublin, has never since voted to it a pound of public money, and in 1873 generously refrained from destroying it by the magnificent majority of three votes. Thus nobly have the English people supported the only institution founded by their own kindred in Ireland, which has achieved an unqualified success, educated for them many of the greatest men who have adorned their history and literature, and thousands who have ably served the State in every division of the Empire.

Besides those already mentioned, most of the less celebrated statesmen of the close of the century in Ireland had graduated in Trinity College. It will be sufficient to mention Luke Fox;[*] Lawless, afterwards

---

[*] Luke Fox, M.P., and afterwards Justice of the Common Pleas, described Ireland as inhabited by three nations, whose feelings,

Lord Cloncurry; Curran, afterwards Master of the Rolls, who like Grattan, Plunket, and most of the other patriots of the time, though a Protestant, was one of the most eloquent advocates of Catholic Emancipation; Sheil, hardly less brilliant as a speaker than any of those already named; Sir Lucius O'Brien, one of the ablest financiers in the House; Corry, the Chancellor of the Exchequer who fought a duel with Grattan; and Lords Mountjoy and O'Neill, both earnest supporters of the cause of Ireland, who during the civil war of ninety-eight fell in battle, O'Neill at Antrim, Mountjoy at New Ross.

Before passing on to mention the more outstanding names among the later members of the College, it may be interesting to record that Wentworth Dillon, Earl of Roscommon, the elegant critic and translator of the Augustan Age, received part of his education in Trinity College, as also, it is said, did Sir John Denham, author of *Cooper's Hill* and other poems well known in their day. Dr. Leland, the eloquent divine, of whom Parr and Johnson speak with enthusiasm, and who carried on a controversy with the redoubtable Warburton, was Fellow in 1746, and afterwards Professor of Oratory. A few years his senior was Philip Francis (father of the more famous Sir Philip), of whose translation of Horace Dr. Johnson made the remark: 'The lyrical part of Horace never can be properly translated, so much of

---

opinions, and requirements were almost irreconcilable. He advocated the foundation of a Catholic College in the University of Dublin, and the transference to the Crown of the patronage of Roman Catholic sees.

the elegance is in the numbers and the expressions. Francis has done it the best; I'll take his, five out of six, against them all.' Madden, one of the founders of the Royal Dublin Society; Delany, the friend of Swift; Sherlock, author of *The Practical Christian;* Hugh Hamilton, the Bishop of Ossory, one of the most distinguished mathematicians of his day, author of a treatise on Conic Sections and of several important scientific papers;* Archbishop Synge, who in 1725 preached before the House of Commons, perhaps the earliest sermon in which toleration for Irish Roman Catholics was boldly advocated, and in an age of bigotry nobly supported the Liberal cause; Matthew Young, the disciple of Newton, author of the brilliant essay on *Sounds and Musical Strings;* Molesworth, William III.'s Ambassador to Denmark, and afterwards the first Viscount Molesworth;† Harris, the learned editor of Ware's *Antiquities;* Gast, the historian of

---

* See p. 174.

† Molesworth was the author of a very remarkable pamphlet, entitled *Some Considerations for the Promotion of Agriculture and Employing the Poor* (1723), which, says Mr. Lecky (*Ireland in the Eighteenth Century,* vol. i., p. 302), 'exposed with a skilful and unsparing hand the gross defects of Irish agricultural economy, and at the same time proposed a series of remedies which, if they had been carried out, might have made Ireland a happy and prosperous country.... With equal boldness and sagacity Lord Molesworth proposed to deal with the question of the position of the priesthood. ... He accordingly proposed that the State should charge itself with the payment of the priests. ... It would do more than any single measure to attach them to the Government. It would improve the economical condition of the country by freeing the cultivators of the soil from an oppressive burden; and, as its benefits would be felt and understood in the meanest hovel, it would do much to create a feeling of loyalty through the Catholic population.'

Greece; Walker, the editor of Livy; Wolfe, the author of the lines on the death of Sir John Moore—

> ' And next he came—as veiled evening falls
> In silence—whose lament for England's brave
> Floats yet o'er ghostly guns and trumpet-calls
> Above Corunna's grave ;'—*

Robert and Christopher Emmet and Wolfe Tone, whose careers occupy so large a space in the history of Ireland, are all names worthy of remembrance, though any such selection must do injustice to men hardly less accomplished to whom reference cannot here be made.

One of the first Roman Catholics to take advantage of the Act of 1793 was Thomas Moore. He records the pride with which he inscribed himself as of Trinity College, Dublin, and preserved throughout his life his early affection for his alma mater. There is no need to appraise the work of Moore as a poet. His place is secure, though it has been denied that he possesses the true Celtic touch, the impetuous Celtic spirit, the wide-eyed Celtic imagination. It has been said of him that he is neither Irish nor English, and has failed to gain a firm hold of the affections of either people. Somewhat similar is the charge not infrequently levied against his University also, a charge it will be time to investigate when the delicate question, Who, then, are the true Irish people? has been answered by some historian of analytic genius.

But if Moore be dethroned from the primacy among Irish poets, Trinity College will suffer no loss, for Thomas Davis or Sir Samuel Ferguson must take his

* *The Tercentenary of Trinity College, Dublin*, by Robert Ashe.

place. Davis, indeed, was hardly a poet by profession, for only during the last three years of his short life was he occupied with verse, and Ferguson has perhaps the best claim to sovereignty among the later Celtic bards. In *Lays of the Western Gael*, in *Congal*, in *Conary*, and in *Deirdre*, he marshals the ancient stories with an epic simplicity and vigour that win the heart, and not unfair, though rapturous, was the remark that he was 'the one man of his time who wrote heroic poetry—one who, among the somewhat sybaritic singers of his day, was like some aged sea-king sitting among the inland wheat and poppies—the savour of the sea about him and its strength.'

Besides Davis, Trinity College educated John O'Hagan, also one of *The Nation* poets, and a number of men who like him, if not widely known, have at least added to the national treasury some exquisite verse. Among them may be mentioned Luke Conolly, the author of the lovely lines beginning 'To Rathlin's Isle I chanced to sail'; George Darley,* the singular poet and mathematician, who counted Tennyson and Browning among his admirers, and author of the well-known poem 'It is not beauty I demand';† John Francis Waller, who contributed to the *Dublin University Magazine* many fine lyrics; Joseph Callanan, the admirable translator of Celtic poetry, best known by the lines 'There is a green island in lone Gougaune Barra'; and George Fox, whose felicitous rendering of

* Author of *Errours of Ecstasie*, *Sylvia* (a fairy drama, 1827), and *Nepenthe* (1839).
† Formerly printed by Mr. Palgrave, in his *Golden Treasury*, as an anonymous seventeenth-century poem.

an Irish song, 'The County of Mayo,' is transcribed here, because, though little known, it is, in its own way, one of the supremely perfect lyrics of the century, and illustrates the singular affection borne by the Irish people for their ancient aristocracy:

'On the deck of Patrick Lynch's boat I sat in woeful plight,
  Through my sighing all the weary day and weeping all the night.
Were it not that full of sorrow from my people forth I go,
By the blessed sun, 'tis royally I'd sing thy praise, Mayo.

'When I dwelt at home in plenty, and my gold did much abound,
  In the company of fair young maids the Spanish ale went round.
'Tis a bitter change from those gay days that now I'm forced to go,
And must leave my bones in Santa Cruz, far from my own Mayo.

'They are altered girls in Irrul now; 'tis proud they're grown and high,
  With their hair-bags and their top-knots, for I pass their buckles by.
But 'tis little now I heed their airs, for God will have it so,
That I must depart for foreign lands, and leave my sweet Mayo.

''Tis my grief that Patrick Loughlin is not Earl in Irrul still,
And that Brian Duff no longer rules as Lord upon the Hill,
And that Colonel Hugh Macgrady should be lying dead and low,
And I sailing, sailing swiftly from the county of Mayo.'

The nineteenth century is too large a field to ear, and agreeable as would be the task of chronicling the names of men still living who have climbed the steep paths to fame, it must be left to the historian of the future. Yet one may not overlook the service done by Trinity College for the world in educating the Irish novelists, Maxwell, Sheridan Lefanu, and Charles Lever; Maginn, the brilliant contributor to *Blackwood* and *Fraser*; Anster, the translator of *Faust*; Howard Russell, the first of 'war correspondents'; Croker, the editor of Boswell; Archer Butler, the first Professor of Moral Philosophy; Hincks,* the Orientalist; Cairnes and Cliffe Leslie among the most original of later political economists; Isaac Butt, the friend of Ireland; Stokes and Graves,† who gave to the Dublin School of Medicine a

---

* 'That great pioneer in Oriental research and discovery, Edward Hincks' (*Professor Tiele of Leyden at the Tercentenary*). Hincks made large advances in the reading of Egyptian hieroglyphics and all forms of cruciform writing, in his day hardly yet deciphered. He takes rank with the most brilliant scholars of any age or country. The following are the titles of some of his more important papers, mainly contributed to the *Transactions* of the Royal Irish Academy: *The Enchorial Language of Egypt* (1833); *On the Egyptian Stele* (1847); *On the Hieroglyphic Alphabet* (1847); *On the Three Kinds of Persopolitan Writing* (1847); *On the Khorsabad Inscriptions* (1850); *On the Assyrio-Babylonian Phonetic Character* (1850); *Assyrian Mythology* (1850); *On the Relation between the Accadian and the Indo-European, Semitic and Egyptian Languages; On the Polyphony of the Assyrio-Babylonian Cuneiform Character* (1863); *Assyrio-Babylonian Measures of Time* (1865).

† In his address at the Tercentenary, Professor Stockvis, Rector of the University of Amsterdam, said: 'If I call to mind the great and illustrious names in the branches of science alone, in which I am myself a scholar, who in this century were some of the leaders of the medical students, I congratulate you with all my heart on being students of that same University in which Graves held his celebrated clinical lectures in that Meath Hospital which is known by all the world through his fame. His lectures, even to this day,

reputation equal to that achieved for it in mathematics by Rowan Hamilton and McCullagh;* or in Irish antiquarian research by Todd, Bishop Reeves, and, to men-

---

are a model of clear, scientific, eloquent, and elegant writing, in which one does not know what to admire most, the French lucidity, the German thoroughness, the English practical sense, all which this graduate of Dublin Trinity School possessed in perfection.

'I congratulate you again that, in the history of your medical school in the nineteenth century, you may name as yours that renowned and skilful physician, William Stokes, the author of the classic *Diseases of the Heart* and *Diseases of the Chest*. He was the first to follow Laennec, and understand all the significance of the great Frenchman's discovery; he was the first to find out all the use that could be made of percussion and auscultation for the exact diagnosis of the circulatory and respiratory organs.

'The history of medicine is proud of these men. They are not national, they are international glories; and so long as human suffering shall be relieved by medicine, so long will the names of Graves and Stokes be honoured all over the world.'

* 'The brief career of McCullagh was yet sufficiently long to place him in the highest rank among the mathematicians of Europe, and to allow him to leave the impress of his powerful mind on the mathematical school of the University of Dublin. Of that school, if not the actual founder, he has always been regarded as the Master, who gave it a mighty impulse, which, it is to be earnestly hoped, will long continue to be felt. Fortunately for science and for the University, Hamilton's career was longer, and has been marked by a series of mathematical works of so high an order that few indeed are able to read them, much less to form an opinion of their merits. The impartial testimony of a distinguished Professor of the University of Edinburgh may, however, be cited, without reserve, as the opinion of one who, from the extent of his own mathematical acquirements, and from the special study he has made of the writings of Hamilton, is perhaps of all men living the most competent to anticipate the verdict of posterity. Speaking of Hamilton, Professor Tait lately remarked: "His name will not only rank with any in the foregoing list (Napier, Maclaurin, etc.), but will undoubtedly be classed with the grandest of all ages and countries, such as Lagrange and Newton."'—T. ANDREWS, F.R.S.: *Studium Generale*, p. 23.

tion the name of one scholar still with us, Whitley Stokes. In theology, Lee, O'Brien, Fitzgerald, and the two Magees, Archbishops of Dublin and York, nobly sustained the reputation of their *alma mater*, while Napier and Whiteside in Ireland, and Cairns and Charles Russell in England enriched her traditions of the Senate and the Bar. Yet these are but names chosen almost at random, and

'they must read many books who seek to know the fortunes and achievements of the graduates of Dublin in recent years, for a record of them will carry the reader into the political, military, and literary history of the English-speaking people in all the continents.'

NOTE.—As an illustration of the close connection which exists between Trinity College, Dublin, and the colonies, the following document may be cited:

'THE ALUMNI OF THE UNIVERSITY OF DUBLIN RESIDENT IN VICTORIA, AUSTRALIA, TO THE PROVOST AND FELLOWS OF TRINITY COLLEGE, DUBLIN.

'We desire to offer to you our hearty congratulations on the occasion of the Tercentenary of the University of Dublin, and to assure you that, although separated from you by many thousand miles of land and sea, we are one with you in love and reverence for our Alma Mater, and in pride for the high place she has long held among the most distinguished seats of learning in Europe, which high place, as we cannot but know, has been made higher still by the achievements of those who are the leaders and teachers of the present generation of her students.

'We have a lively recollection of the days we spent within the walls of our old College, and a deep sense of gratitude for the opportunities afforded us there of making acquaintance with the wisdom and learning of ancient and modern times.

'We beg to inform you that it is our purpose to perpetuate our sense of these benefits by founding in the University of Melbourne, with which many of us are incorporated, a gold medal or medals, to be identified by name with the University of Dublin, and to be annually bestowed as an encouragement here to the pursuit of some of the studies which are so successfully cultivated there. And thus we hope to establish among future generations a living link of sympathy with that great seat of learning where we have had the honour to be students.

'As citizens of Victoria, we remember with pride how large a share men who have been trained in Trinity College, Dublin, have had in the making of this colony. The public careers of Sir William Foster Stawell, Sir Redmond Barry, Sir Robert Molesworth, Mr. Percy Lalor, and Dr. William Edward Hearn, to speak only of those who are no longer living, form no small part of the history of our adopted country; and there is no University of the Old World with which the chief seat of learning in this colony is more closely linked than our own. Of the five Chancellors who have up to the present time presided over the University of Melbourne, three have been graduates of the University of Dublin.

'We ask you to accept the assurance of our heartfelt and respectful regard, in token whereof we here affix our signatures:

    GEORGE HIGINBOTHAM, Chief Justice of Victoria.
    H. B MACARTNEY, B.D., Dean of Melbourne.
    N. FITZGERALD, Member of the Legislative Council of Victoria.
    BRYAN O'LOGHLEN, Bart., Q.C., late Premier of Victoria.
    H. J. WRIXON, Q.C., K.C.M.G., late Attorney-General of Victoria.
    E. B. HAMILTON, Judge of County Courts.
    B. TENLON BEAMISH, D.D., Archdeacon of Warrnambool.
    ROBERT WALSH, Q.C., Crown Prosecutor.
    ALEXANDER LEEPER, LL.D., Warden of Trinity College, University of Melbourne.
    H. E. COOPER, M.A., Archdeacon of Hamilton.
    ROBERT POTTER, B.A. Dub., Canon of St. Paul's, Melbourne, M.A. Melbourne.
    JOHN TREVOR FOX, M.A. T.C.D.
    THOMAS R. LYLE, M.A. T.C.D., Professor of Natural Philosophy in the University of Melbourne.
    W. BUTLER WALSH, M.D. (Dublin and Melbourne), F.R.C.S.I., late Examiner in Anatomy, University of Melbourne.
    H. B. MACARTNEY, jun., M.A., Incumbent of Caulfield, Melbourne.
    B. NEWPORT WHITE, M.A., St. Peter's Vicarage, Mornington.
    EDWARD COLE COGHLAN, Member of Institute of Journalists.

AUSTRALIAN GRADUATES

ALEXANDER MACULLY, M.A., LL.B.
P. P. LABERTOUCHE, Secretary for Victorian Railways.
HERBERT B. FIGGIS, B.A. Melbourne.
GEORGE WILLIAM TORRANCE, M.A., Mus. Doc.
JOHN ERNEST FANNIN EVANS, B.A. T.C.D.,
DR. KELLY, Grosvenor, St. Mornee Ponds.
CHARLES B. M. BARDIN, Vicar of Christ Church, Brunswick.
THOMAS ELMES, J.P., F.R.C.S.I.
ROBERT L. MCADAM, B.A., M.D., Ch.B., D.S.M., St. Kilda.
JOHN WILLIAM O'BRIEN, M.B., B.Ch., F.R.C.S.I., M.A. Melbourne.
EVELYN G. HOGG, M.A., Mathematical Lecturer, Trinity College, Melbourne.
EDWARD FITZGERALD, LL.D. T.C.D.
WILLIAM LEADER, Police Magistrate, Melbourne.
WADE SHENTON GARNETT, B.A., Barrister-at-Law.
PHILIP HOMAN, M.A., late Vicar of Marat.
W. R. MURRAY, late Clerk of Petty Sessions.
JAMES ANTHONY LAWSON, Solicitor.
THOMAS B. HILL, Secretary Melbourne Exhibition, 1880.
J. W. Y. FISHBOURNE, A.B., M.B., Ch.M.
PATRICK WHYTE, M.A. T.C.D.
ALFRED MACHUGH, M.A. T.C.D., Barrister.
W. BEAUCHAMP CLAYTON, B.A., University Tutor.
HENRY LANGTREE, M.A., Barrister-at-Law.
RICHARD PHILP, M.A., LL.D., Inspector of State Schools.
E. S. RADCLIFF, B.A., Canon, Registrar of Ballarat Diocese.
W. A. KIRKPATRICK, A.B., Ex. Sch., Barrister-at-Law.
CHARLES TUCKEY, B.A.
H. H. FLEMING, St. Arnaud, Victoria.
TOWNSEND MACDERMOTT, A.B., Barrister-at-Law, a former Solicitor-General of Victoria.
G. R. MACMULLAN, M.A., LL.D., Barrister-at-Law '

CHAPTER XII

TRINITY COLLEGE TO-DAY

LIKE all resident Universities, Trinity College is a microcosm of the great world, the sphere of so many and varied interests, so much intellectual and physical activity, as to render any description of its life difficult, if not impossible. The newly-fledged undergraduate drifts into the companionship of men with similar tastes and sympathies, and to none is it given to share in all the emotions or gather the fruit of all the proferred experiences of the University world. The rowing man learns the stern joys of the river and its racing crews, but not the green carpet of the park with the wicket and the nets in June; the budding orator is claimed by the competition for office, the honours of the 'Historical' or the 'Phil,' and the high politics of their 'Private Business'; the honour man eschews the seductive company of—let us say—'the Corks,' presided over by the *Lord High Bung,* or other assembly of the wilder spirits, who give their days to contemplative idleness and their nights to revelry; the musician

TRINITY COLLEGE, DUBLIN, 1592

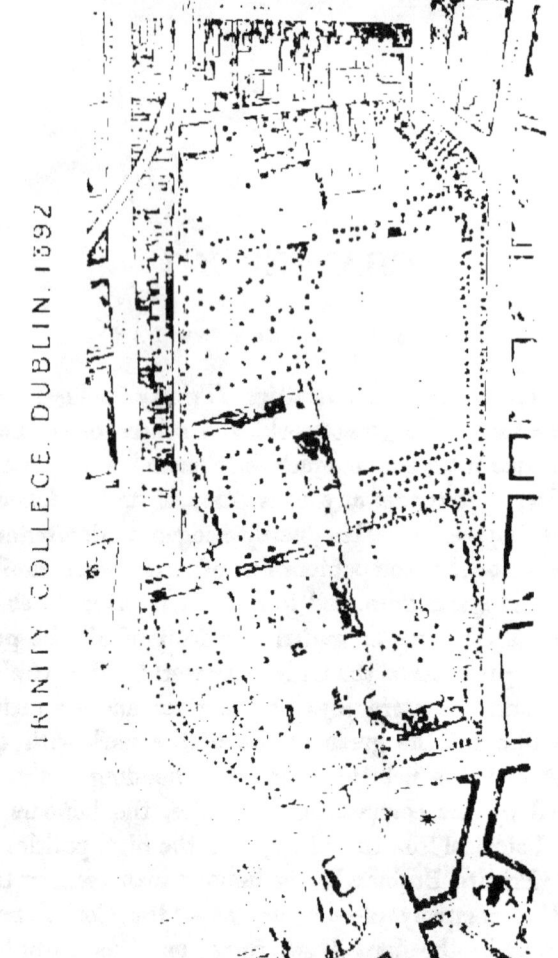

PLAN OF COLLEGE, 1892

frequents the rooms of the 'Choral'; the classical man consorts with his fellows; the poet, it may be, dreams his dreams with the makers of the past. Though they may meet in Hall, and though the inexorable days of examination claim all as victims, yet each man moves in a circle of his own within the wider society. The routine of life is similar to that of an Oxford or Cambridge College—morning chapel, lectures, rowing or football or cricket, the debates in the societies, Hall and night roll, and 'corrections' with the Dean on Saturday mornings for delinquents. The College gates are closed at nine o'clock, after which hour entry or exit is only possible through the wicket, guarded by the sleepless College watch in the lodge.

'On the left side as you enter the vestibule is the porter's lodge, as it is called, and although it is but an humble apartment, and its occupants sober and discreet men, yet its influence is, by a certain class of students, known as *Town-Haunters*, considered more depressing and pestiferous than the vapours of Trophonius's cave, or those of the celebrated *Grotto del Cane*. When Great Tom has ceased to toll the hour of nine, this portal is closed, and then vigilance puts into activity her sharpest features, that none may enter without being *noted down*.'*

After Hall comes in a friend's rooms the glorious College hour of expansion, of wit and wisdom, tale and jest, the hour of coffee and tobacco and disdain of the anxious world. Then across the quadrangle, where the great cross on the campanile threads its nightly course among the wheeling stars, to one's own sacred

* *Taylor's History*, p. 295.

hearthstone and the purple visions that pass the shadowy gates of ivory and horn.

'Up here I sleep in the hawthorn scent:
  It swims through my windows from lawn to lawn,
While June's first nights with their deep content
  Possess my spirit from dusk to dawn.

'I lying here, alone, a king,
  In the centre of pleasances green and sweet;
Hearing the tree-tops murmuring,
  Hearing the far-away sounds of the street;

*   *   *   *   *

'Eastward, westward—spread in the dark
  An acre of grass, an acre of daisies:
Northward a square; to the south, a park;
  Mine is the midmost of pleasant places.

'Here I can see, as the midnight wears,
  The first blue tides of the morning steal
Between shores of cloud, among fleets of stars,
  Blanching the coigns of the campanile.

'And all the divine repose that looms
  Through the College courts as the sweet hours go:
Palatial piles and their cloistered glooms,
  And dormer and terrace and portico.'*

Rooms in College usually reflect the tastes of their owners. The boudoir type finds little favour in Trinity, but books, pictures, oars, bats, weapons of the chase, commonly adorn undergraduate quarters, while some illustrate special eccentricities of character.†

* 'Trinity College, Dublin,' in *Songs of Study*, by William Wilkins
† The freedom of Trinity College from serious fires originating in undergraduate rooms has frequently been the subject of comment.

'A neighbour of mine satisfied his æsthetic instincts by having on his walls the most comprehensive and highly coloured assortment of pictorial advertisements, and such trophies of illicit enterprise as door-knockers. Over his bedroom door were the printed words, "Third Smoking," which had formerly graced a railway carriage, and, regarded as an indication of the comfort to be looked for within, were not wholly inapplicable in their present position. The walls of his sitting-room were adorned with such placards as "None but Guinness kept," "All dogs prosecuted," "Trespassers shot," while on the back of his door was one containing the significant words, "Always on draught." He is gone now, and the place knows him no more; he sleeps beneath the stars of an African sky.'*

On the great day of the *College Races*, the summer festival of Trinity, College rooms are invaded by smart frocks and gay millinery, for the entertainment of ladies is a feature of the event. In the evening a bonfire not unusually illuminates the bay, and beyond the College precincts the undergraduate seldom fails to attract public attention to his proceedings; he may capture the green flag of the city which floats in the garden of the Mansion House, or in force at the theatre, after a scuffle, and cries of 'Throw him over!' precipitate, to

---

But it seems that all Colleges are under special protection. Fuller calls attention to the immunity enjoyed by those of Oxford and Cambridge: 'Here, by the way, whoever shall consider in both Universities the ill-contrivance of many chimneys, hollowness of hearths, shallowness of tunnels, carelessness of coals and candles, catchingness of papers, narrowness of studies, late reading and long watching of scholars, cannot but conclude that an especial Providence preserveth those places.'

* *Student Life in Trinity College, Dublin*, by H. A. Hinkson, p. 8.

the horror of the audience, a dummy policeman from the gallery to the pit.

During Trinity Term, in the early summer days, the delights of College life are at their zenith. Then the old walls lose something of their grayness, the grass and the creepers are softly green, the flower-beds gay, the hawthorn in bloom, and the quadrangles and park bright with flannels and blazers. Even the reading man postpones to the long vacation the thought of coming examinations, and migrates to the park with rug and pipe to watch the cricket, or beyond the walls to the links, or river, or Kingstown Bay.

Since, as is generally known, residence is not a *sine quâ non* for an Arts degree, though indirectly necessary for those in the professional schools, the students are divisible into two classes, the residents and non-residents, or, as they might more correctly be designated, the members of the College and the undergraduates of the University. The graduates in Arts who have never been in residence consist chiefly of masters in secondary schools and Nonconformist ministers of religion for whom the expenses of residence are too great. But from this class honour students are rarely if ever drawn, as is sufficiently proved by the significant fact that no note is taken by candidates for College prizes or distinctions of any possible competitors beyond the circle of men known to the reading world in the College.* Though an abuse, the possibility of

---

* 'As to the origin of the Dublin non-residence system, I have no doubt it is to be traced to the provision in the statute 13 Car. I., that an examination should be held at the beginning of every term on the subjects of the lectures of the preceding term. This was intended merely to promote diligence and attention to lectures, but

obtaining an Arts degree without actual residence has proved a boon to many poor students, and the University policy may be defended. The culture unattainable except by intercourse and companionship with their fellows Dublin offers to all her sons who are fortunate enough to come more directly under her fostering care, while to the class which by circumstances or the demands of hurried modern life is debarred from the social and intellectual gain of academic residence, she does not refuse whatever help in the pursuit of knowledge she can place within its reach.

Many of the terms in use in Dublin are identical with those of Cambridge, such as that of sophister, or pensioner, or sizar,* but many of them are now used in

---

gradually, no doubt, the examinations assumed more and more importance; they became the end, the previous lectures merely a means of preparing for them. Then it came to be reckoned sufficient to pass the examinations, and private study (if it proved to have been sufficient to effect that result) was held an equivalent for attendance on lectures; the state of the country, the difficulty of travelling, and the poverty of the students, made many of them, no doubt, prefer to prepare for their examinations at home; and so the usage would grow up. But, like all abuses, it was, of course, gradually developed.'—REV. J. GWYNN, Regius Professor of Divinity in the University (quoted by T. Andrews, M.D., F.R.S., in his *Studium Generale*, p. 4).

The Universities of Oxford and Cambridge very properly refuse to extend the privilege of incorporation to Dublin undergraduates or graduates who are unable to produce certificates of residence.

* 'My year is so very large that, though I have been half a year Junior Soph, I have not gotten a scholarship' (see Wordsworth's *Schola Academica*, p. 299).

A *pensioner* is one who pays *pensio*, or rent, for his rooms; *sizar* is probably connected with the Oxford *servitor*, and originally meant one who received from the College 'sizings,' or portions of meat and drink

a slightly varying sense. 'Moderator,' for example, an old academic word, is applied in Dublin to the men who attain distinction in the final honour schools, the examinations of which are styled 'moderatorship examinations.' 'Gib' for a freshman is, perhaps, peculiar to Dublin, as are some few other phrases, but the terminology differs little on the whole from that of the English Universities.

The life Fellowship system firmly established in Dublin is accompanied by both advantages and disadvantages. 'The horse is trained to run one splendid race and clear a last fence, which brings him safe into a clover-field.' A single effort takes the place of a strenuous life of effort, and occasionally the holder of a Fellowship does little in after-life to justify the appointment. On the other hand, the value of the prize makes the competition excessively keen, and for the single Fellowship awarded in each year a large number of brilliant mathematical and classical scholars enter. The standard of knowledge is necessarily, therefore, the highest possible, but the severity of the struggle, a course of hard reading seldom lasting in the case of the best men for less than four or five years after degree, limits the competition to possessors of an iron constitution, and frequently the most original minds turn from the slavery with disgust, or find it beyond their physical powers. In late years some of the men of science produced by the University, who afterwards achieved the highest distinction, have been found among those who failed to secure a Fellowship. But the system has one great compensating advantage: it renders the highest prize in the gift of the College, since it is the result

THE FIRST ROWING CLUBS

of a competition open to all comers, beyond the reach of innuendo or suspicion of favour.

At the beginning of the nineteenth century boat-racing was unknown both on the Cam and the Isis, and the first authentic account of rowing in Ireland dates from the year 1836. In September of that year a number of persons met at Radley's Hotel, Dame Street, for the purpose of forming a club (Joseph Hone, Esq., in the chair), and in the minutes of the meeting there appears the resolution, 'That this club be called the Pembroke Club.'* The same year a plot of ground was acquired at Ringsend, and a store-house and club-room erected. In 1837 the Hon. Sidney Herbert was made president of the club, which was first spoken of as the Pembroke *Rowing Club* in his letter accepting the invitation of the committee to become president, and about this time there was a large accession of members, amongst whose names are found those of John Jameson and William Potts, editor of the oldest Irish newspaper, *Saunders' News Letter*. Meanwhile the rowing spirit was gaining in strength, and, still further to encourage its development, two challenge cups were purchased in 1838. There now cropped up a controversy over the definition of the term 'amateur.' The matter was referred by the Victoria Club to the committee of the Pembroke Club for decision, and we find that a member of the former was disqualified on the ground that he had 'worked at manual labour for wages.' In 1839 two crews visited English waters, though, to judge from the following clause in the report of the committee for

* For the information here given of the origin and history of University rowing, I am indebted to Mr. W. R. P. McNeight.

that year, rowing was not considered to be a sport free from danger:

'Your committee consider it to be a subject strongly deserving of congratulation that not the slightest accident has happened during the past year to any member of the club in pursuing the amusements for which your club was established.'

About the year 1840 another club appears to have been formed. Its members were graduates and undergraduates of Trinity College, and its title the *Dublin University Rowing Club*. At first its efforts appear to have been attended with success, but later the University Club, and even to a greater degree the Pembroke Club, fell upon evil days. Early in 1847 the committee of the University Rowing Club made a proposal for amalgamation, which was accepted at a general meeting held at Ringsend on May 15, 1847. The resolution states that the name of the new club was to be the Dublin University Rowing Club, also

'that persons matriculated in the University of Dublin shall henceforth be eligible as members for the Dublin University Rowing Club. Persons not matriculated in that University shall henceforth be ineligible as members, but shall be eligible as associates of that club.'

It was also resolved:

'That associates of the Dublin University Rowing Club shall not be eligible as officers of the club, nor shall they be entitled to vote at general meetings thereof, but in all other respects they shall be entitled to the rights and privileges usually enjoyed by members of that club.'

Finding the old club-house too small for its needs, the new club reclaimed a further stretch of ground on the bank of the Dodder, and added to the accommodation till the premises were almost exactly as they were when the University Rowing Club left them in 1898. At first the members had to be content with races among themselves, their annual regatta being a social function of considerable importance; but as time passed other clubs were started, small regattas were organized, and the club entered crews for them, their racing colours being royal blue. In 1864 the club engaged the services of an English trainer, Richard Clasper, and two years later endeavoured to put rowing on a better footing in Ireland by the organization of a public regatta, which was held at Ringsend, proved a great success, and became an annual fixture under the title of the Dublin Metropolitan Regatta.

About this time a controversy with respect to the constitution of the club arose, and by 1867 had become so keen that secession took place of a considerable number of the members, who formed another club under the title of the Dublin University Boat Club, whose colours were black and white. The rivalry between the two clubs was henceforth very keen, and did much to further the well-being of Irish rowing. Between them the two Trinity clubs won nearly all the principal races held in Ireland for nearly thirty years, and frequently sent crews to compete at Henley also. At the English regattas they secured on different occasions the Ladies' Plate and the Visitors' and Wyfold Cups. A Dublin four also went to Philadelphia to row at the International Regatta held there in 1876. Before leaving

America the Irishmen presented their boat to the Quaker City Boat Club, and it was used two years later by Mr. Ellis Ward and his three brothers, who rowed for Pennsylvania University in 1879, and won the first intercollegiate race ever rowed in America. This was the beginning of the Pennsylvania University Boat Club.

With time old differences were gradually forgotten, and it was generally agreed that the University would be more fitly represented by a single club. On May 7, 1898, a meeting was held at Ringsend, with Dr. J. Kells Ingram, Senior Fellow, in the chair, and a resolution was passed amalgamating the University Rowing and University Boat Clubs under the title of the latter. The colours of the new club are black and white, with the College arms on a royal blue shield. Before this date the transference of the Metropolitan Regatta from Ringsend to the quieter waters of the Upper Liffey had been under discussion, but the committee could not see its way to undertake the labour and expense necessary to make the reach between Chapelizod and Island Bridge suitable for the purpose. It was suggested by Mr. W. G. Towers that the boat club should itself take the step and organize a regatta. The scheme, no light undertaking nor lightly achieved, resulted in the acquisition of land along the river-bank. A great part of the bank was cut away to straighten the racing course, and a club-house and grand-stand erected on the grounds. Immediately after its formation the amalgamated club moved its quarters to Island Bridge, where it held its first regatta on July 7 and 8, 1898.

Since that date the membership of the club has considerably increased, and the annual regattas have proved very successful. The club has been represented at almost every regatta in Ireland, and has met with no little success. In 1900 and 1901 crews were sent to Henley, and in the latter year the club challenged Pennsylvania University to row a three-mile race on the lower lake of Killarney, after their visit to Henley. The challenge was accepted, but the visitors were much too strong for the boat club crew.

The annual income of Trinity College, Dublin, is often the subject of discussion, and it is not infrequently greatly exaggerated. Though magnificent for a College, it is barely adequate for the work of a University, and at the present day, however distributed, is entirely insufficient to provide for the extensions rendered necessary by the developments of modern science. It has not yet been realized either by Government or people that the cost of an education in science is more than treble that of the old education in arts, and that revenues once adequate, or even princely, are now almost beggarly. The value of the land received by Trinity College from the State at various times may be set down at £30,000 per annum, and to this must be added the income derived from private estate, amounting to £6,000 or £7,000 a year. This practically constitutes the whole endowment of the University, which earns in addition in receipts from students about £20,000 per annum. The gross total of the income is therefore usually about £60,000, but probably in the most prosperous times never exceeded £70,000 a year. If compared with Trinity College, Cambridge, it will be found that the income of the latter foundation is about £10,000 or

£12,000 a year less than that of the former; but Trinity, Dublin, since it is a University as well as a College, has vastly greater demands made upon its financial resources. In 1869 Trinity College received, by the Irish Church Act, £122,000 in compensation for the loss of the eighteen advowsons granted to it by letters patent in 1610,* and for three additional advowsons of Killyleagh, Killeshandra and Clogherny, purchased at different times by the Provost and Fellows, in whose hands the College patronage lay. A considerable portion of this sum was spent on building, chiefly in connection with the Medical School.

There are many societies and many clubs in the College to-day. Among them the 'University Philosophical,' founded in 1853, has become a formidable though friendly rival to the renowned 'Historical,' and already possesses a distinguished roll of honorary members. The younger society, at which papers are read and discussed, brings together the students of art and letters; the older draws to its debates the men whose interests lie rather in the domain of politics or history; but both prepare their members for the wider arena of public life, and some enthusiasts have had the hardihood to declare of the training they afford that it constitutes the most valuable part of University education. Such a dictum would not, however, pass unchallenged at the *Athletic Union*, consisting of the various athletic clubs. A record of great doings in the past by cricket and football teams, or their individual members, is here omitted,

* Of the College livings granted by James I., six were in the diocese of Raphoe, five in Armagh, four in Clogher, and three in Derry.

but if written would prove not the least interesting chapter in the history of the College.

Besides *T. C. D.*, the weekly gazette of the little academic kingdom, *Kottabos* and *Hermathena* offer a field to University penmen, the former to the wits and poets, the latter to the savants, the philosophers, and mathematicians. It seems to be generally conceded that whether in the composition of verses or in the more sober region of literary criticism, whether in philosophy or in mathematics, form and style have been happily cultivated in the work of Trinity College men. It would be difficult to find a rival to Congreve, to Berkeley, to Goldsmith, to Burke, in their respective fields. And in *Dublin Translations*,* or in the medical lectures of Stokes and Graves, a similar grace and finish and refinement is to be found. *Kottabos* and *Hermathena* are not widely known except in the world of high scholarship, but their audience, though few, is fit and keenly appreciative. A word may be added on another aspect of Dublin studies. Since the days of Molyneux, who introduced Locke to Dublin undergraduates, logics and ethics have been a staple of their intellectual diet. Here first among English Universities was Kant systematically studied, and to Kant Dublin has been more faithful than her sisters, who at times have wandered after strange gods when their worship was already outworn and abandoned in the land which gave it birth.†

* Edited by Professor Tyrrell.

† It is worthy of note that Dr. Mahaffy's was the first commentary on Kant published in this country, and that of the *Kritik der Praktischen Vernunft* and the *Kritik der Urtheilskraft* the only English translations are by Fellows of the society—Dr. Abbott and Dr. Bernard.

In her philosophical temple Dublin has admitted to a place beside Plato and Aristotle only her own Berkeley, Descartes, Spinoza and Immanuel Kant. The others she knows indeed, but without enthusiasm; they are hardly more to her than deities of the intellectual middle-class.

Thus sketched in barest outline, how unfamiliar to its old members will seem the features of their College, what a pale shadow of the glorious reality! Yet as around Odysseus in the under-world clustered the shades, eager to have word of their fellows who still beheld the light, and to renew again, if only in memory, the days when they, too, were buoyant in blood, valorous of soul, and armed to war with gods, so may we, at the sound of remembered names, rebuild the past, and, escaping for a season from a duller world, drink at the well of youth.

APPENDICES

A.—CELEBRATION OF THE CENTENARY

'Ann. Dñi 1693, Dec. 30. It was order'd that the Bursar shou'd lay out so much money as shou'd be found necessary, in order to prepare matters for the ninth of January.

'Ann. Dñi 169¾, January 9. This being the first secular day since the foundation of this University, it was observed with great solemnity. The order and method of the ceremony was published the day before, in ye following form :*

'In the morning there was a solemn service (*preces solleniores*) in the Chapel and a sermon.

'At 2 p.m., after a musical instrumental performance, an oration was made by Peter Browne, F.T.C., containing a panegyric in honour of Queen Elizabeth : " Dea nobis hæc otia fecit." Dominus Maude, Fellow Commoner, followed with a " Carmen seculare " in Latin hexamaters :

'" Aspice venturo lætentur ut omnia seclo
. . . . sequitur ramis insignis olivæ."

* This and the concluding paragraph are in English in the Register; the rest is in Latin. The version here given is from *Tercentenary Records*.

'Then Benjamin Pratt, F.T.C., followed with praise of King James the First, "Munificentissimi Academiæ auctoris":

'"Pariter pietate vel armis egregii."

'William Carr, F.T.C., commemorated the Chancellors of the University during the preceding century:

'"Nec nos iterum meminisse pigebit Elisæ."

'Sir Richard Gethinge followed with an English poem in memory of the illustrious founders of the College.

'Robert Mossom, F.T.C., delivered a Latin oration in praise of Charles the First and Charles the Second:

'"Heu pietas, heu prisca fides . . .
. . . Amavit nos quoque Daphnis."

'Then followed a recitation of some pastoral verses by Mr. Tighe and Mr. Denny, Fellow Commoners, bearing upon the revival of the University by William and Mary:

'"Jam fides et pax, et honor pudorque
Priscus, et neglecta redire Virtus
Audet. . . ."

'A thanksgiving ode was then sung accompanied by instrumental music.

'A grateful commemoration of the benefits which the City of Dublin had conferred upon the University, by Richard Baldwin, F.T.C.:

'"Laudabunt alii claram Rhodon aut Mitylenen."

'Verses commemorating the hospitality shown to the members of the University when dispersed, by the sister Universities of Oxford and Cambridge, were recited by Benjamin Hawkshaw, B.A.; William Tisdal, B.A.; Jeremiah Harrison, B.A.:

'". . . Quales decet esse Sorores."

'Then there was a Latin debate on the subject, "Whether the Sciences and Arts are more indebted to the Ancients or the Moderns?":

    For the Ancients—Nicholas Foster, B.A.
    For the Moderns—Robert Cashin, B.A.

'Then followed a "Carmen seculare lyricum," recited by Anthony Dopping, son of the Bishop of Meath:

    '"Alterum in lustrum meliusque semper
    . . . . Proroget ævum."

'Concerning the increase of University studies, in an humourous speech by Thomas Leigh, B.A.

'Eugene Lloyde, Proctor of the University, closed the Acts.

'A skilled band of musicians followed the procession as they left the building (*discedentes*).

'The sermon was preach'd by the Provost, Dr. Ashe, upon Matthew xxvi. 13,[*] concerning the duty of Gratitude, which he applied in the commemoration of our Royall Foundress.

'Several of the Senior Fellows assisted at Divine Service. The First Lesson was 1 Chronicles xxix., verses 3-19; the Second Lesson, Ecclesiasticus xxxix., verses 1-16. The Epistle, Ezra vi., verses 7-13; the Gospel, Matthew v., verses 13-17. The Anthem was Revelation vii., verses 9-13. The solemnity was honour'd with the presence of the Lords Justices, accompanied by the Lord Bishop of Meath, Vice-Chancellour (who at ye opening of the Act made a Latin speech concerning the antiquity of learned Foundations, and their usefulness to the publick), and by several other bishops, by ye Lord Mayor, nobility, and most of the gentry

[*] 'Verily I say unto you, Wheresoever this Gospel shall be preached in the whole world, there shall also this, that this woman hath done, be told for a memorial of her.'

of the city. The whole ceremony concluded with the illumination of all the windowes of the college, and of that part of the town next to it.

'The several Exercises are laid up in y* Manuscript Library.'*

B.—CELEBRATION OF THE TERCENTENARY.

The festivities connected with the celebration of the tercentenary occupied four days. A full and official account of the proceedings has been published in a volume entitled *Records of the Tercentenary Festival of Dublin University*. In response to the invitations sent to the four quarters of the globe, seventy-five Universities and learned bodies sent representatives to the celebration.† Between 400 and 500 distinguished persons were also invited to attend, of whom a large number accepted the invitation. A directory was published which gave the names of all the guests and of their hosts in Dublin. The proceedings were opened by the reception of the guests on Tuesday, July 5, by the Provost, followed by an academic procession to St. Patrick's Cathedral, where a sermon was preached by the Dean,‡ and came to a conclusion with the University ball on the evening of Friday, July 8. A copy of the *Book of Trinity College*, written and published for the occasion, was presented to each guest as a memorial of the celebration in which he had borne a part.

Besides the official University guests, students of most

---

* These are not now to be found. Dunton, in his book, *My Conversation in Ireland* (1699), adds some particulars of this celebration, and quotes part of Nahum Tate's (Poet Laureate) ode on the occasion.

† Six Universities declined.

‡ It had originally been intended that the sermon should be preached by Dr. Magee, Archbishop of York, who died, however, before the date fixed for the celebration.

CELEBRATION OF THE TERCENTENARY

British and a number of foreign Universities were also present in response to the invitation of the Students' Representative Committee. A banquet in the College hall on the night of the University banquet in the Leinster Hall, and a smoking concert, were the special features of the programme arranged for the student delegates. Of the concert it was well said by the editor of the *Records* that the students endeavoured ' to compress into "one crowded hour of glorious life" the diffused hilarity of three centuries.' During the week a meeting was held to promote the Graduates' Memorial scheme, towards which over £6,000 had already been contributed. The building which now faces the library commemorates the tercentenary and the affection of the alumni of Trinity College for their *alma mater*.

The success of the festival was very complete. The weather was favourable, the city put on her festal attire, the proceedings were marked by colour, variety, and picturesqueness, and gaiety and enthusiasm were everywhere apparent.

The following was the order of proceedings as set out in the official programme:

Tuesday, July 5.

10 a.m.: Reception of Guests and Delegates by the Provost in the Examination Hall, Trinity College.

11.30 a.m.: Commemoration Service in St. Patrick's Cathedral, to which a procession will start (weather permitting) from the Examination Hall, Trinity College, at 11 o'clock. (Guests and Delegates will be expected to attend in their Academic Robes or Official Costume.)

3 p.m.: Cricket Match in the College Park—Cambridge *v.* Dublin University.

4 p.m.: Garden Party in the Fellows' Garden, Trinity College.
9 p.m.: Performance of Tercentenary Ode by the University Choral Society in the Leinster Hall.
10 p.m.: Reception and Ball in the Mansion House.

WEDNESDAY, JULY 6.

12 noon: The Conferring of Honorary Degrees in the Examination Hall, Trinity College.
3 p.m.: Meeting in connexion with the Graduates' Memorial.
    Cricket Match in the College Park—Cambridge v. Dublin University.
3 p.m.: Garden Party at the Viceregal Lodge.
6.45 p.m.: Tercentenary Banquet in the Leinster Hall.

THURSDAY, JULY 7.

11 a.m.: Procession in Academic Robes or Official Costume from the Examination Hall, Trinity College, to the Leinster Hall.
11.30. a.m.: Presentation of Addresses by the Delegates in the Leinster Hall.
4 to 6 p.m.: Garden Party at the Royal Hospital, Kilmainham.*
8 p.m.: Dramatic Performance in the Gaiety Theatre.

FRIDAY, JULY 8.

11 a.m.: Addresses to the Students by certain of the University Guests in the Examination Hall, Trinity College.
12.30 p.m.: College Races in the College Park.
10 p.m.: University Ball in the Leinster Hall.

* Official residence of the Commander-in-Chief of the Forces in Ireland, then Lord Wolseley.

C.—COLLEGE DISCIPLINE.

The following excerpts from the Caroline charter, dealing with College discipline, are of interest:

'Quinetiam statuimus, ne quis Collegii muros, aut sepimenta transcendat, aut fores, fenestrasve diffringat; qui semel fecerit, si aetate puer, virgis castigetur; qui autem bis, Collegio amoveatur. Eadem poena mulctentur, qui aliorum pomaria expilaverint, vel in domos oppidanorum, aliorumve aliquam viam exercurint. Porro aleae, et chartarum ludo nemo in Collegio omnino utatur, nisi tempore sollenitatis Natalitiorum Domini, idque publice in aula Collegii; secus facientes post tertiam admonitionem a Collegio amoveantur. Nemo canes venaticos, accipitres, aut aves vocales in Collegio nutriat, teneatve; neque aucupio, neque venatione sit deditus; qui contra fecerit, puniatur, ut supra dictum est. Nulli lusus discipulis in area, vel hortis Collegii permittantur; nec discipulorum ulla fiant in area conventicula, nec ibi colloquendi causa moram faciant, neque in aula nisi tempore merendae, dum simul bibunt. Post prandium vero et coenam, ex aula sine mora discedant. . . .

'Statuimus etiam, atque ordinamus, ut Socii, et Discipuli, Commensales, cameram in Collegio possidentes, studentesque omnes, et singuli habeant togam, eaque semper utantur, et in Collegio, et in urbe Dublinensi; ut nemo togatus ocreis utatur, aut vestitu, capillitio, incessu, ad pompam aulicam se componat, sed unusquisque modestiam et gravitatem ordini suo convenientem, et academico dignam sectetur. Permittimus vero, ut singuli studentes cujuscunque gradus, et conditionis (modo non sacris ordinibus initiati fuerint) extra academiam, et urbem Dubliniensem pro arbitratu vestiantur, dummodo decenter, et vestimentis obscuri cujuspiam coloris induti incedant. Quod si quis hoc violaverit, primo, sex denariis mulctetur; secundo duodecim; tertio duobus solidis; quarto, pro qualitate contumaciæ puniatur. Porro statuimus, et ordinamus, ut nullus prædictorum armis, aut telis, veluti gladiis, sicis, aut pugionibus in Collegio, aut in urbe utatur, sub pœna, primo, commeatus duarum hebdomadarum, secundo, menstrui, tertio, amotionis perpetuæ a nostro Collegio. Nemini item licebit, equum intra ambitum, seu situm Collegii alere, seu habere, exceptis Præposito, et Sociis qui ecclesiastica beneficia possideant extra urbem Dubliniensem; qui secus fecerit, puniatur a Præposito quinque solidis hebdomadatim, donec huic statuto morem gerat.'

(*Caput xi.*, *Literæ Patentes*, 13 *Caroli Primi*.)

D.—ARMS OF TRINITY COLLEGE, DUBLIN.

It would appear that the College obtained a grant of arms at the foundation in 1591, but no record of this grant has been preserved. The earliest evidence now extant is that afforded by the seal attached to the document appointing Lord Ormonde first Chancellor of the University, 1612. It should be noted that in the seal the harp is facing towards the sinister; but this is probably due to a mistake on the part of the seal-cutter.

The first mention—if mention it can be called—of the arms in the records of Ulster's Office is a rude 'memorandum' sketch, dating *circa* 1640. This sketch occurs on the back of a leaf in a book which contains many finished drawings, and, although obviously imperfect, is entitled 'The Colledge Arms.' In Ulster's Office is also preserved a book, dating 1720-30, containing a 'tricking' of the coat, and bearing the title 'The Arms of ye Colledg of

Dublin.' This eighteenth-century volume was compiled from older records, now destroyed.

The certificate granted in 1901 is based upon the seal of 1612, and is worded in these terms:

'To all and singular to whom these Presents shall come I, Sir Arthur Edward Vicars, C.V.O., Ulster King of Arms, and Principal Herald of all Ireland, Registrar and Knight Attendant on the most Illustrious Order of St. Patrick, do hereby certify and declare that the Armorial Bearings above depicted—that is to say, Azure, a Bible closed, clasps to the dexter, between, in chief, in the dexter a lion passant, on the sinister a harp, all or, and in base a castle with the towers domed, each surmounted by a banner flotant from the sides argent, the dexter flag charged with a cross, the sinister with a saltire, gules—do of right belong and appertain, as appears from the Records of my Office, unto the Provost, Fellows and Scholars of the College of the Holy and Undivided Trinity of Queen Elizabeth, near Dublin, and their successors, for ever according to the laws of Arms. As witness my hand

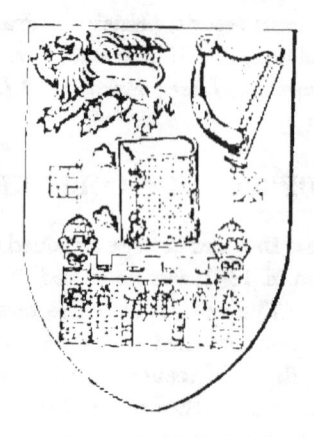

and seal in the sixty-fourth year of the reign of our Sovereign Lady Victoria, by the grace of God of the United Kingdom of Great Britain and Ireland Queen, Defender of the Faith, and so forth, and in the year of our Lord one thousand nine hundred and one.

'ARTHUR E. VICARS, *Ulster.*'

The College colour is royal blue, the old national colour of Ireland. Green is not the true Irish colour, but a comparatively late innovation, dating from about 1798, and without authority. The *light* blue of the St. Patrick's ribbon was adopted at the institution of the Order because royal blue was already associated with the Garter.

INDEX

Abbot, Dr., 224, 225, 228, 280, 282, 277
Abbot, Archbishop, 28
Abercorn, Marquis of, 217
Absentee landlords, 150, 179, 180
Academic dress, 169, Appendix C
Accounts, early College, 11
Acton, Vice-Provost, 59, 68, 66
Addison, Joseph, 99, 164, 247
Advice to the University, 168
Agassiz, L., 191
Alcuin, 2
Allen, Fellow, 59, 62
All Hallows Priory, 6-8, 54, 201
Alvey, Provost, 13
'Anatomies,' bodies for, 146, 147
Anatomy, Chair of, 193
Analysis of Equations, 175
Analysis of Infinities, 174
Analytic Geometry, 184
Anderson, R., 185
Andrews, Dr. T., 269
Andrews, Provost, 108-111, 113
Annals of Ireland, 3
Annesley, case of, 101
Annus Medicus, 190
Anster, R., 259
Apprentice's Vade-Mecum, 170
Arabic, Chair of, 195
Archbishop King's Lecturer, 186
Aristocratic families support College, 92, 100
Armagh, Archbishop of, 4, 5
Armagh, Irish scholars at, 2
Armagh, proposed University of, 25
Arms, College, 9, Appendix D
Army and library, 220, 222
Army Medical Service, 196
Arnold, M., 244, 249
Arthur, Mr., case of, 204

Articles to be observed, etc., 156
Ashbourne, Lord, 185
Ashe, Provost, 79, 94
Ashe, R., 247, 256
Astronomy, Chair of, 113
Astronomy, Ptolemaic system, 20
Astronomer Royal, 114
Athletic Union, 276
Australian graduates, 261-263
Avonmore, Lord, 134

Bacon, Friar, 221
Bailiffs in College, 103
Baldwin, Provost, 94, 97, 103-105, 107, 108, 173
Ball, Lord Chancellor, 185
Ball, Sir R., 108, 114
Barber Surgeons, 190
Barlow, case of, 99
Barrett, Dr. J., 175-177, 181
Barrett's *Life of Swift*, 88
Bath, Countess of, 69
Beaux' Stratagem, Farquhar's, 242
Bedell, Provost, 23, 32, 33, 35, 80, 145, 205
Bedford, Duke of, 109, 110, 148, 215
Bell, the College, 23, 176, 208
Belmore, Lord, 186
Beresford, Lord J., 212
Berkeley, George, 96, 151, 174, 175, 204, 211, 216, 230, 245, 246, 277, 278
Bernard, Dr. J. H., 277
Bernard, Dr. N., 20, 220
Bicentenary, 123
Bicknor, A. de, Archbishop, 3
Bird, Judge, 185
Blackburne, Lord Chancellor, 135
Blacquiere, Sir J., 115
Boat Club, the, 272, 273

19

Bodleian Library, 59, 221, 224
Bodley, Sir T., 221, 239
Body-snatching, 147
Bologna, University of, 22
Book of Armagh, 225, 226
Book of Censures, Temple's, 82
Book of Dimma, 225, 226
Book of Durrow, 225, 226
Book of Hymns, 229
Book of Kells, 225, 226
Book of Lecan, 227
Book of Leinster, 226
Book of Mulling, 225, 226
Book of Trinity College, 17, 57, 64, 80, 85, 89, 108, 117, 122, 185, 190, 191, 194, 199, 208, 212, 216, 217, 218, 225, 228, 230, 232
Botanic Garden, 218
'Botany Bay,' 54, 211
Boulter, Archbishop, 94-96, 101, 104
Bowling-green, 76, 84
Boyle, Hon. Robert, 84
Boyne, Battle of, 62, 69
Brady, Lord Chancellor, 135
Brady, Nicholas, 241
Brereton, Sir W., 24, 231
Brian Boroimhe, 231
Brinkley, Dr., 118
British Association, 191
Brooke, Henry, 243
Brooking's Map of Dublin, 75
Browne, Arthur, 139
Browne, Colonel, 197
Browne, George, Provost, 94
Browne, Peter, Provost, 94, 244
Browning, R., 257
Bruce, Edward, 8
Bruce Joy, 233
Brünnow, Dr. F., 114
'Bucks,' the Dublin, 164, 167
Burdy's *Life of Skelton*, 104, 105, 120
Burke, Edmund, 115, 121, 122, 131, 133, 151, 155, 157, 199, 211, 248, 249, 276
Burke, Ulick R., 199, 213
Burlington, Lord, 215
Bushe, Lord Chief Justice, 134, 250, 251
Butler, W. Archer, 134, 185, 259
Butt, Isaac, 102, 134, 259

CAIRNES, J. E., 259
Cairns, Earl, 215, 261
Caius, Dr., 72
Callanan, J., 257
Cambridge, Caius College, 118
    Christ College, 36
    Emmanuel College, 32
    King's College, 21

Cambridge, Trinity College, 21, 275
    Union, 151, 153
    University, 21, 55, 150, 156, 184, 186, 189, 192, 200, 269
Camden, Lord, 128
Cameron's *History of Royal College of Surgeons*, 147
Campanile, 212
Campbell's *Philosophical Survey*, 204
Caroline charter, 139, 174
Caroline statutes, 32, 33, 40, 44, Appendix C
Carson, Sir E., 135
Carteret, Lord, 108
Carte's *Life of Ormonde*, 50
Cartwright, Thomas, 12
Cary, L., Lord Falkland, 240
Cash, George, 232
Cashel, Irish scholars at, 2
Cassels, architect, 208, 211
Catholyckt Conference, A, etc., 214
'Cautioned,' 80, 171
'Caxtons' in library, 230
Cecil, Lord Burleigh, 6
Celibacy statutes, 33, 112
Celtic MSS., 225-229
Celtic ornaments, 232
Censures, Book of, 82
Chadwich, Bishop, 135
Challoner, Luke, 6, 16, 28, 76, 202, 219, 220
Chambers, Sir W., 204, 210
Chandler, Bishop, 240
Charlemagne, 2
Charlemont, Hardy's Life of, 109
Charnock, Stephen, 50
Chapel, College, 58, 59, 65, 202-204
Chappel, Provost, 36-44
Chesterfield, Lord, 156
Choir, College, 110
Choral Society, 142
Christchurch Cathedral, 91
Christmas play, 87
Chronology, Hales', 175
'Chumming' system, 80
Civil Service, Indian, 196
Clandeboye, Viscount, 15
Clanricarde, Lord, 231
Clare, Lord, 119, 124, 128, 129
Clarendon, Lord, 61, 62
Clasper, Richard, 273
Class distinctions in College, 92, 193
Clement V., Pope, 2
Clock, the College, 209
Clonard, Irish scholars at, 2
Clyn, John, 6

INDEX

Codex Montfortianus, 225
Codex Usserianus, 225
Codex Z, 176, 224
Coghlan, Mr., 66
Coleridge, S. T., 114
College and University, 21, 22
College, Elizabethan, 12
College Examination, The, a poem, 172
College Green, 12, 199
College of Physicians, 145-148, 191
Colleges, foundation of additional, 22-24
Colonial graduates, 261-263
Colonists support College, 8
Columba, St., 226, 228
Commencements, 13-16, 89-91
Commission of 1857, 193
Common Cranks, a poem, 158
'Commonplaces,' 74, 79
Commonwealth and the College, 48-51
Composition, attention to, 157
Conclave Dissected, a poem, 140
Concordatum Fund, 61
Confiscations of Irish land, 18
Congreve, William, 151, 154, 242, 243, 276
Conolly, Luke, 257
Constituency University, 150
Conyngham, W., 231
Cooke, John, 133
Corbett, T., 130
Corbett, W., 130
Cork House, 25
Cork, Lord, 216
Cormac, King-Archbishop, 2
'Corrections,' 81, 265
Corry, Isaac, 135, 254
Council, Academic, 194
Crampton, Dr., 144
Crampton, Mr. Justice, 135
Croker, J. W., 135, 239
Cromwell, Henry, 20, 24, 49-51, 222, 241
Cromwell, Oliver, 239
Crump, case of, 99
Cudworth, Ralph, 49
Curran, J. Philpot, 254
Curriculum, early, 77-80

DANES, invasion of the, 2
Daniel, Archbishop, 34, 240
Darley, George, 257
Davis, Thomas, 134, 256
Dean, the Junior, 171, 211
Deane and Woodward, 212
De Bicknor, Archbishop, 3
Declamations, 74, 79
Degrees for Dissenters, 123, 187, 188

Degrees recognised by Oxford and Cambridge, 21
Degrees, suspension from, 86, 87
Deirdre, Ferguson's, 257
Delany, Dr., 108, 233, 255
De Lanne, Dr., 23
De Morgan, 114
Denham, Sir J., 254
De Origine Mali, King's, 242
Descartes, 184, 277
Desiderata Curiosa Hibernica, 13
Desmonds, the, 10
De Tolly, 191
De Toqueville, 191
Dialogues, Berkeley's, 245
Diarmuid, King of Leinster, 8
Dickson, Dr. B., 233
Diet, College, 76, 163
Dillon, Earl of Roscommon, 254
Dining-hall, 12, 58, 65, 75, 107, 163, 209
Dinner-hour, 74, 163
Discipline, early, 81, 87
Disputations, 79, 152
Dissolution of the monasteries, 7
Divinity, Chair of, 53, 186
Divinity School, 186
Dodwell, Henry, 56, 239
Dominican Friars, the, 3
Dominus, as title, 83
Donegal Lectureship, 51, 54
Donellan, James, 88
Donoughmore, Lord, 118
Donovan, Dr., 233
Dopping, Anthony, 215, 242
Dorset, Duke of, 100
Downes, Chief Justice, 135
Doyle, case of, 61
Doyle, William, 118
Dramatic performances, 87
Drogheda, Parliament of, 3
Dublin, Archbishop of, 2
Dublin, Mayor of, 6, 9, 43
Dublin Translations, 276
Dublin, undergraduate life at, 56
Dublin University Magazine, 176, 177, 257
Dubourg, the violinist, 110
Duels, student, 119, 120
Duigenan, Dr. Patrick, 115, 128, 174
Dunne, Dr., 14, 15
'Dunscope,' 187
Dunsink Observatory, 113
Dunton's *Life and Errors*, 205-207

Ecclesiastica Disciplina, Travers', 12
Edinburgh, Speculative Society of, 133
Editiones Principes in the Library, 231

19—2

INDEX

Edward III., 3
Eglinton, Lord, 197
Election songs, 118
Elections, College, bribery at, 117
Elizabethan college, 12, 26, 204
Elizabethan grants, 10, 194
Ellwood, Dr., case of, 104
Elrington, Provost, 112, 128, 144, 180
Ely, Lord, 34
Emigration from Ireland, 225-228
Emmet, Robert, 126-126, 256
Emmet, T. A., 128
Emmet, Temple, 128, 256
Endowments, the College, 275
Engineering, Chair of, 192, 195
Engineering, degrees in, 195
Engineering, School of, 195, 201
English by birth, English by blood, 1, 95, 96
English literature, Chair of, 196
Equus, 192
Essex, Earl of, 27
Estates, the College, 6, 8, 10, 11, 275
Examination Hall, 106, 121, 210, 211
Examination, hours of, 187
Examination, the College, a poem, 172-174
Examinations conducted in Latin, 191
Examinations, early, 77
Examinations, records of, 92
Expenditure of College, early, 11, 91
Expulsion of students, 82, 99, 130

Fagel Library, the, 228
Falkland, Lucius Cary, Lord, 92, 240
Farmer, Anthony, 61
Farquhar, George, 242
Fatal Marriage, Southerne's, 242
Fawcett Act (1873), 134, 188
Fees for degrees, early, 91
Fellow Commoners, 92, 193
Fellows, attacks on the, 162
Fellowships, 26, 40, 41, 125, 139, 140, 191, 270
Fencing school in College, 116, 118, 119
Ferguson, Sir S., 256, 257
Filius Nobilis, 92, 193
Finch, renewal, 194
Fitzgerald, Lord Edward, 118
Fitzgerald, Professor G., 164
Fitzgerald, Sir J., 64
Fitzgibbon, Earl of Clare, 128, 129, 211, 252
Fitzgibbon, Lord Justice, 135
Fitzwilliam, Lord Deputy, 8
Fitzwilliam, Lord, Viceroy, 133
Flood, Henry, 194, 215, 250-252
Foley, J. H., 199

Fool of Quality, Brooke's, 243
Forbes, Edward, case of, 97
Ford, Edward, murder of, 102, 161
Foster, Lord Oriel, 128, 129, 250, 252
Foundation of College, 1, 5-10
Fox, George, 257
Fox, Luke, 258
Fox, Mr. Justice, 135
Francis, Philip, 254
Frederick, Prince of Wales, 110
Freeman's Journal, 243
Freshmen, junior and senior, 77, 187, 270
Fuller's *Church History*, 9, 21, 267
Fullerton, James, 6, 16

Gainsborough, Sir T., 110, 215
Games in College, early, 75, 76
Gardens, the College, 218
Garrick, David, 111
Gast, Dr., 255
Geology, Chair of, 192, 195
George I., 215
George III., 115, 215
George IV., 181-183
Geraldines, the, 8
'Gib,' 137, 270
Gibbings, Dr., 31
Gibson, Mr. Justice, 135
Gilbert, Dr. C., 222, 228
Gloucester, Duke of, 130
Goldsmith, Oliver, 77, 108, 151, 155, 165, 199, 207, 248, 249, 276
Graces, the College, 209
Graduates' Memorial, the, 207, Appendix B
Grammar School, Dublin, 6
Grammar Schools, Ireland, 144
Grattan, Henry, 115, 188, 215, 250-252
Grattan's Parliament, 133
Graves, Dr., 259, 260, 276
Greek, Chair of, 195, 196
Green, College, 12, 199
Greene, Arthur, case of, 60, 64
Greene, Surgeon, 145
Green's *Oxford Studies*, 163
Griffith, Judge, 135
Griffiths, Colonel, 197
Gulliver's Travels, Swift's, 247
Gustavus Vasa, Brooke's, 244
Gwynn, Rev. J., 269

Halm, William, 175
Hall, the College, 12, 58, 65, 75, 107, 168
Hall, Fellow, 59, 68, 69
Hall, Provost, 122, 180
Hamilton, Edwin, 76

INDEX

Hamilton, Hugh, 174, 255
Hamilton, James, 6, 16
Hamilton, Sir W. Rowan, 114, 124, 192, 260
Hamlet, Garrick's, 111
Hampton, Archbishop, 14, 15
Handel's *Messiah*, 111
Hanoverian policy of college, 97-99
Harding, Fellow, 40
Harp, Brian Boroimhe's, 231
Harris, Dr., 5, 255
Harvard, University of, 50, 241
Harvey, case of, 99
Haughton, Dr. S., 184
Hawking, 84
Hearne's *Diary*, 168
Hearth-tax, 149
Hebrew, Chair of, 78, 111
Hebrew, study of, 20, 78
Helsham, Dr., 145
Henley regatta, 273, 275
Henry VIII, 8
Herbert, Hon. S., 271
Hermathena, 276
Hermit, Parnell's, 243
Heron, D. C., case of, 187
Heron's *Constitutional History of the University*, 5, 124, 183
Herschel, 114
Hibernian Journal, 168
Hibernian Magazine, 164
Hincks, Edward, 232, 259
Hindustani, Chair of, 196
Hinkson's *Student Life in Trinity College, Dublin*, 127, 183, 267
Historical Society, 127, 131-136, 169, 180, 248, 250, 276
History, Ancient, Chair of, 193
History, Chair of, 111, 144, 158, 159
Hoggin Green, 23, 201, 202, 204
Holy Offices Book, 31
Holy Well of St. Patrick, 214
Hone, J., 271
Honour lectures, 152
Honour schools, 153, 185
Hopkins, case of, 141
Hoyle, Joshua, 28
Hoyle, Vice-Provost, 48, 52
Huntingdon, Provost, 34, 59, 202
Hutchinson, Hely F., 118
Hutchinson, Hely, Provost, 115-122, 157

Ingram, Dr. J. K., 274
Inquisition, Papal, in the College, 30
Ireland Ninety Years Ago, 107, 126, 129, 136-139, 164, 165

Ireton, Henry, 49
Irish, Chair of, 84
Church Act, 275
lectures, 26, 84
lectureship, 60
oratory, 151, 250, 251
printing, 34
schools, early, 2
Irishmen United, the, 127-130
Iveagh, Lord, 216

Jacobitism in College, 94, 97, 99
James I., 11, 16, 27, 90
James II., 60-62, 64
Jameson, John, 271
Jebb, John, 134
Jellett, Provost, 184, 196
Jesuit seminary in Dublin, 24
John XXII., Pope, 3
Johnson, Dr., 243, 254
Jones, Elizabeth, case of, 86
Jones, Lord Chancellor, 14
Jones, Vice-Chancellor, 50

Kant, Immanuel, 277
Kearney, Provost, 143, 180
Kells, Book of, 200
Kelly, case of, 166
Kerdiffe, Fellow, 40
Kerney, William, 18, 84
Kildare Hall, 24
Kildare, Lord, 167
King, Archbishop, 34, 64-66, 99, 211, 242
Kinsale, Battle of, 220
Kneller, Sir G., 215
Knox, George, 139
Kottabos, 209, 276
Kyle, Provost, 164, 181, 182

Lachrymæ Academicæ, 115, 119
Lambeth degrees, 145
Latimer, Bishop, 72
Latin, examinations conducted in, 191
Latin, lectures in, 20
Laud, Archbishop, 30, 36, 37, 39, 41, 45
Laudian statutes, 77
Law, Civil and Canon, Chair of, 53, 194 195
Constitutional and Criminal, Chair of, 195
Feudal and English, Chair of, 195
Regius Professorship of, 194
School, 194
Lawless, Valentine Lord, Cloncurry, 134, 190, 254

Lay Fellows, 127, 174
Lech, Archbishop, 2
Leckey, William, 52
Lecky, W. E. H., 135
Lecky's *History of Ireland in the Eighteenth Century*, 18, 25, 50, 95, 111, 115, 139, 151, 179, 180, 208, 211, 226-238, 244, 246, 249, 251-255
Lectures in the sixteenth century, 20
Lectures in the seventeenth century, 78, 85
Lee, Dr., 261
Lefanu, Sheridan, 134, 259
Lefroy, Thomas, 134
Leinster, Duke of, 109
Leland, Dr., 111, 165, 174, 254
Leslie, Charles, 241
Leslie, Cliffe, 259
Letter on the Present Condition of University (1734), 161
Letter to the Students (1734), 100, 161
Lever, Charles, 108, 211, 259
Lever, Thomas, 73
Lhuyd, E., 223
'Liberty Boys,' 105, 106
Library, the College, 58, 205, 220-233
Lightfoot, Bishop, 240
Limerick, Treaty of, 70
Livings, College, 276
Lloyd, Bartholomew, Provost, 123, 149, 183-185, 189, 191
Lloyd, Humphrey, Provost, 185, 195, 198, 211, 238
Locke's *Essay*, 79, 152, 172
Loftus, Adam, Provost, 4-7, 215, 216
Loftus, Dudley, 48, 56, 85, 239
Logic, study of, 77, 85, 171, 172
Logics and Ethics, School of, 185
Lutteral, Colonel, 65
Lydiate, T., 240
Lyon, Dr. J., 232

MACARTHY, Teigue, 64, 66
Macaulay, Lord, 154, 243
McCullagh, J., 184, 185, 260
McDonnel, Provost, 195, 196
Mace, the College, 216, 217
MacGeoghan's *Annals of Ireland*, 228, 237
Mackay, J. T., 218
Macklin, H. G., 196
Macmillan's Magazine, 179
McNeight, W. R. P., 271
McNeill, Sir J., 195
Madden, Mr. Justice, 135
Madden, Samuel, 156, 202, 255
Madden's *Life of Emmet*, 181

Magee, Archbishop (Dublin), 134, 139, 171, 174, 216, 261
Magee, Archbishop (York), 134, 261, Appendix B
Maginn, W., 259
Maguire, Sir R., 135
Mahaffy, Dr. J. P., 17, 57, 64, 80, 85, 89, 117, 123, 179, 216, 217, 277
Malone, Anthony, 249
Malone, Edmund, 249
MSS. in library, 224-230
Marsden, J., 50
Marsh, Provost, 56-59, 80, 202
Marshall, Fellow, 40
Martin, Provost, 14, 43
Mason, H. Monck, 232
Mater Universitatis, 6
Mathematics, Chair of, 111, 184
Mathematics, study of, 20, 79, 184, 260
Mather, I., 50, 241
Mather, N., 50, 241
Mather, S., 50, 241
Maxwell, W., 259
Mayo, County of, 258
Mayor of Dublin, 6, 9, 43
Mazarin Bible, 225
Mazarin, Cardinal, 222
Meds, Fellow, 32
Medical degrees, 147-149
  Fellows, 145
  licenses, 145, 148
  School, 144-149, 189, 190, 212, 213, 276
Medicus, 174
Medicus Annus, 190
Mendicant Friars, 3
Merryman, University, 88
Metropolitan regatta, 273, 274
Miller, Dr., 124
Mills, case of, 164
Moderatorships, 152, 185, 186, 270
Modern Language Chairs, 120
'Mohocks, The,' 164
Molesworth, Lord, 255
Molyneux, W., 57, 104, 147, 152, 244
Montalembert, 191
Moore, Dr. M., 66, 68, 94
Moore, Thomas, 129, 134, 136, 256
Moral Sciences, Chair of, 185
Mornington, Earl of, 110, 215, 249
Mountjoy, Lord, 254
Mulgrave, Earl of, 192
Munster rebellion, 10, 220
Murray, Provost, 111, 121, 122, 142, 172
Music, Chair of, 110, 249
Musical taste in Dublin, 110

INDEX

Nagle, Sir R., 64
Napier, Sir J., 261
Nation, The, poets of, 257
'Natives,' provision for, 26
Natural Philosophy, Chair of, 111, 144, 158, 159
New College, 24
Newman, Cardinal, 113
Nicholson, Dr., 217
Night roll, 162
Nobilis, 92, 193
Noblemen in College, 92, 100
Nonconformists and the College, 45, 50
Norbury, R., 50
North, Lord, 115
Novelists, Irish, 259
Nunan, J. J., 236

O'Brien, Dr., 261
O'Brien, Sir L., 254
Observatory, astronomical, 113
Observatory, magnetical, 211
O'Curry, Eugene, 228
O'Donovan, P., 228
O'Farrihy, Thaddæus, 80, 81
O'Gorman, Chevalier, 231
O'Grady, S., Lord Guillamore, 185
O'Hagan, John, 257
O'Malley, Charles, 103
O'Neill, Lord, 254
O'Neill, Phelim, 46
O'Neill, Shane, 5,
O'Neill, Sir Thurlough, 60
O'Neills, the, 10
Orange societies, 129
Orange, William of, 69, 70, 94, 148
Oratory, Chair of, 111, 144, 158, 159
Oratory, Irish, 151, 250-252
O'Regan's *Address to the Fellows*, 162
O'Reilly, E., 232
O'Reilly, Phelim, 85
Organ, the Spanish, 142, 210
Organist, the College, 110
Oriental Languages, Chair of, 144
Ormond Boys,' 105, 106
Ormonde, Duke of, 141, 142, 216
Ormonde, Marquis of, 48, 52, 96
Oronooko, Southerne's, 242
Ossory, Earl of, 89
Ould, Sir F., 148
Oxford, *customs of*, 21
    Magdalen College, 61
    Merton College, 59
    St. Alban's Hall, 56
    Studies, Green's, 163
    Union, 131, 133, 135

Oxford, University College, 45
    University of, 21, 55, 150, 156, 163, 179, 189, 192, 200, 269

Pale, the, 26
Palgrave, F. T., 257
Palliser, Archbishop, 215, 223, 241
Palliser, Fellow, 104
Papal Universities in Dublin, 2-4
Paris, University of, 2, 22
Park, the College, 75, 207, 218
Parliament, English, and the College, 48, 49, 150, 253
Parliament, Irish, and the College, 42-44, 66, 97, 98, 109, 123, 133, 136-139, 148-150, 207, 208, 210, 223
Parliamentary representation, 17, 66, 150
Parliament Square, 210
Parnell, H., 155
Parnell, T., 243
Parsons, L., Earl of Rosse, 134
Patrick, St., 226
Pavia, University of, 2
Pechell, Vice-Chancellor of Cambridge, 61
Pembroke Rowing Club, 271
Pennefather, Baron, 185
Pennefather, Chief Justice, 185
Pennsylvania Boat Club, 274, 275
Pensioner, 269
Perrin, Louis, 185
Perrot, Sir J., 4
Petre, Father, 67
Petty, Sir W., 50, 57
Philadelphia regatta, 273
Philology, Comparative, Chair of, 193
Philosophical Society, 264, 276
'Physic Garden,' the, 217
Physicians, College of, 145-148
Physics, Experimental, Chair of, 196
Plate, the College, 47, 61, 216, 217
Plummer, Mr., case of, 209
Plunket, W. C., Lord, 134, 250-253
Poisson's *Mechanics*, 134
Portland, Duke of, 25
Portraits, 211, 215, 216
'Post-Graduate' study, 78
Potts, W., 271
Prancerriana, 116
Pratt, Provost, 94, 97
Precedence, University, 181
Premiums, Madden, 156
Press, the University, 18, 19, 211
Principles of Human Knowledge, Berkeley's, 245
Printing in Dublin, 4, 18, 19, 34, 211
Prison, College used as, 65

Prizes at examinations, 156, 157
Professorships, mode of appointment to, 194
Provosts: Adam Loftus (1592), 6
  Walter Travers (1594), 12
  Henry Alvey (1601), 13
  William Temple (1609), 27
  William Bedell (1627), 32
  Robert Ussher (1629), 35
  William Chappel (1634), 36
  Richard Washington (1640), 45
  Anthony Martin (1645), 48
  Samuel Winter (1651), 49
  Thomas Seele (1661), 52
  Michael Ward (1674), 56
  Narcissus Marsh (1678), 56
  Robert Huntingdon (1683), 59
  Michael Moore (?) (1689), 66
  St. George Ashe (1692), 94
  George Browne (1695), 94
  Peter Browne (1699), 94
  Benjamin Pratt (1710), 94
  Richard Baldwin (1717), 94
  Francis Andrews (1758), 108
  John Hely Hutchinson (1774), 115
  Richard Murray (1795), 122
  John Kearney (1799), 148
  George Hall (1806), 180
  Thomas Elrington (1811), 180
  Samuel Kyle (1820), 181
  Bartholomew Lloyd (1831), 182
  Franc Sadleir (1837), 192
  Richard McDonnell (1852), 195
  Humphrey Lloyd (1867), 196
  John Hewitt Jellett (1881), 196
  George Salmon (1888), 196
Provostship, the, 32, 94
Pulpit, the College, 209
Pump, the College, 54, 102, 165, 202
Punishments, early, 81-86
Puritanism of early College rulers, 13, 27, 30

Querist, Berkeley's, 246
Quin, H. G., 223, 231

Races, the College, 267
Ramsay, Allan, 215
Rathmore, Lord, 185
Rebellion, O'Neill's, 46
  O'Reilly's, 85
  Tyrone's, 10
  of '98,' 127
  of 1641, 43, 46-48
Recruiting Officer, Farquhar's, 242
Reeves, Bishop, 260

Reform Act of 1832, 150
Reformation in Ireland, 17
Regattas, 273, 275
Regent House, 202, 206
Register, Bedell's, 33, 34, 90
Register, College, 62-65, 68, 69, 87, 144
Reid Professorship, 195
Relief Act of 1788, 124
Representation in Parliament, 17, 66, 104, 117
Residence system, 30, 268
Revenue, College, 11, 275
Richardson, Dr., 13-15
Richelieu, Cardinal, 239
Ridgeway, Sir T., 14
Riding-school, 116, 119
Rigby, Secretary, 109
Riots and disorders in College, 101-103, 161
Riots and disorders in the city, 105-107
Roberts, Dr., 184
Roman Catholics and College, 17, 44, 45, 70, 123-125, 188
Roman Catholic petitions, 67, 124
'Root and Branch' Bill, 46
Rosse, Earl of, 184, 215
Rosse, Lord, 167
Ross, Irish school at, 2
Ross, Mr. Justice, 185
Rotunda Hospital, 148
Roubiliac, 233
Rowan, A. B., 60
Rowing, 271-275
Royal College of Surgeons, 23
Royal Commission, 133, 192
Russell, Howard, 259
Russell of Killowen, Lord, 261

RADLER, Provost, 159, 192, 195
St. Andrews, University of, 6
St. Patrick's Cathedral, 3, 4, 105
St. Patrick's Well, 214
St. Stephen's Hall, 24
Salmon, Provost, 184, 196
Sanskrit, Chair of, 193, 195
Saunders' News Letter, 271
Saurin, Attorney-General, 185
Scholæ Academicæ, Wordsworth's, 20, 269
Scholarships, 134, 187
Scholarships, examination for, 153, 155
Schoolmasters, College advice to, 154
'Schools,' the, 201, 212, 213
Scotus, Erigena, 2
Sebright, Sir J., 223
Seele, Provost, 52-54
Selden, John, 221, 239

INDEX

Senior and junior Fellows, 28
Shackleton, R., 155
Sheas, the, 212, 213
Sheil, Lalor, 184, 254
Sheridan, Bishop, 241
Sherlock, Dr., 255
Sibbes, R., 31, 32
Sidney, Lord-Deputy, 5, 27
'Silent Sister, The,' 179
Silken, Thomas, 8
'Sir' as the title of Bachelor, 83
Sixtus IV., Pope, 8
Sisar, 269
Sizarships, 158
Skelton, Life of, Burdy's, 104, 105
'Skip,' 137
Sloane, Sir Hans, 215
Smith, Erasmus, 139, 143, 144, 157, 210, 223
Snagge, Judge, 135
Societies, secret, in College, 129
Songs of Study, Wilkins', 266
Sophister, 77, 269
Sounds and Musical Strings, Young's, 143
Southerne, Thomas, 242
Spinosa, 277
Squire, case of, 112
Stainhurst, Speaker, 5
State aid to College, 194
Statutes, Bedell's, 33, 35
Statutes, Caroline, 26, 40-45, 174, Appendix C
Stearne, Dr. J., 23, 50, 52, 145, 204, 223
Steeple, the College, 201, 203
Stocks, the College, 81
Stokes' *Medical Education*, 189
Stokes, Dr. W., 259, 260, 276
Stokes, Whitley, Fellow, 129, 130, 145, 174
Stokes, Whitley, Mr., 261
Strafford, Viscount, 36, 37, 85, 92
Stubbs' *History of the University*, 16, 19, 23, 24, 75, 76, 86, 91, 99, 124, 160, 164, 185, 202, 208, 210, 248
Students, nationality of, 92
Students, number of, 80, 160
Studium Generale, 22
Sullivan, Edward, 135
Sumptuary laws, 84
Surgeons, Royal College of, 23, 147
Surgery, degrees in, 190
Swift, Jonathan, 88, 95, 108, 151, 211, 233, 242, 246, 247
Swift, Theophilus, 112, 171
Synge, Archbishop, 98, 255

Taite, Dr. Faithful, 47
Talbot, Captain, 63
Tara, 200
Tate, Nahum, 241
Taylor, Fellow, 82
Taylor, Jeremy, 52, 53
Taylor's *History of the University*, 96 108, 168, 181-188, 265
'T. C. D.', 276
Temple, Provost, 27-31, 92
Temple's *Book of Censures*, 82
Tennyson, 257
Tercentenary, 76, 196, 217, 233, 261, Appendix B
Terms, length of, 186, 187
Terræ Filius, 88
Text-books, earliest, 85
Themes, 79
Theological Acts, Moderator of, 14
Theological Controversies, Chair of, 28, 79
Theory of Vision, Berkeley's, 245
Thewles, Fellow, 59, 63, 69
Thomond, Earl of, 231
Todd, Dr., 260
Tone, Theobald Wolfe, 126, 184, 256
Toplady, Augustus, 251
Torrens, Robert, 135
Tours, Council of, 145
Towers, W. G., 274
'Town and Gown,' 105, 165
Town-Haunters, 265
Townsend, Dr., 184
Travers, Fellow, 84
Travers, Provost, 12
Trinity Hall, 22, 145
Tripos, Cambridge, 152, 186
Tripos, Sir Jones', 88
Tyrconnel, Lord, 60-62
Tyrone, rebellion of, 10
Tyrrell, Professor, 276

Ulster, College lands in, 11
Union, Act of, 139, 150, 250, 252
United Irishmen, 127, 129, 130
University and College, 21, 22, 29
University of Dublin, medieval, 2-4
Unpopularity of Fellows, 100-108
Upington, Sir T., 135
Urwick's *Early History of Trinity College*, 24
Ussher, Dr. Henry, 113
Ussher, H., Archbishop, 6, 239
Ussher, James, Archbishop, 25, 211, 215, 220, 221, 238, 239
Ussher, Provost, 85, 87

INDEX

Vankey, Peter, 202
Vesey, Archbishop, 241
Victoria, address from graduates in, 261-268
Victoria Rowing Club, 271
Visitations, 119, 128
Volunteers, College, 127

Wages of College Servants, early, 91
Walker, Dr. 256
Walker, John, 143, 174
Walker, Lord Chancellor, 135
Waller, J. F., 257
Walpole, Sir H., 238
Walsh, Bishop, 34
Walsh, E., Master of the Rolls, 135, 166
Walsh, J. E., 133
Walsh, Robert, 133
Ward, Ellis, 274
Ward, Provost, 56
Wards, Court of, 98
Ware, Sir J., 33, 240
Washington, Provost, 45
Webb, Judge, 135
Wellington, Duke of, 110, 118
Wentworth, Lord Strafford, 36, 37, 85, 92

Wesley, Earl of Mornington, 110, 215, 249
Wesley, John, 105
Whig policy of College, 97, 98
Whiteside, Chief Justice, 261
Wilder, Dr. T., 165
Wilkins, W., 206
William III., 69, 70, 94
Williamson, Cæsar, 52, 222
Willibrord, 2
Wills, Freeman, 135
Wills' *Lives of Illustrious Irishmen*, 177
Wilson, Bishop, 241
Winter, Provost, 49
Wolfe, Charles, 134, 256
Wordsworth, W., 114
Wordsworth's *Scholæ Academicæ*, 30, 269
Wrixon, Sir A. J., 135
Wyse, Thomas, 125

Yelverton, Barry, Lord Avonmore, 134
Young, Mathew, 143, 255

Zoology, Chair of, 193
Zu chero, 215

Printed in the USA
CPSIA information can be obtained
at www.ICGtesting.com
LVHW100156290823
756585LV00004B/41